C000182928

GUIDE TO THE

river thames & the
southern waterways

Also available:

Nicholson Guide to the Waterways
1. **Grand Union, Oxford & the South East**
2. **Severn, Avon & Birmingham**
3. **Birmingham & the Heart of England**
4. **Four Counties & the Welsh Canals**
5. **North West & the Pennines**
6. **Nottingham, York & the North East**
8. **Scotland – the Highland and Lowland Waterways**

Nicholson Inland Waterways Map of Great Britain

Published by Nicholson
An imprint of HarperCollins*Publishers*
77–85 Fulham Palace Road
Hammersmith, London W6 8JB

www.collins.co.uk
www.collinsbartholomew.com

First published by Nicholson and Ordnance Survey 1997
Reprinted 1998
New edition published by Nicholson 2000, 2003
Reprinted 2003, 2004
Copyright © HarperCollins*Publishers* Ltd 2003

Researched and written by David Perrott and Jonathan Mosse.
Designed by Bob Vickers.

The publishers gratefully acknowledge the assistance given by British Waterways and
their staff in the preparation of this guide.

Grateful thanks is also due to the Environment Agency and members of the
Inland Waterways Association, CAMRA representatives and branch members.

Photographs reproduced by kind permission of Derek Pratt Photography.

Printed in Hong Kong.

ISBN 0 00 713670 6
RJ11695 03/4/64

The publishers welcome comments from readers. Please address your letters to:
Nicholson Guides to the Waterways, HarperCollins Reference,
HarperCollins Publishers, Westerhill Road, Bishopbriggs, Glasgow, G64 2QT or
email nicholson@harpercollins.co.uk

Wending their quiet way through town and country, the inland navigations of Britain offer boaters, walkers and cyclists a unique insight into a fascinating, but once almost lost, world. When built this was the province of the boatmen and their families, who lived a mainly itinerant lifestyle: often colourful, to our eyes picturesque but, for them, remarkably harsh. Transporting the nation's goods during the late 1700s and early 1800s, negotiating locks, traversing aqueducts and passing through long narrow tunnels, canals were the arteries of trade during the initial part of the industrial revolution.

Then the railways came: the waterways were eclipsed in a remarkably short time by a faster and more flexible transport system, and a steady decline began. In a desperate fight for survival canal tolls were cut, crews toiled for longer hours and worked the boats with their whole family living aboard. Canal companies merged, totally uneconomic waterways were abandoned, some were modernised but it was all to no avail. Large scale commercial carrying on inland waterways had reached the finale of its short life.

At the end of World War II a few enthusiasts roamed this hidden world and harboured a vision of what it could become: a living transport museum which stretched the length and breadth of the country; a place where people could spend their leisure time and, on just a few of the wider waterways, a still modestly viable transport system.

The restoration struggle began and, from modest beginnings, Britain's inland waterways are now seen as an irreplaceable part of the fabric of the nation. Existing canals are expertly maintained while long abandoned waterways, once seen as an eyesore and a danger, are recognised for the valuable contribution they make to our quality of life, and restoration schemes are integrating them back into the network.

This series of guides offers the most comprehensive coverage of Britain's inland waterways, all clearly detailed on splendid Ordnance Survey® maps. Whether you are boating, walking, cycling or just visiting, these books will give you all the information you need.

▐ CONTENTS

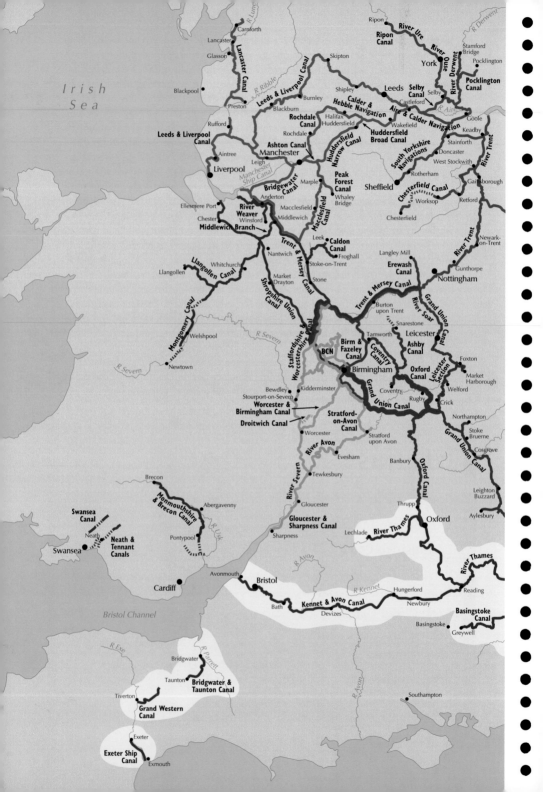

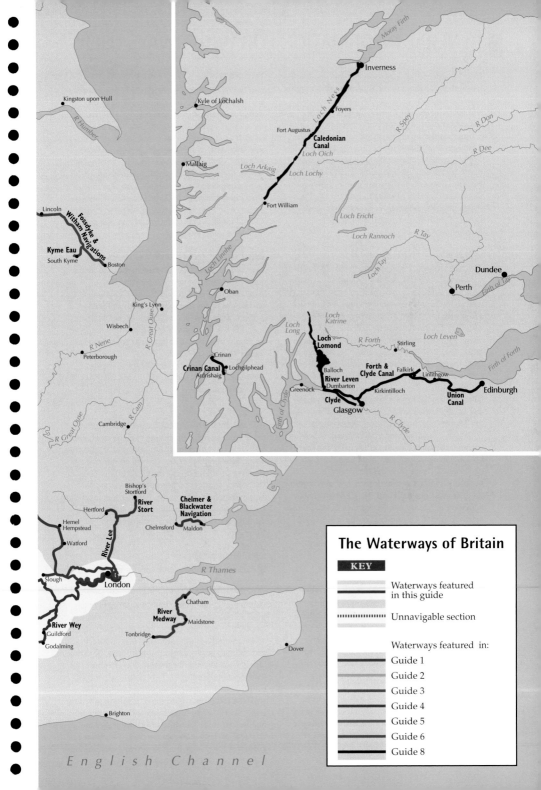

Kingston upon Hull

R Humber

Lincoln

Fossdyke & Witham Navigations

Kyme Eau

South Kyme

Boston

King's Lynn

Wisbech

R Nene

Peterborough

R Great Ouse

R Cam

Cambridge

R Great Ouse

Kyle of Lochalsh

Mallaig

Loch Arkaig

Fort William

Loch Linnhe

Oban

Crinan

Crinan Canal

Ardrishaig

Lochgilphead

Loch Long

Inverness

Foyers

Loch Ness

Fort Augustus

Caledonian Canal

Loch Oich

Loch Lochy

Moray Firth

R Spey

R Don

R Dee

R Tay

Loch Ericht

Loch Rannoch

Loch Tay

Dundee

Perth

Firth of Tay

Loch Katrine

Loch Lomond

Balloch

River Leven

Dumbarton

Greenock

Clyde

Glasgow

Firth of Clyde

Kirkintilloch

R Forth

Stirling

Loch Leven

Forth & Clyde Canal

Falkirk

Linlithgow

Union Canal

Edinburgh

Firth of Forth

R Clyde

Bishop's Stortford

Hertford

River Stort

Chelmer & Blackwater Navigation

Chelmsford

Maldon

Hemel Hempstead

Watford

River Lee

Slough

London

Chatham

River Medway

Maidstone

Tonbridge

Dover

River Wey

Guildford

Godalming

Brighton

R Thames

English Channel

The Waterways of Britain

KEY

━━━ Waterways featured in this guide

▬▬▬ Unnavigable section

Waterways featured in:

━━━ Guide 1

━━━ Guide 2

━━━ Guide 3

━━━ Guide 4

━━━ Guide 5

━━━ Guide 6

━━━ Guide 8

GENERAL INFORMATION FOR WATERWAYS USERS

Boaters, walkers, fishermen, cyclists and gongoozlers (on-lookers) all share in the enjoyment of our quite amazing waterway heritage. British Waterways and the Environment Agency, along with other navigation authorities, are empowered to develop, maintain and control this resource. It is to this end that a series of guides, codes, and regulations have come into existence over the years, evolving to match a burgeoning – and occasionally conflicting – demand. Set out below are key points as they relate to everyone wishing to enjoy the waterways. Please see the inside front cover for details on how to contact British Waterways (BW) and the Environment Agency (EA).

LICENSING – BOATS

The majority of the navigations covered in this book are controlled by BW and the EA and are managed on a day-to-day basis by local Waterway Offices. All craft using the inland waterways must be licenced and charges are based on the dimensions of the craft. In a few cases, these include reciprocal agreements with other waterway authorities (as indicated in the text). BW and the EA now offer an optional Gold Licence which covers unlimited navigation on the waterways of both authorities. Permits for permanent mooring on BW waterways are issued by BW. You can download licence fees and charges and an application form from the BW website. For the Thames telephone EA Craft Registration.

BW and the EA operate the Boat Safety Scheme, setting technical requirements for good and safe boat maintenance. A Boat Safety Certificate or, for new boats, a Declaration of Conformity, is necessary to obtain a craft licence. BW also requires proof of insurance for Third Party Liability for a minimum of £1,000,000 for powered boats. Further details from BW Customer Services or EA Craft Registration. Other navigation authorities relevant to this book are mentioned where appropriate.

LICENSING – CYCLISTS

Not all towpaths are open to cyclists. Maps on the BW website show the stretches of towpath open to cyclists, and local offices can supply more information. A cycle permit is required, and this is available free of charge (except for the Kennet & Avon Canal, where a charge is made) from BW Customer Services. The Waterways Code gives advice on taking care and staying safe, considering others and helping to look after the waterways. Cycling along the Thames towpath is generally accepted, although landowners have the right to request that you do not cycle. Some sections of the riverside path, however, are designated and clearly marked as official cycle ways. No permits are required.

TOWPATHS

Few, if any, artificial cuts or canals in this country are without an intact towpath accessible to the walker at least and the Thames is the only river in the country with a designated National Trail along its path from source to sea (more information is available on www.nationaltrails.gov.uk or 01865 810224). However, on some other river navigations, towpaths have on occasion fallen into disuse or, sometimes, been lost to erosion. The indication of a towpath in this guide does not necessarily imply a public right of way or mean that a right to cycle along it exists. Motorcycling and horse riding are forbidden on all towpaths.

INDIVIDUAL WATERWAY GUIDES

No national guide can cover the minutiae of detail concerning every waterway, and some BW Waterway Managers produce guides to specific navigations under their charge. Copies of individual guides (where they are available) can be obtained from the BW Waterway Office detailed in the introduction. Please note that times – such as operating times of bridges and locks – do change year by year and from winter to summer. For a free copy of *A Users Guide to the River Thames*, please telephone EA Craft Registration.

STOPPAGES

BW and the EA both publish winter stoppage programmes which are sent out to all licence holders, boatyards and hire companies. Inevitably, emergencies occur necessitating the unexpected closure of a waterway, perhaps during the peak season. You can check for stoppages on individual waterways between specific dates on the BW website, lockside noticeboards or on Canalphone; for stoppages on the Thames telephone the EA Navigation Information Line or visit the EA website).

STARTING OUT

Extensive information and advice on booking a boating holiday is available on the BW website, or from the EA's website for the Thames, www. visitthames.co.uk. Please book a waterway holiday from a licenced operator – only in this way can you be sure that you have proper insurance cover, service and support during your holiday. It is illegal for private boat owners to hire out their craft. If you are hiring a holiday craft for the first time, the boatyard will brief you thoroughly. Take notes, follow their instructions and don't be afraid to ask if there is anything you do not understand. BW have produced a short video giving basic information on using a boat safely, copies of which are available free of charge from BW Customer Services. *The Boater's Handbook* is available from all navigation authorities and sections of the *Boater's Safety Toolkit* can be downloaded from the internet at www.aina.org.uk.

GENERAL CRUISING NOTES

Most canals and rivers are saucer shaped, being deepest at the middle. Few canals have more than 3-4ft of water and many have much less. Keep to the centre of the channel except on bends, where the deepest water is on the outside of the bend. When you meet another boat, keep to the right, slow down and aim to miss the approaching craft by a couple of yards. If you meet a loaded commercial boat keep right out of the way and be prepared to follow his instructions. Do not assume that you should pass on the right. If you meet a boat being towed from the bank, pass it on the outside. When overtaking, keep the other boat on your right side.

A large number of BW and EA facilities – pump outs, showers, electrical hook-ups and so on – are operated by pre-paid cards, obtainable from BW and EA Regional Offices, local waterways offices (see introductions to individual navigations), lock keepers and some boatyards within the region. Cards are available in £5, £6, £10 and £15 denominations. Weekend visitors should purchase cards in advance.

Speed
There is a general speed limit of 4 mph on most BW canals and 5 mph on the Thames. There is no need to go any faster: if your wash is breaking against the bank or causing large waves, slow down. Slow down also when passing moored craft, engineering works and anglers; when there is a lot of floating rubbish on the water (and try to drift over obvious obstructions in neutral); when approaching blind corners, narrow bridges and junctions.

Mooring
Generally speaking you may moor where you wish on BW property, as long as you are *not causing an obstruction*. On the Thames, generally you have a right to anchor for 24 hours in one place provided no obstruction is caused, however you will need explicit permission from the land owner to moor. There are official mooring sites along the length of the river; those provided by the EA are free, the others you

will need to pay for. All are listed in the free booklet *A Users Guide to the River Thames*. Your boat should carry metal mooring stakes, and these should be driven firmly into the ground with a mallet if there are no mooring rings. Do not stretch mooring lines across the towpath. Always consider the security of your boat when there is no one aboard. On tideways and commercial waterways it is advisable to moor only at recognised sites, and allow for any rise or fall of the tide.

Bridges
On narrow canals slow down and aim to miss one side (usually the towpath side) by about 9 inches. *Keep everyone inboard when passing under bridges*, and take special care with moveable structures – the crew member operating the bridge should be strong enough and heavy enough to hold it steady as the boat passes through.

Tunnels
Make sure the tunnel is clear before you enter, and use your headlight. Follow any instructions given on notice boards by the entrance.

Fuel
Hire craft usually carry fuel sufficient for the rental period.

Water
It is advisable to top up daily.

Lavatories
Hire craft usually have pump out toilets. Have these emptied *before* things become critical. Keep the receipt and your boatyard will usually reimburse you for this expense.

Boatyards
Hire fleets are usually turned around on a Saturday, making this a bad time to call in for services.

LOCKS AND THEIR USE

A lock is a simple and ingenious device for transporting your craft from one water level to another. When both sets of gates are closed it may be filled or emptied using gate or – on canals – ground paddles at the

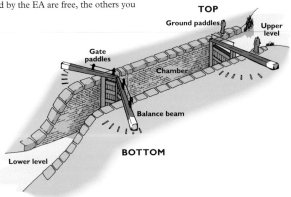

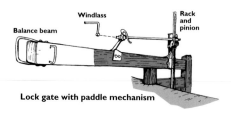

Balance beam **Windless** **Rack and pinion**

Lock gate with paddle mechanism

top or bottom of the lock. These are operated with a windlass. On the Thames, the locks are manned all year round, with longer hours from April to October during the boating season. You may operate the locks yourself at any time.

General tips

- Make safety your prime concern. *Keep a close eye on young children.*
- Always take your time, and do not leap about.
- Never open the paddles at one end without ensuring those at the other end are closed.
- Never drop the paddles – always wind them down.
- Keep to the landward side of the balance beam when opening and closing gates.
- Never leave your windlass slotted onto the paddle spindle – it will be dangerous should anything slip.
- Keep your boat away from the top and bottom gates to prevent it getting caught on the gate or the lock cill.
- Be wary of fierce *top gate* paddles, especially in wide locks. Operate them slowly, and close them if there is *any* adverse effect.
- Always follow the navigation authority's instructions, where given on notices or by their staff.

PLANNING A CRUISE

Don't try to go too far too fast. Go slowly, don't be too ambitious, and enjoy the experience. Mileages indicated on the maps are for guidance only.

A *rough* calculation of time taken to cover the ground is the lock-miles system:

Add the number of *miles* to the number of *locks* on your proposed journey, and divide the resulting figure by three. This will give you an approximate guide to the number of *hours* your travel will take.

TIDAL WATERWAYS

The typical steel narrow boat found on the inland waterways system is totally unsuitable for cruising on tidal estuaries. However, the adventurous will inevitably wish to add additional 'ring cruises' to the more predictable circuits of inland Britain. Passage is possible in most estuaries if very careful consideration is given to the key factors of weather conditions, tides, crew experience, the condition of the boat and its equipment and, perhaps of overriding importance, the need to take expert advice. In many cases it will be prudent to employ the skilled services of a local pilot. Within the text, where inland navigations connect with a tidal waterway, details

are given of sources of both advice and pilotage. It is also essential to inform your insurance company of your intention to navigate on tidal waterways as they may very well have special requirements or wish to levy an additional premium. This guide is to the inland waterways of Britain and therefore recognizes that tideways – and especially estuaries – require a different approach and many additional skills. We do not hesitate to draw the boater's attention to the appropriate source material.

GENERAL

Most inland navigations are managed by BW or the EA, but there are several other navigation authorities. For details of these, contact the Association of Inland Navigation Authorities at www.aina.org.uk or BW Customer Services. The boater, conditioned perhaps by the uniformity of our national road network, should be sensitive to the need to observe different codes and operating practices.

BW is a public corporation, responsible to the Department of Environment, Food and Rural Affairs and, as subscribers to the Citizen's Charter, they are linked with an ombudsman. BW has a comprehensive complaints procedure and a free explanatory leaflet is available from Customer Services. Problems and complaints should be addressed to the local Waterway Manager in the first instance. For more information, visit their website.

The Environment Agency is the national body, sponsored by the Department of Environment, Food and Rural Affairs, to manage the quality of air, land and water in England and Wales. For more information, visit its website. Queries about the Thames can be directed to the Waterway Manager (*see* the start of the Thames section).

The Inland Waterways Association campaigns for the 'conservation, use, maintenance, restoration and development of the inland waterways', through branches all over the country. For more information contact them at PO Box 114, Rickmansworth, WD3 1ZY, telephone 01923 711114, fax 01923 897000, email iwa@waterways.org.uk or visit their website at www.waterways.org.uk.

BRITISH WATERWAYS EMERGENCY HELPLINE

Emergency help is available from BW outside normal office hours on weekdays and throughout weekends via British Waterways Emergency Helpline (see inside front cover). You should give details of the problem and your location.

ENVIRONMENT AGENCY INCIDENT LINE

Emergency assistance is available on the Thames for boat fires and explosions and emergencies at locks and weirs, and nationally for any pollution incident. Please call the Agency incident line on 0800 807060.

BASINGSTOKE CANAL

MAXIMUM DIMENSIONS

Length: 72'
Beam: 13' 6"
Headroom: 5' 9"

MILEAGES

WOODHAM JUNCTION (River Wey) *to:*
Woodham Top Lock: 1 mile
Goldsworth Bottom Lock: 5 miles
Pirbright Bridge: 8 miles
Deepcut Top Lock: 10 miles
Mytchett: 13 miles
Ash Lock: 16 miles
Pondtail Bridges: 20 miles

Crookham Wharf: 23 miles
Barley Mow Bridge: 27 miles
Odiham Wharf: 29 miles
Limit of navigation: 30¾ miles
Greywell Tunnel: 31 miles

29 locks

LICENCES

Basingstoke Canal Office
Mytchett Place Road
Mytchett
Surrey GU16 6DD
01252 370073
info@basingstoke-canal.co.uk

An Act of Parliament for the building of this canal was passed in 1778, and the navigation opened to Basingstoke in 1794. Intended as an artery to and from London for mainly agricultural produce – timber, grain, fertilizers, chalk and malt – it was never a financial success. Built by the great canal contractor, John Pinkerton (who issued his own tokens or coins as payment to his navvies), it was originally estimated to cost £86,000. By 1796 £153,463 had been spent. Tonnages of goods carried averaged about 20,000 per annum, 10,700 tons below what was anticipated, and profit forecasts of £7,783 8s 4d proved wildly optimistic, the best figure achieved being £3,038 4s 2d in 1800.

The Napoleonic Wars, and the danger they brought to coastal shipping, benefited the Basingstoke Canal, which could transport goods bound for Portsmouth and Southampton in safety. But with the advent of peace, trade slumped – the canal managers commenting that 'some considerable injury must be sustained by the Canal'. There was a minor boom in goods carried in 1839 to build the London & South Western Railway, but when this opened it was clear that the navigation had been instrumental in its own demise. Trade flourished for a while in 1854 with the building of the barracks at Aldershot, but this was short-lived. Plans for a revival by building a link canal from Basingstoke to the Kennet & Avon Canal at Newbury came to nothing, and the company went into liquidation in 1866. A dissolution order followed in 1878. Purchased by new owners in 1896, and renamed the Woking, Aldershot & Basingstoke Canal, a considerable amount of money was spent on improvements, to link with the new brickworks at Up Nately, but all to no avail, and by 1904 it was once again offered for sale. In 1913, *Basingstoke*, the last narrowboat to almost reach Basingstoke, carried 5 tons of moulding sand. The canal was owned by A.J. Harmsworth between 1923 and 1947, and he did much to ensure its ultimate survival, despite the collapse of Greywell Tunnel in 1934. Munitions were transported on the canal during World War II, and the last commercial traffic, 50 tons of timber on *Gwendoline*, came to Woking in June 1949. In 1950 the canal was auctioned and sold to the Inland Waterways Association but due to insufficient funds being raised the canal was sold on to what was to become the New Basingstoke Canal Company. Now owned by the County Councils of Hampshire and Surrey, its restoration represents a magnificent achievement by both councils, the Surrey & Hampshire Canal Society and the IWA.

Woking

The Basingstoke Canal leaves the River Wey Navigation at Woodham Junction, near a large electricity sub-station and overshadowed by the M25 motorway. Its course is immediately lined with a fine mixture of mature trees, a feature which is to persist throughout most of its route, isolating the canal from much of its surroundings. The new pump house, which back pumps water on the Woodham flight of six locks, and alleviates a long-standing water supply problem, is passed before you reach the peaceful, almost secret, houseboat world which still exists between Locks 1 and 3. There is easy access to shops, banks and pubs from Lock 2 – walk south west into West Byfleet; and to the south of Chobham Road Bridge. Above Woodham Top Lock the waterway maintains its seclusion, with the large private gardens of a smart residential area backing onto the canal. Horsell Common provides more open views before Woking is reached, where the last commercial traffic on the canal was a load of timber in 1949.

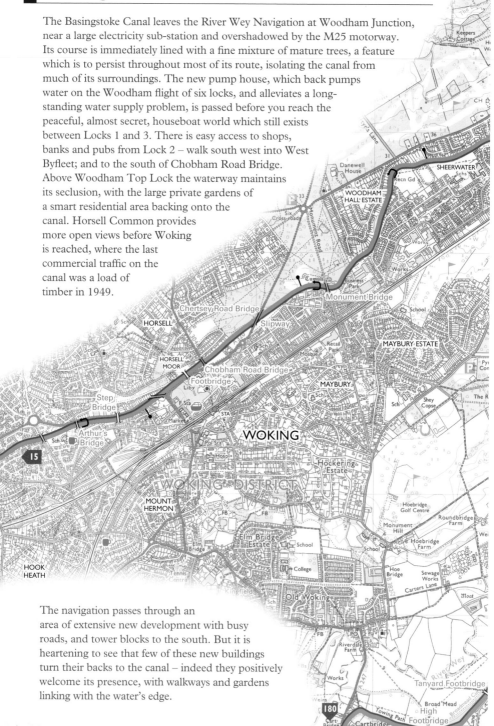

The navigation passes through an area of extensive new development with busy roads, and tower blocks to the south. But it is heartening to see that few of these new buildings turn their backs to the canal – indeed they positively welcome its presence, with walkways and gardens linking with the water's edge.

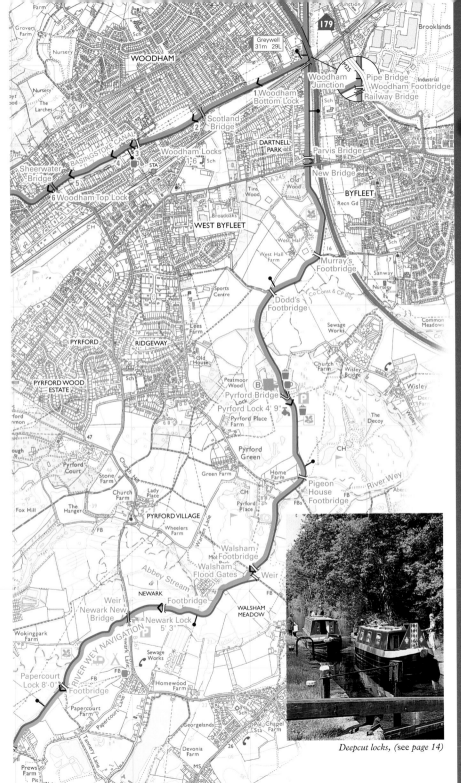

WOODHAM

Grovers Farm
Nursery
Sch

Greywell
31m 29L

Woodham
Junction

Pipe Bridge
Woodham Footbridge
Railway Bridge

Nursery
Loyt wood
The Larches

BASINGSTOKE CANAL

1 Woodham
Bottom Lock

Industrial

2 Scotland Bridge

Woodham Locks 1'6

STA

DARTNELL PARK

Parvis Bridge

New Bridge

BYFLEET

Recn Gd

Sheerwater Bridge

6 Woodham Top Lock

WEST BYFLEET

West Hall

West Hall Farm

Murray's Footbridge

Sanway

Nursery

PYRFORD

RIDGEWAY

Sports Centre

Lees Farm

Dodd's Footbridge

Sewage Works

Church Farm

Wisley Bridge

Wisley

Common Meadows

PYRFORD WOOD ESTATE

Old House

Peatmoor Wood

Pyrford Bridge
Lock

Pyrford Lock 4'9"

Pyrford Place Farm

The Decoy

Pyrford Court
Stone Farm

Green Farm

Pyrford Green

Home Farm

Pigeon House Footbridge

River Wey

Church Hill

Church Farm

Lady Place

PYRFORD VILLAGE

Wheelers Farm

Pyrford Place

CH

Fox Hill
The Hanger

FB

Walsham Footbridge

Walsham Flood Gates

Weir

Abbey Stream

NEWARK

Footbridge

WALSHAM MEADOW

Weir
Newark New Bridge

Newark Lock 5'3"

RIVER WEY NAVIGATION

Wokingpark Farm

Sewage Works

Homewood Farm

Papercourt Lock 8'0"

Footbridge

Papercourt Farm

Georgelands

Devonia Farm

Prews Farm Pit

Chapel Sta

Deepcut locks, (see page 14)

1 Facilities for boaters are fairly limited on the Basingstoke Canal. There is water available at Mytchett, Ash Lock, Fleet and Odiham (BW key required for all sites) together with pump out facilities at Mytchett and Odiham. There are many garages close to the route.

2 Slipways are available at Chertsey Road Bridge, Woking; Potters Steak House, Mytchett; Farnborough Road, Aldershot; and Barley Mow Bridge, Winchfield. A BW key is required to unlock the barriers. To use the Woking slipway first contact the Leisure Services Officer on (01483) 755855.

● **Woking**
Surrey. All shops and services. Surrey's largest town, built around the railway, which came here in 1838. The original village, Old Woking, lies 2 miles to the south. Development carries on apace, making dormitory homes for the thousands of commuters who rush up to the city daily. It is, however, worth walking south from Monument Bridge, and taking the third turning on the right, Oriental Road, to see the Shah Jehan Mosque, built in 1889 and reminiscent of the Taj Mahal in India with its onion-shaped dome. Built by the enormously rich Begum Shah Jehan, ruler of Bhopal State in India, its design, by W. I. Chambers, is honest and dignified. A P&O captain was employed to take bearings to ensure an exact orientation towards Mecca. It is now the main centre for Muslims in England.

Brooklands Museum Brooklands Road, Weybridge (01932 857381; www.motor-software.co.uk/brooklands). A museum assembled around what remains of the Brooklands race track, the world's first purpose-built circuit, constructed by wealthy landowner Hugh Locke King in 1907. Its heyday was in the 1920s and 30s, when records were being set by the likes of Malcolm Campbell and John Cobb, driving vehicles with wonderfully evocative names, such as the Napier, Delage, Bentley and Bugatti. It became very fashionable, and was known as the Ascot of Motorsport. It was also an aerodrome, and it was here that A.V. Roe made the first flight in a British aeroplane. The Sopwith Pup and Camel were developed here, and later the Hawker Hurricane and the Vickers Wellington were built here – the only surviving Wellington, salvaged in 1985 from Loch Ness and restored, is on display. The outbreak of war in 1939 brought an end to racing, and aircraft production ceased in 1987. Now you can walk on part of the legendary circuit, and see historic racing cars and aircraft in the museum. The clubhouse is listed as an ancient monument. A new addition is the Raleigh Cycle Museum, a reminder that cycle races were also held at Brooklands. *Open Tue–Sun 10.00–17.00 (16.00 winter). Closed G Fri, B Hol Mons and Xmas.* Charge.

Elmbridge Museum Church Street, Weybridge (01932 843573; info@elm-mus.datanet.co.uk). Above the public library. A collection established in 1909 and refurbished in 1996, covering local and social history and featuring items relating to Oatlands Palace, near Weybridge, which was built by Henry VIII in 1537. Also finds from a Romano-British bath-house near Cobham. *Open Mon–Wed and Fri 11.00–17.00, Sat 10.00–13.00 and 14.00–17.00.* Buses or train to Weybridge.

New Victoria Theatre Peacocks Centre, Woking (Box office 01483 545900; www. theambassadors.com/woking/newvic). Situated in the Peacocks Arts & Entertainments Centre and providing a 1300-seat venue for drama, musicals, opera and ballet. Also big screen cinemas, bars, cafés and restaurants. Disabled access.

Woking Leisure Centre Woking Park, Kingfield Road (01483 771122). Aerobics, gym, health suite, squash, badminton, children's activities, a multisensory suite and a 1930s Wurlitzer organ. Disabled access.

Woking Visitor Information Centre Crown House, Crown Square (01483 720103; tourist@woking.gov.uk).

● **Woodham**
Surrey. All shops and services. A typical commuter conurbation of dull, closely packed houses, only pretty in the more expensive areas, where large, spacious houses and gardens nestle among trees. Definitely at its best and most characterful by the canal.

● **Horsell**
Surrey. Indistinguishable from Woking (*see* above), although if you look hard enough, you will find a few original cottages.

UPS AND DOWNS ON THE BASINGSTOKE

The Basingstoke Canal was at one time often portrayed as a restoration failure, but this was borne entirely out of a misconception. At the outset the objective of the two county councils involved was to create a 32-mile, linear country park for the benefit of a wide variety of potential users, of which boaters were to be but one (albeit significant) group.

Two barge movements a day was the average traffic when the waterway was opened and water supply was always constrained by an undertaking not to tap existing watercourses, jealously guarded by millers and landowners alike. Apart from springs and rainwater run-off – plentiful during the winter months – the only other water source is limited to two pumped supplies: one at Woking and a second at Frimley, lifting storm water from a drainage sump on the trackbed of the mainline railway.

Now a new pumping station at the bottom of Woodham Locks serves to stop water losses to the River Wey, and maintains the level in the pound above the flight. Springs work on more or less a six month cycle so a good time to visit the canal is between February and mid June when water supplies should be at their maximum.

It has aptly been described as a sleepy backwater of a canal and navigating it is more akin to boating in the 1950s: locks fill slowly and require care, and the waterway itself is not to be rushed along. Herein lies its real charm and to appreciate it – together with the abundant wildlife and SSSIs – visitors must understand its constraints, together with the way in which it has successfully fulfilled all the aims of its restorers and delighted one-and-a-half million diverse visitors annually.

WALKING & CYCLING

The towpath is in excellent condition throughout the entire length of the navigation, including the disused section west of Greywell Tunnel as far as Penny Bridge. The short section across Greywell Hill, however, may be uneven and overgrown. The towpath is well used by walkers and cyclists alike and in conjunction with the numerous British Rail stations, situated at regular intervals close to the canal, it is fairly easy to plan excursions without having to double back.

Pubs and Restaurants

There are plenty of pubs and restaurants in Woking and West Byfleet but only one is adjacent to the canal.

The Claremont West Byfleet (01932 345048). Large, lively pub opposite West Byfleet Station, south of Lock 3. Real ale. Meals (V) *Mon–Sat, L and E*. Children welcome *until 20.00*. Pool and games. Large garden.

✕ **The Bridge Barn** Woking (01483 763642). Tastefully converted 17th-C timbered barn by Arthur's Bridge, housing 'Out and Out' restaurant. Meals (V) *L and E*. Real ale. Children welcome. Canalside garden with play area. Moorings outside. Venue for the Basingstoke Canal Festival, held *each Easter*.

Wetherspoons 51-57 Chertsey Road, Woking (01483 722818). Popular, town centre pub. Real ale. Meals (V) *all day*. Outside seating.

Brookwood

Woking is gradually left behind as the canal rises through the five Goldsworth Locks to Kiln Bridge, where there are good moorings above the bridge. Here there is easy access to shops, Indian and Chinese restaurants, and a laundrette. The railway, which accompanies the canal to Frimley Green, comes very close at Knaphill, and is then replaced by the trees of Brookwood Lye. Houseboats moored here, by Hermitage Bridge, add a picturesque touch. A collection of used cars are parked almost at the edge of Brookwood Bottom Lock, but the remaining two locks are pleasantly situated and once again the trees reappear. An old overgrown pill box still guards Pirbright Bridge – beyond the bridge

is the first of the Deepcut, or Frimley, flight of locks. The canal now climbs steadily up the 14 locks in a superb, tree-lined, setting. Even the vast Pirbright Army Camp to the north hardly intrudes. Between many of the locks there are wide pools – check the depth of these carefully if you intend to stray off the direct course. Each of the locks has a footbridge, and a ladder in the chamber, but not all have an easy means of landing below the bottom gates, so it is a good idea for a member of the crew to walk ahead to open the gates while ascending. Above the top lock is a dry dock, rebuilt in 1984. The building here was once a workshop and forge.

● **St John's**
Surrey. PO, tel, stores, takeaways, chemist, laundrette. Swallowed up by Woking, the area around Kiln Bridge somehow, against all odds, manages to retain the feel of a village centre. Notice the well-restored building topped by a clock tower, right by the bridge.

● **Knaphill**
Surrey. Basically a large Victorian village around the barracks and the site of the gaunt Brookwood Mental Hospital, a mid 19th-C asylum which was once entirely self-sufficient, generating its own electricity and running its own farm in the grounds. To the west is Bisley,

famous for its annual rifle shooting competitions.
Brookwood Cemetery A superbly landscaped expanse of heathland covering 2,400 acres, to the south of Brookwood Station, where mature trees and eccentric mausoleums coexist harmoniously. Founded by the London Necropolis Company in 1854, when the numbers of dead Londoners were becoming increasingly difficult to accommodate, it was once served by a railway – indeed one of the station buildings still survives. There is a military cemetery in the south west corner, where British and American soldiers are buried.

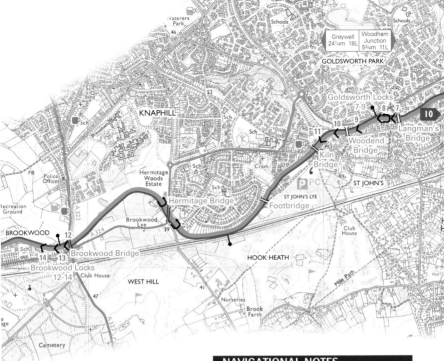

NAVIGATIONAL NOTES

Do not stray from the direct course of the canal without first checking the depth. Many of the wide pools are quite shallow.

Pubs and Restaurants

The Rowbarge St John's, Woking (01483 761618). Real ales and inexpensive bar food (V) *L and E (not Sun E)*. Children welcome. Traditional pub games. Canalside garden.

The Robin Hood 88 Robin Hood Road, St John's (01483 472173). A fine pub majoring on conversation and good beer. Real ale. Food (V) *L*. Children's indoor play area. Large garden and spontaneous entertainment *B Hols*.

✕ ♀ **Vojon Indian Restaurant & Takeaway** St John's (01483 725354/715611). 50 yds south of Kiln Bridge. Indian food.

The Hunter's Lodge Knaphill (01483 798101). Attractive and welcoming pub north of Brookwood Bridge. Real ale. Traditional English bar food (V) *all day*. Free from loud music – and it has a *silent* fruit machine. Children welcome. Garden. *Open all day*.

Hooden Takes a Knap (Hooden Horse) 136 High Street, Knaphill (01483 473374). Ten-minute walk from Brookwood Bridge along Bagshot Road. Real ale in a bistro-style bar. Mexican and traditional English food (V) *L and E*. Children welcome. Large garden with play area. Regular theme nights. *Closed afternoons Mon–Thur*.

♀ **Shooters Wine Bar** 42-44 High Street, Knaphill (01483 480071). ½ mile north of Hermitage Bridge, then left along Queen's Road. Wine bar with warm and cosy atmosphere. Bar snacks *L and E*. Children welcome, and there is a patio.

✕ The Brookwood Hotel Beside Brookwood Station (01483 472109). Well-preserved and friendly Victorian pub. Real ale. À la carte restaurant and inexpensive bar meals (V) *L and E*. Children welcome. Large beer garden. Children's play area. Traditional pub games.

Mytchett

Having climbed 90ft, the navigation now enters the dramatic Deepcut cutting, 1000yds long and up to 70ft deep. Lined with large, mature, deciduous trees, it is pleasantly shady and remote. Beyond Wharfenden Lake, now part of a country club, and the supposedly lead-lined aqueduct over the railway, the canal turns sharply south towards Mytchett, with woods and heathland rising to the east. Mytchett Lake, owned by the army and renowned amongst anglers for the size of its pike, adjoins the canal, but is closed to navigation. The canal continues south, enclosed by the railway and thick woods on one side, and leafy gardens on the other. Just beyond the railway bridge at Ash Vale is the corrugated iron boathouse, dated 1896, where 15 barges were built between 1918 and 1935, and repairs were undertaken until 1947. There is a post office here (by the station), an off-licence and easy access to shops. Great Bottom Flash, which contains the sunken remains of *Basingstoke*, the last narrowboat to almost reach Basingstoke, is surrounded by trees. It was here that Samuel F. Cody came to test his early seaplanes, prior to World War I. It is now a Danger Area, used by the army. Large houses with gardens landscaped to the water's edge face a busy road at Ash Vale before the navigation resumes its general westerly course, passing handy shops, another post office and Chinese takeaway at Ash Wharf Bridge. It then crosses Spring Lake on an embankment and the Blackwater Valley Road on an aqueduct, leaving Surrey and entering Hampshire. There are good moorings above Ash Lock, opposite the Canal Depot (slipway). The reappearance of army property – barrack blocks behind high wire fences – announces the approach to Aldershot. The canal has now climbed 195ft since leaving Woodham Junction. Queen's Avenue Bridge is notable for its modestly ornate iron balustrades, bringing a little light relief from the army camps which now completely enclose the waterway. Beyond Eelmoor Bridge, the canal widens at Eelmoor Flash, a Site of Special Scientific Interest (SSSI) due to its exceptional dragonfly population.

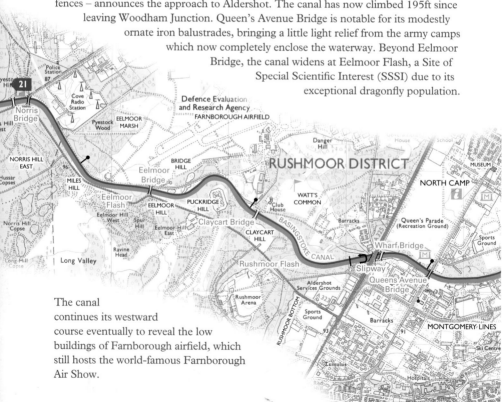

The canal continues its westward course eventually to reveal the low buildings of Farnborough airfield, which still hosts the world-famous Farnborough Air Show.

NAVIGATIONAL NOTES

1 Do not stray from the direct course of the canal without first checking the depth. Many of the wide pools are quite shallow.

2 Wharf Bridge is very low – 5ft 10in – so keep to the non-towpath side for maximum headroom.

WALKING & CYCLING

There are excellent waymarked trails for walkers in Lakeside Park (*see* below).

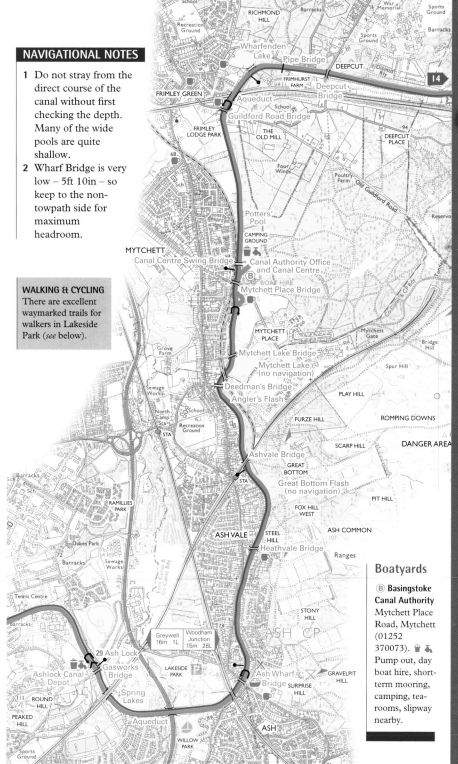

Boatyards

Ⓑ **Basingstoke Canal Authority**
Mytchett Place Road, Mytchett (01252 370073). Pump out, day boat hire, short-term mooring, camping, tea-rooms, slipway nearby.

Royal Logistic Corps Museum Deepcut, Camberley (01252 340871; query@rlcmuseum. freeserve.co.uk). North of the canal, on the B3015. Built as a museum in 1995, this collection depicts the last 500 years of history of the Royal Corps of Transport, the Royal Pioneer Corps, the Army Catering Corps and the Postal and Courier Services of the Royal Engineers. Tableaux depict scenes from the Crimea to Northern Ireland. *Open Mon–Fri 10.00–16.00 and Sat 10.00–15.00. Closed Sun and B Hols.* Free.

Basingstoke Canal Museum Mytchett Place Road, Mytchett (01252 370073). Visitor centre with an exhibition showing 200 years of canal history. Model of a barge cabin and a reconstruction of the Greywell Tunnel. Shop. *Summer boat trips (Easter–Sep weekends 11.30– 17.00 and Tue–Sun during school holidays)*, picnic facilities, camping, caravanning. Tearoom *(summer only)*. Visitor Centre *open summer, Tue–Sun and B Hols 10.30–17.00; winter Tue–Fri 10.30–16.30.* Charge.

● **Ash and Ash Vale**
Surrey. PO, tel, stores. Villages which are now enclosed by the sprawl of Aldershot. St Peter's Church, Ash, is early medieval and retains a Norman window, a finely detailed south door, c.1200 and a 17th-C wooden font.

Army Medical Services Museum Keogh Barracks, Ash Vale (01252 340320). East of Mytchett Lake. The achievements of the army medical services in war and peace – see the Duke of Wellington's hearing aids, Napoleon's dental instruments, and branding and flogging equipment which was used on soldiers. Fine medal collection. Undergoing redevelopment. *Open Mon–Fri 10.00–15.30.* Free.

Queen Alexandra's Royal Army Nursing Corps Museum Keogh Barracks, Ash Vale (01252 340294). The history of army nursing from Florence Nightingale to the Gulf War conflict. Photographs, diaries, albums and scrapbooks. Shop. *Telephone for opening times.*

Lakeside Park Parks and Countryside Division (01483 444705). Gravel extraction during the 1950s created the fine landscape of lakes and woods we see today. Remnants of the original field system still remain, and common spotted and bee orchids flower annually. Dragonflies are prolific during the summer months, and on warm evenings bats can be seen.

● **Farnborough**
Hants. All shops and services (but they are some distance north of the canal). A name synonymous with the famous biennial air show *(see below)*, Farnborough is now just a northerly extension of Aldershot, the original village having been

engulfed by light industry, housing and the military. Almost 2 miles north of Wharf Bridge is St Peter's Church, dating from around 1200, with a wooden porch and weatherboarded tower. A short walk further north of this is Farnborough Hill, the former home of the Empress Eugenie, wife of Napoleon III of France, from the time of her exile to England in 1871 until her death in 1920. The building is now a convent school but is occasionally open to the public *(see* below for details). The Empress built an extravagantly French mausoleum for her husband, her son and herself in 1871, as well as an abbey, known as St Michael's, now occupied by English Benedictine monks.

DERA Farnborough. This aerodrome was set up in 1905 as His Majesty's Balloon Factory. The American showman, Samuel Cody, and a Red Indian friend, made the first powered flight in Britain at Laffan's Plain, Farnborough, in 1908, when Cody was Chief Kiting Instructor at the Balloon School here. Cody died in an air crash in 1913. During the two World Wars extensive research into developing military aircraft was carried out at the airfield, and this continues today, although it has now broadened into the sphere of civil aviation. Much of the design and development work on *Concorde* was executed here. The world-famous Farnborough Air Show is held here biennially in *September,* and attracts over 200,000 visitors with its static exhibitions and dramatic flying displays. Considering the orientation of the main runway, you should get a good view from the canal.

Farnborough Hill Farnborough Road (01252 545197;www.farnborough-hill.org.uk). A mid-Victorian Gothic house, completed in 1863, and once home to Empress Eugenie, the wife of Napoleon III. It is now an independent girls' school. *Open Aug Mon, Wed and Fri. Tours at 14.30, 15.30 and 16.30.* Charge.

● **Aldershot**
Hants. All shops and services, cinema and theatre (but some distance south of the canal). In 1854 the army bought 10,000 acres of heathland surrounding the rural hamlet of Aldershot, bringing building materials on the Basingstoke Canal and descending upon the area in force. It has never been the same since. In spite of a great deal of redevelopment it is still, for the most part, an uninspiring place, with the military being all pervasive. What is left of the original village, and it is not much, is to the south east of the station. The spectacular biennial army display, held in *June,* attracts over 250,000 visitors.

The Parachute Regiment & Airborne Forces Museum Browning Barracks, Alison Road, Aldershot (01252 349619). Smaller exhibits include briefing models; outside there is a Dakota aircraft and various guns spanning the period from Arnhem to Suez and the Falklands. *Open daily 10.00–16.30.* Charge.
Aldershot Military Museum Queen's Avenue, Aldershot (01252 314598). North of Queen's Avenue Bridge. Military history spanning 130 years, including a Victorian barrack room, photographs, models and personal mementoes. Armoured vehicles and guns outside. Also the history of Aldershot. *Open Mon–Sat 10.00–17.00.* Charge. Shop.

Army School of Physical Training Museum Fox Lines, Queens Avenue, Aldershot (01252 347168). Records, equipment, medals and history of the corps since its inaugural course held at Oxford University in 1860. *Open Mon–Fri 09.00–16.30, Sat 09.00–12.30.* Free.
Princes Hall Barrack Road, Aldershot (01252 329155). Theatre, concerts, wrestling and other events.
West End Centre Queens Road, Aldershot (01252 330040; www.andco.co.uk/westend). Comedy, music, jazz, theatre and other events.
Tourist Information Centre 35-39 High Street, Aldershot (01252 320968).

BOAT TRIPS

Merlin Buffet cruises for parties up to 40, operating from the Canal Centre, Mytchett. Also celebration cruises, cream tea cruises and private charter. Booking essential. For further details telephone (01252) 378779.

Daydream provides skippered trips for up to a day's duration for small groups. Operates from the Canal Centre, Mytchett. Details as above.

Astra Self-drive day hire (or skippered) for small groups. Details as above.

Pubs and Restaurants

▯ ✕ **The King's Head** Old Guildford Road, Frimley Green, Camberley (01252 835431). By King's Head Bridge, Frimley Green. A Harvester restaurant with a large garden. Food (V) such as spit roast chicken and smoked ribs *L and E, daily.*

▯ **The Rose & Thistle** 1 Sturt Road, Frimley Green (01252 834942). West of the King's Head overlooking the village green. Real ale, good choice of wine and Belgian beers. Meals (V) *L and E.* No-smoking conservatory. Garden and patio.

▯ **The Old Wheatsheaf** 205 Frimley Green Road (01252 835074). South of the Rose & Thistle along A321. Traditional village local with panelled alcoves. Real ale. Home-made food (V) *L and E (not Sun and Mon E).* Outside seating on patio. Skittle alley and traditional pub games. *Open all day Sat.*

✕ **Canal Centre Tearooms** Visitor Centre, Mychett Place Road, Mychett (01252 370073). Friendly, welcoming establishment. Inexpensive and enticing array of home-baked cakes and light meals (V). Tea, coffee, soft drinks and ice creams. Garden. *Open as for the visitor centre – see page 18.*

▯ ✕ **Potters Steak House** Mytchett Place Road, Camberley (01252 513934). Above Mytchett Place Bridge. Large pub with garden overlooking the canal. Real ale. Bar snacks and restaurant (V) *L and E.* Public slipway in garden and good off-line moorings. *Slipway users must park their cars at the Canal Centre opposite.*

▯ **The Swan** Heath Vale Bridge Road, Ash Vale (01252 325212). At Heathvale Bridge. Warm, welcoming, candle-lit Victorian-style pub with three log fires. Real ale. Meals (V), including fresh fish and autumn and winter game, *all day.* Canalside garden. Children welcome *until late evening. Open all day.*

✕ ▯ **Ashram Tandoori** 2 Wharf Road, Ash Hill (01252 313638). By Ash Wharf Bridge. Indian food *Tue–Sun E.*

▯ ✕ **Standard of England** 158 Ash Hill Road, Ash Hill (01252 325539; judithdickinson@cs.com). East of Ash Wharf Bridge. Friendly local. Real ale. Extensive range of inexpensive food (V) *L and E.* Children welcome. Garden and patio seating. Darts, dominoes and crib. Music and karaoke *Fri and Sat.*

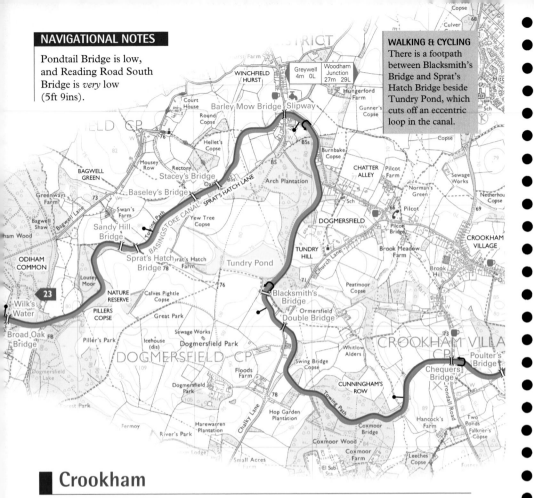

NAVIGATIONAL NOTES

Pondtail Bridge is low, and Reading Road South Bridge is *very* low (5ft 9ins).

WALKING & CYCLING
There is a footpath between Blacksmith's Bridge and Sprat's Hatch Bridge beside Tundry Pond, which cuts off an eccentric loop in the canal.

Crookham

The course of the navigation is now rural and isolated and, notwithstanding all the military presence, approaches Fleet in a richly wooded cutting through Pyestock Hill. There is an excellent licensed supermarket at Pondtail Bridges, selling fresh meat and vegetables as well as the usual things – this marks the eastern extremity of Fleet. Houses and gardens back on to the canal and generally seem to appreciate it being there. A canoe slalom course is marked out (slow down and take care) and there are some moored craft. Shops are close at hand to the north west of Reading Road South Bridge. Between Chequers and Double Bridges old World War II anti-tank barriers still stand by the waterway, and pill-box defences can be seen gently crumbling away in the undergrowth.

- **Fleet**
  Hants. All services. Useful for its shops and services, but little else of interest.
  Tourist Information Centre The Harlington Centre, 236 Fleet Road, Fleet (01252 811151).
- **Crookham Village**
  Hants. PO, stores.

- **Dogmersfield**
  Hants. A well-preserved village with pretty thatched and timbered houses.
- **Winchfield**
  Hants. Walk north from Barley Mow Bridge to see the church of St Mary, a Norman building dating from c.1170. There are three original windows in the tower, and boldly decorated doorways.

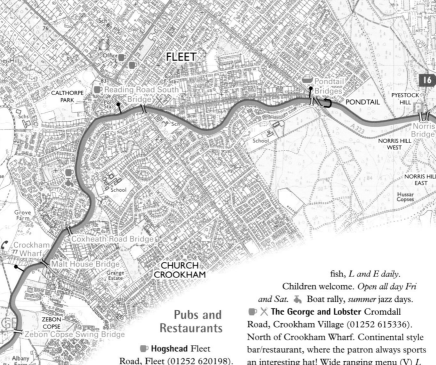

Pubs and Restaurants

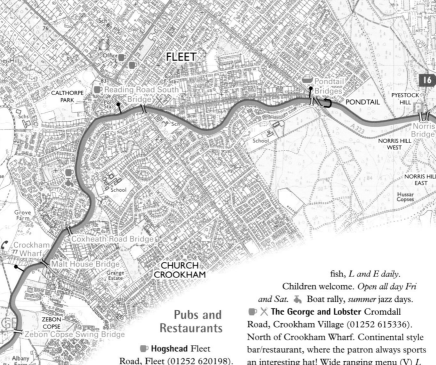 **Hogshead** Fleet Road, Fleet (01252 620198). Large variety of real ales, beers and ciders available in this committed beer drinkers pub. Bar food (V) available *all day.*

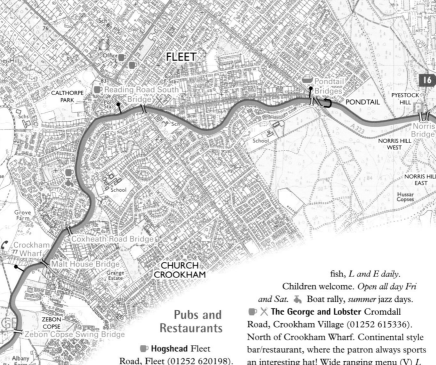 **Old Emporium** Fleet Road, Fleet (01252 816797). Young persons pub, described as an Ale Café. Real ale. Interesting selection of snacks and bar meals (V) *all day.* Garden and patio seating.

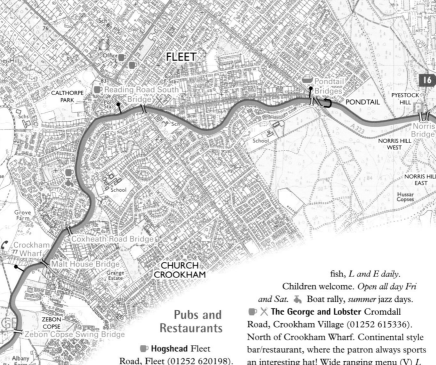 **The Oatsheaf** Crookham Road, Fleet (01252 819508). Large main road pub at the Oatsheaf crossroads, north of Reading Road South Bridge. Real ale and meals (V) *all day.* Large garden. Quiz *Tue and Sun.*

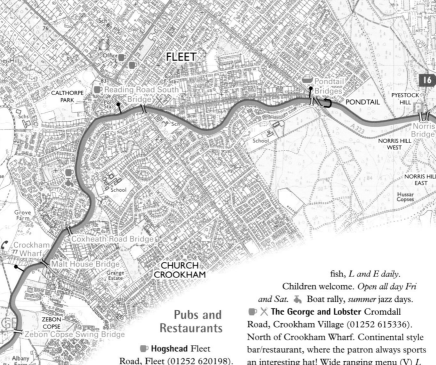 **The Fox & Hounds** Crookham Road, Crookham (01252 615980; www.foxandhoundschurchcrookham.co.uk). Friendly pub with large canalside garden and landing stage. Real ale. Menu (V) includes fresh fish, *L and E daily.* Children welcome. *Open all day Fri and Sat.* Boat rally, *summer* jazz days.

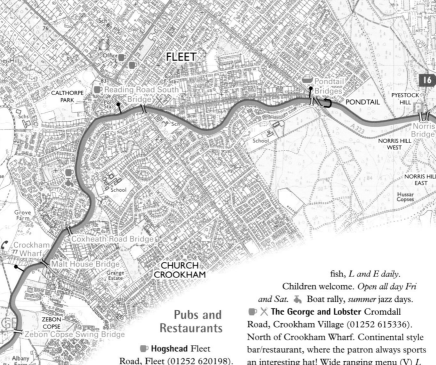 ✕ **The George and Lobster** Cromdall Road, Crookham Village (01252 615336). North of Crookham Wharf. Continental style bar/restaurant, where the patron always sports an interesting hat! Wide ranging menu (V) *L and E*, fresh fish always available. Children welcome. Garden and patio. *Closed Tue.*

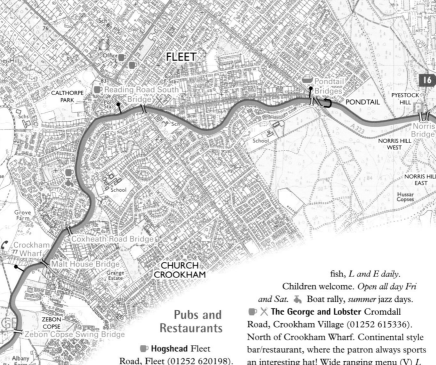 **The Black Horse** The Street, Crookham Village (01252 616434). Beamy village local. Real ale. Inexpensive bar meals (you could try the 'Dustbin Omelette') (V) *L Mon–Sat.* Children welcome *L.* Garden with Wendy house.

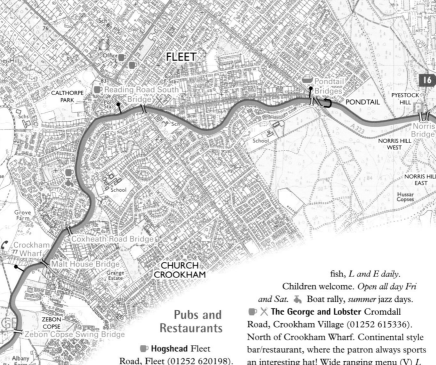 **The Queen's Head** Dogmersfield (01252 613531). Fine 17th-C country pub, where Catherine of Aragon met Arthur, Henry VIII's brother. Real ale. Extensive range of meals (V) *L and E.* Children welcome. Patio and large garden.

 ✕ **The Barley Mow** The Hurst, Winchfield (01252 617490; cbarleymow@aol.com). Large country pub, with an intriguing central fireplace. Meals (V) *L and E (not Sun E).* Garden. The home of the local cricket team.

BOAT TRIPS
Canoeing: Basingstoke Canal Canoe Club Fleet. A type of boating very popular on this canal.
North East Hants Water Activity Centre Fleet. Canoeing for the disabled with specially adapted boats and hoists as required.
Details of both the above from The Canal Centre (01252 370073).

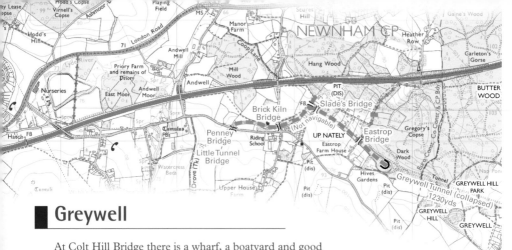

Greywell

At Colt Hill Bridge there is a wharf, a boatyard and good moorings. The course of the canal now becomes more open as it makes its approach to Greywell Tunnel. The few houses and gardens of North Warnborough are followed by a lift bridge, beyond which is the limit of navigation for cruisers, by Odiham Castle. The last commercial boat reached Odiham in 1916. It is then just a short walk to the eastern portal of the collapsed Greywell Tunnel (1230yds), passing the remains of Lock 30. This was built to raise the water level above here by 12ins, to give increased draught and aid navigation. A footpath leads over the tunnel portal to Greywell village, and the Fox & Goose pub. It is possible to follow rough paths over Greywell Hill to see what remains of the western entrance to the tunnel and a short isolated stretch of the canal passing the village of Up Nately. Greywell Tunnel is well known for its colony of some 12,500 bats, including the largest known colony of Natterer's bats.

NAVIGATIONAL NOTES

1 The lift bridge at North Warnborough is operated with a BW key.
2 The limit of navigation is a few yards beyond Odiham Castle. Do not attempt to take your boat any further than this. *Turn here.*

TRIP BOATS

John Pinkerton This is a 50-seater boat operated by the S & HCS for public trips and private charter *Easter–Oct*. Telephone (01962) 713564 for details.
Dawn is a 12-seater dayboat with toilets, heating, tea-making facilities, a lift and power-assisted steering, able to take up to six wheelchairs, designed for the disabled and based at Odiham. Bookings and further details on (01252) 622520/683778.

WALKING & CYCLING

The path over Greywell Hill connects with other footpaths through Butter Wood. You can, if you wish, make a circular route back to Warnborough Green, where there are a couple of pubs.

Boatyards

Ⓑ **Galleon Marine** Colt Hill Bridge, Odiham (01256 703691; galleonmarine@hotmail.com).
🚿 🚽 ♿ D Pump out, gas, narrowboat hire, day hire craft, overnight mooring (by arrangement), winter storage, slipway, boat sales and repairs, engine sales and repairs, chandlery, books, maps and gifts, solid fuel, ice cream. Hire of rowing boats, canoes and punts by the hour, or longer.
Madame Butterfly This is a 7-berth, 63ft long, broad beam craft, fitted with wheelchair lifts fore and aft and available for holidays – the minimum hire is 4 days. Based at Odiham. Bookings and further details on (01252) 622520/683778.

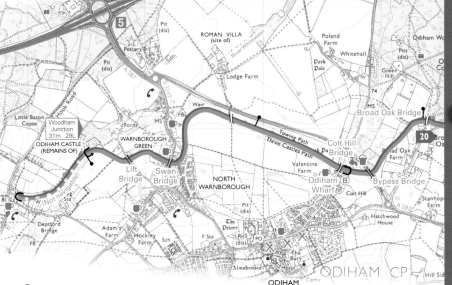

● **Odiham**
Hants. PO, tel, stores, butcher, off-licence, take-aways, chemist, bakery. It's a pleasant walk up the road from Colt Hill Bridge, past May's Model Cottages (1862) to the broad High Street, rich with 17th- and 18th-C buildings.

● **North Warnborough**
Hants. A group of attractive houses, some thatched and dating from the 15th C. There is no church, the village being virtually an extension of Odiham.

Odiham (King John's) Castle
Dating from 1207, this picturesque pile of flint is all that remains of the only octagonal keep in England, a three-storeyed building used by King John as a stopping place between Windsor and Winchester.

● **Greywell**
Hants. A village of charming red-brick houses around the pub and tunnel entrance.

Pubs and Restaurants

⬤ ✕ **The Water Witch** Colt Hill Bridge, London Road, Odiham (01256 702778). Comfortable beamed pub with rustic bar decorated with canal artefacts. Vast waterside garden with children's play area. Real ale together with excellent food (V) *L and E.* Children welcome when dining. *Open all day in Summer.*

✕ ♀ **The Kings** 65 High Street, Odiham (01256 702559/703811). Smart restaurant in converted pub, serving Peking and Szechuan cuisine – not cheap, but good value *L and E (closed Sun and Mon L).* Takeaway service.

✕ ♀ **La Forêt** High Street, Odiham (01256 702697). Family-run restaurant specialising in French and modern European cuisine using only fresh produce, bought in daily. *Open L Mon–Fri and E Mon–Sat (closed Sun).* Children's menu.

⬤ ✕ **The George Hotel** High Street, Odiham (01256 702081; www.georgehotelodiham.com). Handsome 16th-C hotel with a Georgian façade. Inside are beams and an Elizabethan fireplace taken from Old Basing House. Bar food (V) and real ale. Restaurant specialising in seafood, *L*

and E. Patio garden and orchard. Café/bar next door.

✕ ♀ **Grapevine Bistro & Restaurant** 77 High Street, Odiham (01256 701122; info@ grapevine-gourmet.com). Organic produce, fresh bread and vegetables daily, cheeses and ready meals (V) and children's portions. *L Mon–Fri and E Mon–Sat.* Bargain meals *18.00–19.00.* No dogs.

⬤ ✕ **The Swan** Swan Bridge, North Warnborough (01256 702727). Dark, cosy local dating from the 16th C. Real ale. Varied menu (V) of home-made food, *L and E.* Garden. Children welcome. *Open all day.*

⬤ **The Anchor** The Street, North Warnborough. (01256 702740). Cheerful 18th-C village pub. Real ale. Inexpensive meals *L and E (not Mon L). Sat* is Burger Night. Live music once a month. *Open all day Fri and Sat.*

⬤ **The Fox & Goose** The Street, Greywell (01256 702062). Comfortable 16th-C country pub with two open fires. Real ale. Meals (V), including game in season, *L and E.* Large garden with play area. Children welcome.

▌BRIDGWATER & TAUNTON CANAL

MAXIMUM DIMENSIONS	MILEAGE
Length: 50'	*TAUNTON* Firepool Lock to:
Beam: 9' 10"	Creech St Michael: 3 miles
Headroom: 5' 6"	Durston: 6 miles
Draught: 2' 6"	North Newton: 8 miles
	BRIDGWATER DOCK: 14 miles
MANAGER	
01873 830328	6 locks
email:	
enquiries.govilon@britishwaterways.co.uk	

The Bridgwater & Taunton Canal represents a small part of a far more ambitious scheme, the Bristol & Taunton Canal Navigation, for which Rennie gave a quotation in 1811 of no less than £429,990. This was to be part of a ship canal from Bristol to Exeter where it would join up with the long-established Exeter Ship Canal. However, although this sum was forthcoming, very little work seems to have been undertaken and instead, in 1824, an Act of Parliament was obtained to 'abridge, vary, extend and improve the Bristol & Taunton Canal Navigation', which resulted in the much briefer line between the River Parrett at Huntworth (just south of Bridgwater) and Taunton being adopted. The ship canal scheme was abandoned. Although the total cost of the canal on its opening was £71,000, toll receipts in the early days averaged £7,000 per year; most of this, however, was drawn from traffic passing to and from the Chard and Grand Western canals which the Bridgwater & Taunton Canal joined at Creech St Michael and Taunton respectively.

The size of the locks was unorthodox at 54'x13' with a theoretical draught of 3' 0", which meant a normal craft load of 22 tons. The distance as originally constituted from Firepool Lock, Taunton, to Huntworth was 13$^{1}/_{2}$ miles. Prior to the building of the Bridgwater & Taunton Canal, there already existed a navigation of sorts on the rivers Parrett and Tone (i.e. an alternative route between Taunton and Bridgwater). This route suffered from drought in summer and floods in winter and so was not particularly reliable; but it was good enough to cause the shareholders of the Bridgwater & Taunton Canal great embarrassment and they were forced to purchase the river navigation in 1832, five years after their own opening.

In 1837 a further Act was obtained authorising the extension from Huntworth to Bridgwater and the building of the dock and its entrance lock from the River Parrett. This led to the curious anomaly of there being two sets of milestones in close juxtaposition. At the time of its jubilant opening on 25 March 1841, this extension had cost fully £175,000, leaving the proprietors badly out of pocket when the whole waterway and dock complex was sold to the Bristol and Exeter Railway Company for £64,000 in 1866. When control of the waterway eventually passed to the Great Western Railway, little attempt was made to maintain commercial traffic and the last barge tolls were collected in 1907.

In 1940, at the behest of the War Office, the Bridgwater & Taunton Canal, like the Kennet & Avon, was turned into a line of defence against the possibility of enemy invasion and pill boxes were erected at strategic points along it. The bridges were fixed and strengthened to carry military vehicles.

Little interest was shown in the waterway after nationalisation in 1947, although the Bridgwater Docks continued to operate under the Railway Executive of the British Transport Commission. In 1958 the Bowes Committee Report on waterways put the canal into category 'C', i.e. suitable for redevelopment, and various surveys were carried out, seemingly without any concrete results. The canal passed to the British Waterways Board (as was) in 1963 but Bridgwater Docks remained in Railways Board ownership. In the meantime the south western branch of the Inland Waterways Association had begun to consider the canal in terms of restoration and in 1965 the Bridgwater & Taunton Canal Restoration Group was formed. A year later this group became the Somerset Inland Waterways Society, which was formed to work towards restoration of the canal for amenity purposes. A subsequent arrangement negotiated by BWB allowed for the extraction of 3 million gallons of water a day from the canal, to provide much needed revenue. Eventually a partnership between Somerset County Council and British Waterways, encouraged by the Inland Waterways Society, saw full restoration of the navigation and it was opened throughout in 1994. Bridgwater Docks have been developed into a marina, surrounded by new housing, shops and a pub.

*Bridgwater Docks (*see *page 30)*

Bridgwater & Taunton Canal Introduction

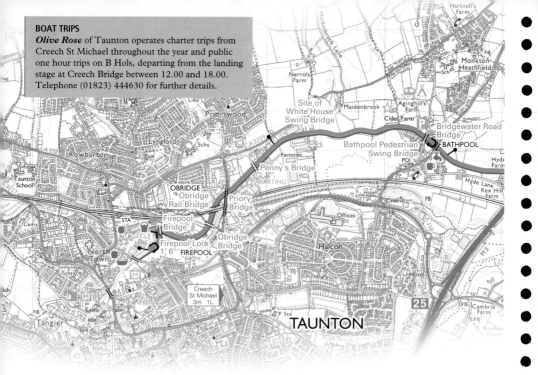

BOAT TRIPS
Olive Rose of Taunton operates charter trips from Creech St Michael throughout the year and public one hour trips on B Hols, departing from the landing stage at Creech Bridge between 12.00 and 18.00. Telephone (01823) 444630 for further details.

Taunton

The Bridgwater & Taunton Canal runs through attractive rolling scenery, typical of rural Somerset. It starts at Firepool Lock, at a junction with the River Tone. In the 18th- and 19th-C the Tone, which passes through Taunton before meeting the canal, was navigable from Taunton to its junction with the River Parrett. Firepool Lock, pleasantly situated beside the Tone weir, is the first stage of the canal's north easterly journey towards Bridgwater and the estuary of the Parrett. The lock is reached from Taunton by following signs to the cattle market, or by crossing the footbridge over the Tone from the town's Firepool district, on the river's south bank. The canal curves past the railway station, passing under the main Bristol to Exeter line, which follows it closely to Bridgwater. The tall railway warehouse is built on the site of the old junction with the Grand Western Canal. Taunton is quickly left behind as the waterway continues through flat pasture land to Bathpool, where the towpath runs briefly through the churchyard of a small corrugated iron church. Bathpool Swing Bridge used to be the first obstacle to restoring the navigation east of Taunton, being one of the structures fixed closed during the invasion scare of 1940, when the War Office destroyed the swinging mechanisms on all the navigation's swing bridges. Today it operates as a pedestrian bridge only. Contrary to popular opinion, this measure was not so much to prevent navigation by German forces, as to create lines of defence along natural barriers. The Bridgwater & Taunton, like the Kennet & Avon and Basingstoke Canals, was hastily turned into a fortified line of resistance. Leaving Bathpool the country becomes hilly and more wooded and a modern housing estate accompanies the canal into Creech St Michael. Before the village is the site of the junction with the Chard Canal. There is little to be seen of the junction itself but to the south the long embankment crossing the Tone flood plain is still visible.

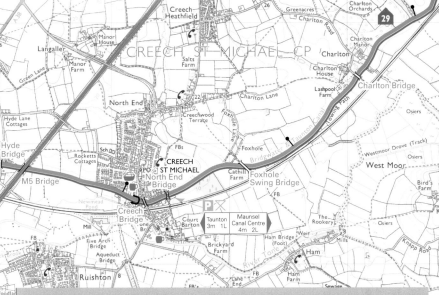

WALKING & CYCLING

This detached and often isolated waterway, just 14½ miles in length, is ideal for walking and cycling. Railway stations at each end make one-way trips possible and well sign-posted car parks along its entire length mean that 'bite-sized' chunks can be tackled by the less energetic. The Somerset Space Walk adds a unique dimension to the experience (*see* page 29 for details). In Taunton there are walkers' trails (available from the TIC) covering the town's heritage and its wealth of non-conformist chapels. For the cyclist, a range of trail guides take one further afield on a variety of interesting quests. The towpath forms part of the West Country Way, National Cycle Network Route 3, from Padstow to Bristol. Route 33 is planned to link Taunton to the South Coast Route 2 at Axminster and Seaton. The South Somerset Cycle Ride is a waymarked route around the byways of South Somerset, centred on Taunton.

NAVIGATIONAL NOTES

1 When using the locks please leave bottom gates open after use.
2 Do not tamper with the settings of the paddle gear.
3 Report any problems to BW on (01873) 830328 or phone the emergency helpline on 0800 47 999 47.
4 Slipways for the use of visiting trail boaters are located at: Bridgwater YMCA HQ (01278 422511), Bathpool Car Park, Firepool Lock, Taunton.
5 Boat licenses are available from: Bridgwater YMCA HQ, John Swayne Huntworth, Bridgwater (01278 662188); Maunsel Canal Centre (01278 663160).
6 Beware of reduced headroom at the following bridges: O'Bridge, Whites, Dairy and Huntworth.
7 Canal wardens can be contacted on (01278) 662188.

● **Bathpool**
Somerset. Tel, garage. A straggling village, running into the outskirts of Taunton, much improved by severe traffic calming measures.
Creech St Michael
● *Somerset. PO, tel, stores, garage.* Although now surrounded by modern housing, the old part of the village still survives. The largely 13th-C church is a sturdy and attractive building; inside there are fine waggon roofs.

● **Chard Canal**
The Chard Canal was one of the last to be built in England and was one of the shortest-lived of all canals. Work began in 1835 and the 13½ mile line to Chard from Creech St Michael on the Bridgwater & Taunton Canal was opened in 1842. The canal included three tunnels, two major aqueducts, two locks and four inclined planes. It suffered from immediate railway competition and never made any

money. Bought by the Bristol and Exeter Railway Company in 1867, it closed down the next year. It is possible to follow the line of the canal on foot, although there are few rights of way that correspond with its original bed.

Taunton

Somerset. All services. Taunton has long been a rich agricultural market town and an important point on the old trunk route to the West Country. The skyline is dominated by the towers of the churches of St Mary Magdalene and St James. The first, rebuilt in 1862, is 163ft high; its ornamental splendour rather dwarfs the double aisled church. In Middle Street there is an octagonal 18th-C Methodist chapel. Wesley preached here when it was opened. The centre of the town contains an interesting mixture of buildings; 15th-C municipal buildings, the 18th-C Market House, the Victorian Shire Hall and the 20th-C County Hall. Remains of the medieval town can be seen, including fragments of the 13th-C priory.

Brewhouse Theatre and Arts Centre Coal Orchard, Taunton (01823 283244; brewhouse@btconnect.com). Entertainment including folk, comedy, classical music, dance and drama. Box office *open Mon–Sat 10.00–20.00 (18.00 on non-performance nights)*. Restaurant *open on performance nights.*

Chapels in Taunton It was observed in the 17th C that Taunton was 'the vineyard of the Lord of Hosts and the inhabitants his precious plants'. A trail around the town's chapels has been laid out

and a leaflet is available from the TIC in Paul Street, where non-conformity was founded in 1662. Less local trails are also available from the TIC and depict such oddities as Towers & Hunkypunks and Bench Ends & Pulpits.

Cycle Hire Bike Park Coal Orchard, Taunton (01823 365917). Showers, cycle lockers and all types of bicycle hire.

Farmers Market Taunton. *Held on last Thur of month, 09.00–16.00,* in the centre of the town.

Somerset County Museum Castle Green, Taunton (01823 320201; www.somerset.gov.uk/museums). The museum displays artefacts from pre-historic and Roman Somerset together with fine collections of ceramics, glass, silver, toys and dolls. Also fossils, minerals, medieval almshouse and depictions of the Somerset Light Infantry. Shop. Charge.

Somerset Cricket Museum 7 Priory Avenue, Taunton (01823 275893). Memorabilia from the Somerset County Cricket Club, bat making demonstrations, cricket shop, refreshments. *Access is restricted on match days.* Charge.

Tacchi-Morris Arts Centre School Road, Taunton (01823 414141). Theatre venue offering a range of shows, workshops and classes for adults and children. Box office *open Mon–Fri 10.00–12.00 and 14.00–16.00. Also 18.30–19.30 on performance nights.* Bar and roof terrace *open daily 19.00 onwards.*

Tourist Information Centre Paul Street, Taunton (01823 336344; tautic@somerset.gov.uk).

Pubs and Restaurants

Royal Mail 78 Station Road, Taunton (01823 331567). Real ale and meals (V) served *E.* No children or dogs. Karaoke *Sat,* live music *Sun afternoon.* Pool and darts. Useful shops opposite.

Crown & Sceptre 74-76 Station Road, Taunton (01823 333384). Large, welcoming town pub serving food (V) *L and E, daily. Sunday* roasts. Children welcome. Beer garden. Regular karaoke and bands. Sports TV.

✕ Harpoon Louies 75 Station Road, Taunton (01823 324404). Seafood is the speciality of this intimate pub-cum-restaurant which only opens *E.* Real ales and cider.

Bathpool Bridgwater Road, Bathpool,

Taunton (01823 272545). Low beamed, comfortable family pub. Real ales. Home-cooked food (V) *L and E (not Sun E).* Garden, children's play area. *Open all day.*

Bell St Michael's Road, Creech St Michael, Taunton (01823 443703). Traditional village pub serving real ale. Children and dogs welcome. Darts, pool and skittle alley. Garden.

Riverside Tavern Bull Street, Creech St Michael, Taunton (01823 442257). Peaceful village pub overlooking the river, offering a friendly welcome and home-cooked food (V) *L and E (not Sun E or Mon L and E).* No children. Dogs welcome. Garden. Quiz *Sun.*

North Newton

This section is typical of the quiet agricultural nature of the whole canal. The canal is slightly raised above the land on a low embankment, with views to the north across farmland and to the south across the low-lying flood plain of the River Tone. The canal leaves the river to the south, passing through marsh and moorland. Several small agricultural hamlets flank the waterway. At Durston, where the BW maintenance yard is located, the busy A361 crosses. Beyond, the canal reaches the first lock which starts the descent to Bridgwater. The paddle gear is quite unique, composed of ball-shaped weights and chains to form a counter-balance mechanism.

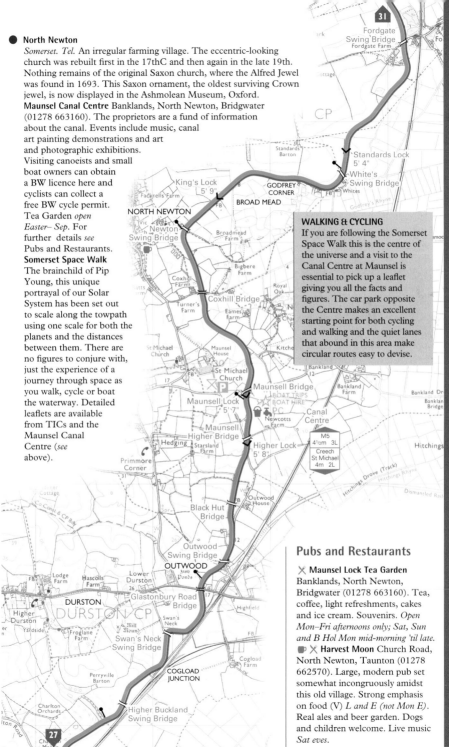

● **North Newton**
Somerset. Tel. An irregular farming village. The eccentric-looking church was rebuilt first in the 17thC and then again in the late 19th. Nothing remains of the original Saxon church, where the Alfred Jewel was found in 1693. This Saxon ornament, the oldest surviving Crown jewel, is now displayed in the Ashmolean Museum, Oxford.
Maunsel Canal Centre Banklands, North Newton, Bridgwater (01278 663160). The proprietors are a fund of information about the canal. Events include music, canal art painting demonstrations and art and photographic exhibitions. Visiting canoeists and small boat owners can obtain a BW licence here and cyclists can collect a free BW cycle permit. Tea Garden *open Easter– Sep.* For further details *see* Pubs and Restaurants.

Somerset Space Walk
The brainchild of Pip Young, this unique portrayal of our Solar System has been set out to scale along the towpath using one scale for both the planets and the distances between them. There are no figures to conjure with, just the experience of a journey through space as you walk, cycle or boat the waterway. Detailed leaflets are available from TICs and the Maunsel Canal Centre (*see* above).

WALKING & CYCLING

If you are following the Somerset Space Walk this is the centre of the universe and a visit to the Canal Centre at Maunsel is essential to pick up a leaflet giving you all the facts and figures. The car park opposite the Centre makes an excellent starting point for both cycling and walking and the quiet lanes that abound in this area make circular routes easy to devise.

Pubs and Restaurants

✕ **Maunsel Lock Tea Garden** Banklands, North Newton, Bridgwater (01278 663160). Tea, coffee, light refreshments, cakes and ice cream. Souvenirs. *Open Mon–Fri afternoons only; Sat, Sun and B Hol Mon mid-morning 'til late.*
▪ ✕ **Harvest Moon** Church Road, North Newton, Taunton (01278 662570). Large, modern pub set somewhat incongruously amidst this old village. Strong emphasis on food (V) *L and E (not Mon E)*. Real ales and beer garden. Dogs and children welcome. Live music *Sat eves.*

Bridgwater

Following the contours of the land, the waterway continues northwards towards Bridgwater. To the west, low hills rise gradually away from the canal; to the east low-lying farm and marsh land separates the navigation from the River Parrett. This tidal river, a vital drain for the whole area, swings ever nearer to the canal as they approach Bridgwater. To the east the railway line stays close to the navigation until just before Bridgwater, when it turns away to pass east of the town. The course of the waterway is quiet and isolated. There are no villages near the canal, although there is easy access for Fordgate and Huntworth. Standard's Lock drops the navigation to the Bridgwater level. Nearing the town civilisation returns with a vengeance as traffic roars overhead on the M5. After the motorway the towpath crosses to the west and the canal enters Bridgwater. South of Taunton Road Bridge there is a useful parade of shops including PO, laundrette and take away; to the north, there is a large supermarket. The waterway passes through the town in a cutting, swinging in a wide arc to the west before turning back to the docks and the junction with the Parrett estuary. Access to the town is easy from the many bridges. The canal enters the dock through a stop lock which passes it into the large inner basin, laid out marina-fashion with floating pontoons. Toilets and showers are available in the Bonded Warehouse, now converted into flats. The smaller outer basin is entered through a twin-bascular lift bridge and then a ship lock and a canal lock used to allow access to the River Parrett and thus the sea. The river locks have been replaced with concrete barriers and so the Bridgwater & Taunton Canal remains just that: an isolated navigation linking its two eponymous towns and nothing else.

● **Bridgwater**
Somerset. All services. Bridgwater is an old market town straddling the River Parrett. Formerly the town was an important centre for the cloth trade, which encouraged development of the port from the Middle Ages onwards. The old quay, despite redevelopment, still has an attractive 18th-C flavour. It suffered severely during the Civil War and, in an artillery bombardment in July 1645, lost the greater part of its commercial and domestic buildings, many of which were of timber-frame construction. Elsewhere in the town are signs of 18th-C wealth: the handsome houses in Castle Street, built c.1725, were sponsored by James Bridges, first Duke of Chances. Little of the medieval town survives. The 13th-C castle was destroyed by the Roundheads as a reprisal for the town's resistance. The watergate, on the west quay, is the only remaining relic of the castle and has a wall 12ft thick. Glass-making briefly flourished in the town when, in 1725, James Bridges built the 125ft Chandos Glass Cone. The venture failed within nine years and the cone, built from rubble from the derelict castle, was converted first to brick making and then to tile manufacture, only closing down during World War II.

Battle of Sedgemoor, 6 July 1685 When Charles II died, he was succeeded by his brother, James II, unpopular due to his Catholic faith. The Duke of Monmouth, an illegitimate son of Charles II, declared himself king in 1685 in Bridgwater. He landed at Lyme with a few supporters and soon raised an army 4000 strong, including 800 horsemen under Lord Grey. They moved to Bridgwater, while a Royalist army commanded by Lord Feversham and John Churchill (later the Duke of Marlborough) camped near Westonzoyland, 3 miles east of the town. Monmouth decided on a night attack but lost the element of surprise when caught crossing the Langmoor Rhine, one of the many drainage ditches in the area. A fierce battle broke out in which the artillery played a dominant part. Grey's cavalry tried to outflank Feversham but were prevented by the Bussex Rhine, another deep ditch. Although firing continued all night, Monmouth's cause was already lost. The leaders of the rebellion escaped for a while but the ill-armed rebel army was rounded up, many to be transported or executed on the orders of Judge Jeffreys. To find the site of the battle take the A372 east from Bridgwater; turn left in Westonzoyland. There are signs to the Sedgemoor Memorial Stone.

Admiral Blake Museum Blake Street, Bridgwater (01278 456127; www.somerset.gov.uk/muse-ums). Robert Blake was born in Bridgwater in 1598 and represented the town as a Member of Parliament. After a distinguished army career he

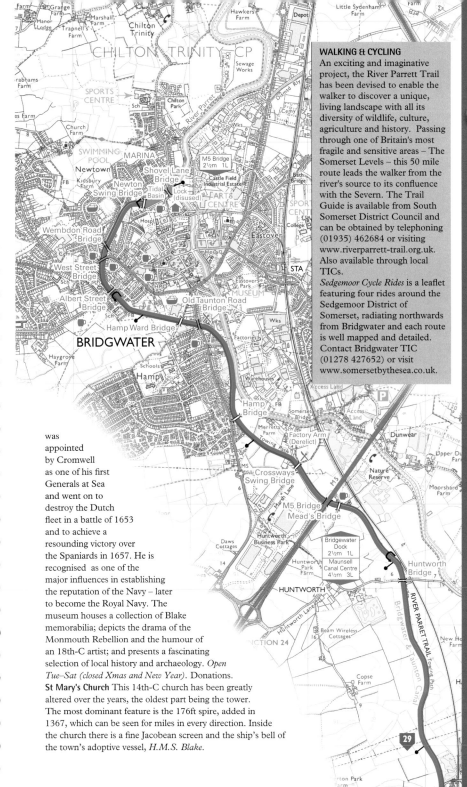

WALKING & CYCLING

An exciting and imaginative project, the River Parrett Trail has been devised to enable the walker to discover a unique, living landscape with all its diversity of wildlife, culture, agriculture and history. Passing through one of Britain's most fragile and sensitive areas – The Somerset Levels – this 50 mile route leads the walker from the river's source to its confluence with the Severn. The Trail Guide is available from South Somerset District Council and can be obtained by telephoning (01935) 462684 or visiting www.riverparrett-trail.org.uk. Also available through local TICs.

Sedgemoor Cycle Rides is a leaflet featuring four rides around the Sedgemoor District of Somerset, radiating northwards from Bridgwater and each route is well mapped and detailed. Contact Bridgwater TIC (01278 427652) or visit www.somersetbythesea.co.uk.

was appointed by Cromwell as one of his first Generals at Sea and went on to destroy the Dutch fleet in a battle of 1653 and to achieve a resounding victory over the Spaniards in 1657. He is recognised as one of the major influences in establishing the reputation of the Navy – later to become the Royal Navy. The museum houses a collection of Blake memorabilia; depicts the drama of the Monmouth Rebellion and the humour of an 18th-C artist; and presents a fascinating selection of local history and archaeology. *Open Tue–Sat (closed Xmas and New Year)*. Donations.

St Mary's Church This 14th-C church has been greatly altered over the years, the oldest part being the tower. The most dominant feature is the 176ft spire, added in 1367, which can be seen for miles in every direction. Inside the church there is a fine Jacobean screen and the ship's bell of the town's adoptive vessel, *H.M.S. Blake*.

Sedgemoor Splash Mount Street, Bridgwater (01278 425636; commercial.services@sedgemoor.gov.uk). Thriving leisure centre swimming pool. *Open daily.* Telephone for further details.

Somerset Brick and Tile Museum East Quay, Bridgwater (01823 320200; www.somerset.gov.uk/museums). The last surviving brick kiln at the former Barham Brothers brickyard – a poignant reminder of an industry which once dominated the area. Exhibits about the history of the industry alongside a workshop demonstrating brick and tile making processes. *Open Thur–Fri 09.00–12.30 and 13.00–16.00.* Shop. Donations.

Westonzoyland Pumping Station Museum of Steam Power and Land Drainage Westonzoyland, Bridgwater (01823 275795; wzlet@btinternet.com). A display of pumping engines, both static and in steam, housed in old pumping station buildings dating from the 1830s. *Open as a static display Sun 14.00–17.00 and Thur Jun–Aug 14.00–20.00. In steam first Sun in month; every B Hol Sun–Mon (except Xmas and Boxing Day); New Year's Day 14.00–17.00.* Shop and tearoom. Charge.

Tourist Information Centre 50 High Street, Bridgwater (01278 427652; bridgwater.tic@sedgemoor.gov.uk). *Open Mon–Sat Easter–Nov and Mon, Wed, Fri in winter.*

BOAT TRIPS

Peggotytom I is a 40-seat narrowboat operating charter trips from the YMCA in Bridgwater. *Peggotytom II* is a 5-berth narrowboat available for hire and based in Bridgwater Docks. For further details about both boats telephone (07778) 750974 or (01278) 451523 (answerphone).

Pubs and Restaurants

Boat & Anchor Huntworth, Bridgwater (01278 662473). Six separate cottages, now all knocked into one, this pub serves home-cooked food (V) – specialising in fresh fish – *L and E daily.* Real ales and *Sunday* Carvery. Children and dogs welcome. Large canalside garden. Mooring. B & B.

Hope Inn 82 Taunton Road, Bridgwater (01278 424239). Home-made pub grub (V) *L and E (not Tue)* and real ales served in a town pub. Children and dogs welcome. Outside courtyard. Pool, darts and skittles. *Monthly* music/disco.

Korean BBQ The Acorns Lodge Hotel, 61 Taunton Road, Bridgwater (01278 445577). Korean Restaurant serving à la carte and set meals (V) *E.* Beside Taunton Road Bridge.

Horse and Jockey 1 Durleigh Road, Bridgwater (01278 424283). Plush, newly refurbished establishment beside the racecourse, serving real ale and food *L and E.* Quiz *first Sun in month.* Regular live music. Darts etc.

Green Dragon 84 Friarn Street, Bridgwater (01278 446936). Reputed to be the oldest pub in town. No dogs, real ale, food, children or garden but the friendliest landlord and locals you are ever likely to meet. Darts and pool.

Annie's Bar 21 North Street, Bridgwater (01278 433053). Atmospheric café/bar with a wealth of exposed beams and stonework, old world decoration and artefacts galore, and no machine. Excellent food (V) *L and E (not Mon–Wed L)* from a European, bistro style menu. Real ales. No children or dogs. Large garden and fish pond. *Monthly* jazz evenings.

Maltshovel 2 Wembdon Road, Bridgwater (01278 422496). Real ale and inexpensive pub grub (V) served *L and E (not Tue E).* Children welcome. Beer garden. Live music *twice a month.* Darts and pool.

Old Market 8 Penel Orlieu, Bridgwater (01278 424944). Varied pub food (V) with a Mexican leaning served *L and E, daily.* Children welcome *during day* if eating. Patio. *Weekend* discos. Skittles, pool, darts and big screen TV.

Old Vicarage Hotel and Restaurant 45–51 St Mary Street, Bridgwater (01278 445297; oldvicaragehotel@aol.com). Charming old establishment opposite the church serving fresh, locally grown food (V), flavoured with their own organically grown herbs. Inexpensive two course set menu. À la carte menu *L and E.*

Admiral's Landing The Docks, Bridgwater (01278 422515). Real ales and food (V) served *L and E (not Sun E)* in an old warehouse, latterly used as a mushroom factory. Children welcome if dining. Dockside seating.

British Flag 77–83 Chilton Street, Bridgwater (01278 422537). Real ales and food (V) served *L and E.* Children and dogs welcome. Large garden. Pool, darts, skittles.

GRAND WESTERN CANAL

MAXIMUM DIMENSIONS

As there are no locks on this navigation the following measurements refer to the overall canal dimensions.

Length: Unlimited
Width: 40' except Waytown Tunnel: 12'
Draught: variable between 2' and 5'
Headroom: 7'

Realistically boats with a beam greater than 7' should not try to navigate throughout this waterway.

Powered craft are only permitted to use the section between Tiverton Basin and Fossend Bridge, Burlescombe. Unpowered craft may navigate the entire waterway.

Permits are required for all boat use and may be obtained from:

Canal Ranger's Office
The Moorings, Canal Hill,
Tiverton, Devon
EX16 4HX
01884 254072; gwcanal@devon.gov.uk

MILEAGE

Tiverton to:
Halberton: 2 miles
Sampford Peverell: $5^1/2$ miles
Ayshford: 8 miles
Lowdwells: $10^1/2$ miles

Originally conceived as part of a proposal to link the English and Bristol Channels, the Grand Western Canal was to run from Taunton to Exeter, with branches to Tiverton and Cullompton. Subsequently an expanded scheme was floated to include a canal from Bristol to Taunton, linking in with the Kennet & Avon, to give a through navigation from London to Exeter.

After much delay and conflicting advice from many engineers, including William Jessop and John Rennie, work started in 1810, on an 11-mile section which included the Tiverton branch and a small portion of the main line from Lowdwells to Burlescombe. This was completed four years later at a cost – for an entirely lock-free length – of £224,505; more than the original estimate for the entire canal. During the course of construction it had been decided to lower the planned level at Holcombe, necessitating an additional 16ft cutting, thereby setting the Tiverton branch on the summit level as a lock-free, contour canal. This was largely responsible for the considerable escalation in cost but subsequently proved beneficial to the large tonnages of limestone transported into Tiverton.

After another delay, work started on the main line in 1827. The section from Taunton to the Tiverton branch was finally opened in 1838 and included seven vertical lifts and one inclined plane: the site of the incline, at Wellisford, $1/2$ a mile north of Thorne St Margaret, can still be seen. The construction of the lifts and the inclined plane was in the hands of James Green who, at the time, was engaged in enlarging the Exeter Canal and building a terminal basin in the city. However, his work on this navigation was less than satisfactory, and he was eventually replaced by Captain John Twisden, Royal Navy retired. The canal was never completed to Exeter. It was a financial disaster, suffering from its over-ambitious engineering, together with railway competition almost from its opening day. The canal was leased to the Great Western Railway in 1854, and they gradually absorbed most of the canal traffic. The predictable pattern of minimal maintenance, coupled with an inevitable decline ensued and the main line was closed in 1867. It has largely disappeared.

However, the trade in limestone persisted and boats continued to ply between Burlescombe and Tiverton until 1924, when a major leak developed, severing the navigation into two separate sections. At this point the canal was finally abandoned as a commercial carrying enterprise.

Some 50 years later, in a joint venture with Mid Devon District Council, Devon County Council purchased the waterway and set about restoration. Today it offers an attractive, linear country park, well patronised by boaters, walkers and cyclists alike.

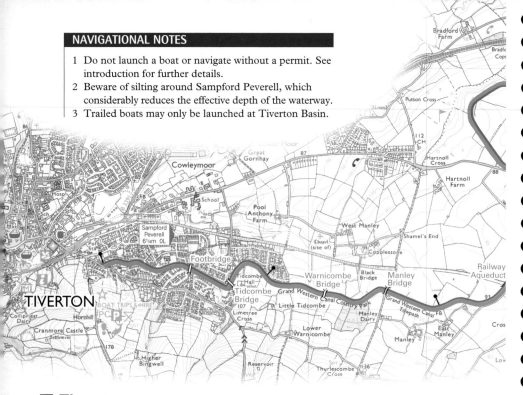

NAVIGATIONAL NOTES

1 Do not launch a boat or navigate without a permit. See introduction for further details.
2 Beware of silting around Sampford Peverell, which considerably reduces the effective depth of the waterway.
3 Trailed boats may only be launched at Tiverton Basin.

Tiverton

The canal occupies an elevated position above Tiverton and is set some way out of the town. The terminal basin is cut into the hill on the south side while to the north, limekilns form a sturdy embankment, squatting solidly beside the towpath. Positioned thus, they serve the function of retaining wall and are also ergonomically placed for direct loading from arriving tub boats. These were towed in chains of three, carrying the waterway's dominant cargo of limestone and coal; the former being burnt in the kilns to produce a soil conditioner-cum-fertiliser for the local acid soils. Nearby is a pretty thatched cottage, now a tearoom but originally the lime-burner's dwelling. Heading west out of the basin, the waterway soon wanders beyond Tiverton's suburbs before bending sharply to the north under Tidcombe Bridge. Here it skirts Tidcombe Hall, originally called Rectory House and once the home of the Bishop of Exeter. In 1810 the then incumbent refused to allow the navigation to come any nearer to the house than 100yds, hence its exaggerated course at this point. Soon all housing is left behind and the canal winds through pasture, lined by mature trees. At Manley Bridge it passes East Manley Farm, which is mentioned in the Domesday Book. More recently it was home to the Victorian Jesuit priest, Gerard Manley Hopkins. Following the road round to the north, the waterway crosses an aqueduct 40ft above the disused trackbed of the old Tiverton Junction to Tiverton line. It consists of a cast iron trough, supported by brick-encased cast iron arches, the structure being wide enough to span the original broad gauge line. At Crownhill bridge the towpath changes over to the east side of the navigation where it remains, almost to Lowdwells. Tiverton Road Bridge heralds an old wharf, now a picnic site; another sharp bend and mile marker number three. The next mile of the canal bed, running over badly fissured rock, was a constant source of leakage during the waterway's commercial usage and has now been sealed

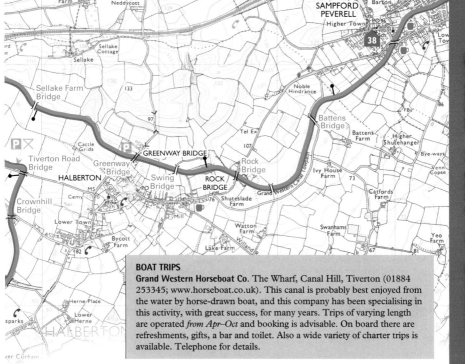

BOAT TRIPS
Grand Western Horseboat Co. The Wharf, Canal Hill, Tiverton (01884 253345; www.horseboat.co.uk). This canal is probably best enjoyed from the water by horse-drawn boat, and this company has been specialising in this activity, with great success, for many years. Trips of varying length are operated *from Apr–Oct* and booking is advisable. On board there are refreshments, gifts, a bar and toilet. Also a wide variety of charter trips is available. Telephone for details.

with an artificial membrane. Beyond, the navigation comes suddenly upon a delightful side valley, the upper side frequented by browsing deer. Then Greenway Bridge is approached, providing the best access to Halberton village. Crossing another diminutive valley, the canal runs through old sandstone quarries; these were the source of much of the material used to build the attractive bridges seen throughout the navigation. Standing beside Rock Bridge is an intriguing house built for Captain John Twisden, who completed the main line of the canal to Taunton. Complete with Doric columns and somewhat eccentric detailing, Rock House is thought to have been constructed to a design of the Captain's, along with the gardener's cottage nearby. Leading out of the cutting, the waterway now heads for Sampford Peverell – the only settlement of any significance along its length. There are fine views to the east over the Blackdown Hills.

● **Tiverton**
Devon. All services (station at Tiverton Parkway). The town grew up on a narrow spit of land between the Rivers Exe and Lowman; its name derived from Twyford, meaning two fords. The oldest part of the settlement is probably around the castle and church and the main street pattern, as seen today, would have developed beside the Exe bridge in the 14th C. By the beginning of the 13th C the town was recorded as having a market and three fairs. Throughout the Middle Ages it quietly prospered, its wealth based on the local cloth trade, becoming one of the key centres in the county by the 16th C. Few buildings from before this time remain

due to a serious of disastrous fires spanning a period 1598–1731, after which legislation was enacted decreeing that all roofs were to be of a tile, slate or lead construction. Surviving houses from the 18th and 19th C testify to the town's wealth and the Industrial Revolution was heralded by the arrival of John Heathcoat's lace factory in the town. This arrested the decline that was setting into other cloth towns in the area and brought Tiverton renewed prosperity. In the 100 years between 1790 and 1891, the population more than doubled as Heathcoat's new bobbin net lace machine placed the town at the forefront of the country's lace production. He had attempted to install this machine in a factory in Loughborough, in 1816, whereupon it was destroyed by a mob from Nottingham. His response was to move to Tiverton where, with a few skilled workers recruited from the Midlands, he established production in a closed cloth-weaving factory. Here, for the first time, water power was harnessed to lace-making machinery. Heathcoat went on to become a significant benefactor to the town, providing housing and community facilities.

Knightshayes Court Bolham, Tiverton (01884 254665; www.nt.org.uk). A house designed by William Burges combining medieval romanticism with lavish Victorian decoration in a series of rich interiors. The well-known garden features rare shrubs, fine specimen trees, a water lily pond and topiary. Woodland walks. Shop and plant centre. Licensed restaurant. House *open daily (except Fri) 11.00–17.30 Apr–Sep; daily (except Thur–Fri) 11.00–16.30, Oct.* Garden *open daily 11.00–17.30 Apr–Oct.* Charge. Located 2 miles north of Tiverton.

Mid Devon Bus Information Traveline (0870 608 2 608; www.devon.gov.uk/devonbus).

Pannier Market Tiverton (01884 234272). Friendly local market operating *Mon–Sat.* Farmers market *every 3rd Wed in the month.*

Tiverton Castle Tiverton (01884 253200; www.tivertoncastle.com). Originally built in 1106 by Richard de Redvers, later the home of the Courtnays and besieged by Fairfax in 1645 during the Civil War. It fell to him after a chance shot hit a drawbridge chain. It was subsequently modernised by a rich Tiverton merchant, Peter West, although the early gatehouse remains one of its most striking features. *Opening times vary so telephone for details.* Charge.

Tiverton Museum of Mid Devon Life Beck's Square, Tiverton (01884 256295; www. tivertonmuseum.org.uk). Reputed to contain the largest social history collection in the south west, housed in a listed building that was once the National School. The collection is displayed in a variety of galleries on a site covering half an acre. *Open Feb–Xmas, Mon–Fri 10.30–16.30 and Sat 10.00–13.00.* Charge.

Tourist Information Centre Phoenix Lane, Tiverton (01844 255827). *Open Mon–Sat.*

Pubs and Restaurants

The Canal Basin is some way from the town centre and the waterway is, arguably, better served by pubs and restaurants at Sampford Peverell.

✕ **Canal Tearooms and Gardens** The Wharf, Canal Hill, Tiverton (01884 252291). The one exception being right on the wharf! Once the lime-burner's dwelling, this 16th-C thatched cottage serves cream teas, home-made cakes, coffee and light lunches. Covered seating area and canalside gardens. *Open daily 10.00–18.00, Easter–Oct.*

🍺 **Racehorse** Wellbrook Street, Tiverton (01884 252606). Busy local, close to Heathcoat's Mill serving real ales and food (V) *L.* Children welcome. Garden and mini-zoo. *Open all day.*

🍺 **White Ball** Bridge Street, Tiverton (01884 251525). A wealth of exposed beams, friendly welcome and food (V) available *L and E.* Real ales and open fires in winter make this a cosy, town pub with no jukebox. No smoking area. Children welcome in garden only.

✕ **l'Opera** 10 Bridge Street, Tiverton (01884 253988). Italian restaurant serving traditional dishes, freshly prepared from local produce. *Open 11.00–14.00 and 19.00–23.00 Mon–Sat.*

🍺 **Barge** 93 High Street, Halberton, Tiverton (01884 820316). Friendly, locals pub serving real ales and food (V) *L and E (not Tue E or Wed L and E).* Open fires. Children welcome if eating. Pool, skittles and darts. Patio garden. Dogs welcome.

WALKING & CYCLING
National Cycle Route 3, otherwise known as The West Country Way, makes use of the towpath throughout. Whilst the route can be entirely off-road (by remaining on the towpath) the official route diverts through villages along the way. It links in with the 1-mile Tiverton Parkway Station to Grand Western Canal route, a combination of off- and on-road tracks. It also connects with the 3-mile Tiverton Parkway to Culm Valley route. Other connected (or nearby) routes include the Exe Valley Cycle Route, Lowman Valley Cycle Route and eight routes in the Blackdown Hills. Detailed leaflets (charge) are available from local TICs or by telephoning Devon Holiday Line (0870 60 85 531). *Mid Devon Country Walks and Villages* are a series of walks detailed in leaflets produced by Mid Devon District Council and available from local TICs. Leaflet No 4 covers walks based on the canal. On a more local level, the District Council also publish a Tiverton Town Trail, available from the TIC.
See Burlescombe, page 39 for further information.

Burlescombe

The village of Sampford Peverell was bisected by the newly-dug canal with the loss of several buildings and the re-alignment of the main road. It also cut through land belonging to the old Rectory and, in 1841, a new Rectory was constructed by the Canal Company in Regency Gothic style with stone mullioned windows, as recompense. This was again replaced in 1993 by a modern building. An attractive skew brick bridge crosses the waterway in the village centre, close to the old wharf situated on the north bank. Beyond Buckland Bridge there is an example of a syphon culvert, not uncommon on this navigation, which carries a stream beneath the canal bed. Where an intersecting water course 'crosses' a canal at a similar level, the more usual culvert is unworkable and the water has to be dropped vertically to a point below the canal bed. It is then led up the other side, via a curved masonry tube, to resume its course across the adjoining fields; the water being effectively syphoned under the navigation. On the offside, just beyond Boehill Bridge, lies the overgrown 'Engineers Clay Pit': in past times a source of the clay puddle material used to seal the canal bed against leaks. At Ayshford, one of the waterway's architectural gems appears in the form of Ayshford Court and Chapel. The rendered front of the house conceals a medieval manor, dating from the 17th C, complete with two-bay hall and evidence of its central open fire witnessed by the smoke-blackened ridge purlin supported on jointed cruck trusses. On the chimney stack is the inscription 'Built 1607, restored 1910'. The adjoining chapel is a small, freestanding, Perpendicular construction complete with tiny pierced quatrefoils, set into its side walls. The plain roof is topped with a pleasing, simple belfry. The building was restored in 1847 and contains some striking Victorian stained glass. The navigation continues, bounded by open countryside but with higher ground beyond. Soon the main Bristol to Exeter railway line is approached and the waterway bends sharply to the north. This marks the point at which it was originally intended that the Tiverton branch would meet the main line. It was to have continued southwards to meet the River Exe at Topsham, running down the Clyst valley and with a branch to Cullompton. Ahead is the tramway bridge that used to lead from the limestone quarries at Westleigh to the main line railway, now swinging away to the east. On the offside, just before Fenacre Bridge, there was a spring which provided a feed for the canal; two others remain, in the vicinity of Whipcott and near Waytown Tunnel. The discovery of these natural water sources, when plans were modified and the navigation was 'dropped' into a 16ft deep cutting, eliminated the need to construct storage reservoirs in the Lowdwells area. It also did away with the proposed locks on the Tiverton branch, making it the contour canal we see today. Beyond Whipcott Bridge is a quarry which, during the early 20th C, was an important source of roadstone for the area, the material being regularly transported along the waterway to wharves at Tiverton Road Bridge and Halberton. There are also limekilns in the area so that limestone could be burnt for local use. At Waytown Tunnel the towpath crosses on the south portal and ducks into the trees. A length of chain attached to an iron ring was the means of propulsion through the tunnel and probably an improvement on the alternative of legging. The navigation terminates at Lowdwells lock, beside the restored lock keeper's cottage, from whence it would have continued to the first lift, crossing the nearby lane on an aqueduct.

Pubs and Restaurants

🍺✗ **Globe Inn** 16 Lower Town, Sampford Peverell, Tiverton (01884 821214; theglobeinn @bigfoot.com). Traditional country pub with two comfortable bars and a restaurant serving an appetising range of home-made food (V) *L and E, daily*. Bar and restaurant menus and a range of real ales. Beer garden and children's play area. Dogs welcome. Canalside seating and moorings. Quiz *last Tue in month*. B & B.

✗ **Merriemeade** Lower Town, Sampford Peverell, Tiverton (01884 820270). Restaurant and hotel, close to the canal, serving meals and snacks (V) *L and E*. Children welcome. Garden.

✗ **Parkway House Hotel** 32 Lower Town, Sampford Peverell, Tiverton (01884 820255; kim@ex167bjfsnet.co.uk). Country hotel with restaurant and bar with views over the Culm

Valley. International cuisine (V) served *L and E*. Real ales. Children's play area in open grounds. Dogs welcome. Jazz evenings *first Fri in month*.

🍺 **Ayshford Arms** Burlescombe, Nr Tiverton (01823 672418). Country pub serving real ales and traditional, home-cooked bar meals (V) when open Sunday roasts. Children and dogs welcome. Garden. Darts, pool and skittles. *Open evenings, and lunchtimes Fri–Sun.*

🍺 **Prince of Wales Inn** Holcombe Rogus, nr Tiverton (01823 672070). Delightful 17th-C country pub serving real ales and home-cooked food (V) *L and E when open*. Log fires in winter, children's room and garden. Real cider available in summer. Darts, pool and skittles. Worth the additional walk or ride from the canal. *Closed lunchtimes Mon–Thur, Oct–Mar.*

● **Halberton**
Devon. PO, tel, stores. A village strung out along the Tiverton road, set a little way away from the canal, containing a mix of old and new housing.

● **Sampford Peverell**
Devon. PO, tel, stores, garage, farm shop, station (1 mile away). A village of character ranged around the canal which clearly led to the demolition of some properties and a diversion to the approach from Tiverton. The church was founded in the 13th C by Sir Hugh Peverell, with later work on the tower and nave and the addition of the porch and south aisle in 1498. Restored in Victorian times, there remains a Norman font and a 17th-C brass.

● **Westleigh**
Devon. Tel, stores. A quarry village.

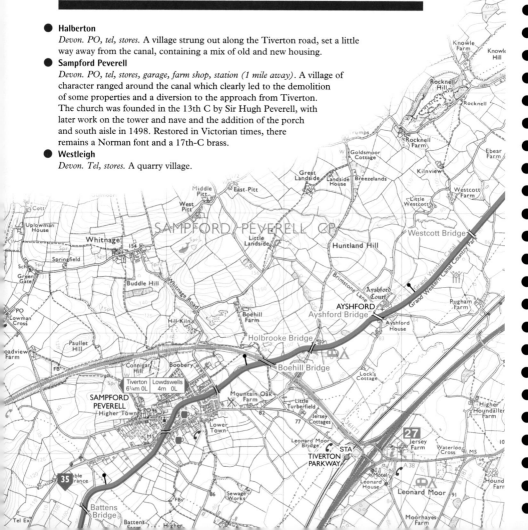

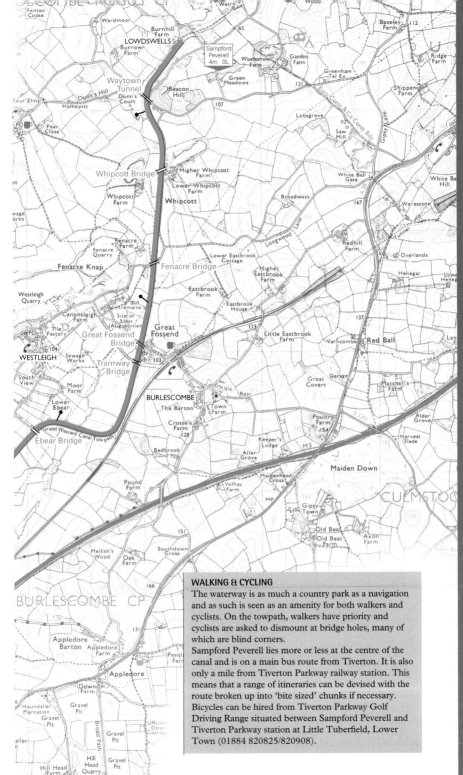

WALKING & CYCLING

The waterway is as much a country park as a navigation and as such is seen as an amenity for both walkers and cyclists. On the towpath, walkers have priority and cyclists are asked to dismount at bridge holes, many of which are blind corners.

Sampford Peverell lies more or less at the centre of the canal and is on a main bus route from Tiverton. It is also only a mile from Tiverton Parkway railway station. This means that a range of itineraries can be devised with the route broken up into 'bite sized' chunks if necessary.

Bicycles can be hired from Tiverton Parkway Golf Driving Range situated between Sampford Peverell and Tiverton Parkway station at Little Tuberfield, Lower Town (01884 820825/820908).

EXETER SHIP CANAL

MAXIMUM DIMENSIONS	MILEAGE
Length: 122'	*Turf Lock to:*
Beam: 26' 3"	Topsham Lock (closed): 1¹/2 miles
Headroom: 32' 9"	Double Locks: 3¹/2 miles
Draught: 9' 9"	Kings Arms: 4¹/2 miles
	St David's Station: 6¹/2 miles
MANAGER	
01392 274306; river–canal@exeter.gov.uk	Locks: 2
Operating Authority	
Exeter City Council	
Civic Centre	
Paris Street	
Exeter	
EX1 1RQ	
www.exeter.gov.uk	

The Exe estuary is up to 1¹/2 miles wide, although it narrows considerably between Exmouth and Dawlish Warren. Its deep water channel can be tortuous and it has proved difficult for shipping since vessels first traded to Topsham and Exeter. Seaborne trade with the city was further constrained by the construction of a weir - by Isabella de Fortibus, Countess of Devon - during the reign of Edward I. This was built above Topsham and ensured that all craft had to unload downstream of the city until an Inquisition, held in 1290, decreed that a 30ft gap be formed in the obstruction. 30 years later the Earl of Devon, whose successors went on to establish a thriving Quay at Topsham, blocked the hole and all goods to Exeter passed through the town, attracting considerable shipping dues in the process.

Towards the middle of 16th C, Exeter Corporation obtained an Act of Parliament to remove what were now three weirs across the river and in 1539 unsuccessfully attempted to remove a series of shoals which had built up in the river and estuary. Passage into the city remained all but impossible so John Trew, of Glamorgan, was engaged to dig a canal, parallel to the river on its west bank. This opened in 1566, at a cost of £5000. For this he received £225 and a percentage of the tolls. This original navigation ran from just below the city walls to a connection with the Exe at Matford Brook, and shipping still had to pass Topsham, attracting dues, despite the quays not being used. The navigation was 16ft wide, 3ft deep and enabled vessels to carry 16 tons. It is reputed to be the first navigation constructed in this country with pound locks; three in total, with guillotine gates. Boats loaded direct from sea-going craft anchored in the estuary but had to contend with an awkward entrance into the canal that was only possible at high tide. Silting in both the estuary and the canal remained an additional problem, as did opposition from quay owners in Topsham who still collected dues from passing barges. This was temporarily overcome when Exeter Corporation bought the Topsham Quay lease, but this was not renewed when it expired in 1614.

After the Civil War the waterway was in poor condition, suffering water shortages from unauthorised mill abstraction, silting and continuing rivalry with Topsham. In 1676 the Corporation decided on improvements, dredging the canal and extending it south by half a mile thereby eliminating one mile of awkward river navigation. They built a larger entrance lock and an adjoining transhipment basin able to handle 60-ton craft.

Exeter was becoming an increasingly prosperous city, its wealth founded on the cloth-making industry and again it found the need to enlarge its waterway. In 1698, the Corporation put in hand a scheme to improve the navigation but the engineer in charge absconded with the city funds, leaving an unnavigable canal and the Corporation to complete the task on its own. Completed in 1701, the enlarged waterway measured 50ft wide, 10ft deep and could carry coasters up to 150 tons. The three old locks were removed and replaced by Double Locks, and flood gates were installed at King's Arms. However, it was still approached up a narrow, winding side channel and was only accessible to larger vessels on spring tides.

In the first part of 18th C an average of 310 craft used the canal per year; by the end of the century this had risen to 448. Notwithstanding this modest increase, the decision was taken in 1825 to further improve and extend the canal and under the direction of James Green, work commenced. He had previously dredged and straightened the navigation and his new strategy was a two mile extension to Turf; raised banks to allow passage by vessels of 14ft draught and the construction of a deep-water basin in Exeter. The old entrance lock was blocked up and as a result of representations from Topsham, a new side lock opposite the port was built in 1829. The total cost was £113,355, more than a fifth being absorbed by Turf Lock which was built on piles driven through clay and bog to the underlying bedrock. Although silting continued to be a problem, the largest ship recorded as using the improved navigation was of 350 tons, drawing 13ft 6ins. The new basin, measuring 900 x 120ft, came into its own – handling paper, leather, wheat, oats and manganese.

In the 1840s steam-driven vessels appeared on the canal but because their speed exceeded the 5 mph limit and their wash threatened the banks, they were prohibited from using their own power and had to be towed by horses. This unpopular move was a turning point for the navigation and the tonnage handled began to decline, as shipping unloaded at nearby coastal ports for onward carriage by rail. In the first half of 20th C traffic stabilised but then steadily dropped off with a single sludge tanker the only vessel finally left. With an end to the estuarine dumping of raw sewerage, this tanker is now no longer visible from the elevated section of the M5, berthed beside the city's sewerage works. Today Exeter is working hard to exploit the leisure potential of the navigation and her once commercially vibrant and historic quays.

WALKING & CYCLING

It is unlikely that many readers of this guide will be navigating the estuary in their own craft, so the section south of Turf Lock is mainly covered with the cyclist and walker in mind. To make the most of this section you will need to use a combination of towpath, ferry and train (or bus). It is straightforward to follow the estuary path north, from either Dawlish Warren or Starcross, both of which offer car parking and a regular train service. At Turf Lock you will join the Ship Canal towpath and via the riverside path through Exeter, both walker and cyclist can reach St David's Station. Alternatively you can visit the city and make use of Exeter Central Station. A frequent train service connects both city stations to villages along the east side of the estuary and to its terminus at Exmouth. Lympstone makes a good point for walkers to leave the train and complete the journey to Exmouth along the waymarked path. Cyclists are faced by a busy section of road. In Exmouth follow signs from the station to the docks and catch the ferry over to Starcross (cycles carried) to complete the circuit. *See* Starcross Ferries pages 43 and 44 for further details. This circuit can be followed in either direction and any permutation and starting point is possible.

At the Countess Weir Road Bridges National Cycle Route 2 – The South Coast Route – joins the Ship Canal and follows it into Exeter on the east bank. Plans are in hand to extend southwards, along the estuary, but routing through the SSSI may take some time to finalise.

In Exmouth there is the Exmouth to Budleigh Salterton Cyclepath along the old railway line; a quiet and almost level route. For the keen off-roader there is the challenging terrain of Woodbury Common. Details of both these possibilities can be obtained from Knobblies Bike Hire (*see* page 44), who will also help you plan a route.

Running south from Exeter, along the estuary and around Torbay, is the South West Coast Path, a challenging walk that can be followed all the way to Lands End.

The 40-mile East Devon Way starts at Lympstone and runs to the county border at Lyme Regis. There are four circular linking paths that tie in with it and detailed leaflets are available from TICs.

Powderham

At Starcross the road is set somewhat below the level of the
railway track, separating it from the Exe estuary. Motorists are thus
initially greeted with a view of gleaming carriage bogies as trains race
backwards and forwards to and from the West Country. The railway is
very much a central feature of the village, as it was here that Brunel built a
pumping station to create vacuum for his ill-fated atmospheric railway.
The Italianate building survives today and now houses the local yacht
club. The route north closely follows the trackbed, which from the road
interrupts views out across the river into east Devon, 1½ miles away at this
point. The ferry operates from a pier in the village and is accessible by crossing
the railway. Soon a minor road leaves the main A379 and walkers and cyclists
can proceed in relative peace, broken only by the passing trains: a mix of the new,
futuristic Voyagers; the still elegant High Speed 125s and a regular procession of
local, stopping DMUs. Pre-Beeching there were two routes into Cornwall; a more
northerly one via Okehampton and this route, perched precariously on the sea wall,
prone to the vagaries of foul weather and high tide. The most spectacular section,
to the south of Dawlish, is also the most vulnerable, and services can be interrupted
during storms; the cost of its upkeep is particularly high. Powderham Castle
nestles, immediately to the west on raised ground, looking out across the estuary.
It is passed not long before the route leaves the road for good, ducking under the
railway to join the foreshore. After a mile Turf Lock and its attendant and very
isolated hotel are approached: this is the beginning of the Exeter Ship Canal. It
is an excellent spot to linger, to enjoy the views and the wildlife and to
wonder at this unusual location (more solitary in winter than in summer).
The railway finally diverges from the towpath and makes a beeline for the
distant suburbs of Exeter, to ultimately follow the river to St David's as
it loops round the city's western boundary. The path leads through
Exminster Marshes, an SSSI and nature reserve administered by
the RSPB; home to geese, curlew and widgeon in winter and
lapwings, redshank and warblers in summer. River and canal run
now in close partnership, only separated (in varying degrees
according to the state of the tide) by mudflats as walker and cyclist
approach Topsham which is spread out along the river's east bank.
Walkers setting out from Exminster are confronted by a mix of track,
road, footpath and foreshore and are accompanied throughout by the
bustling, single-track railway line. Views across the estuary are at all times
uninterrupted and the sea and mudflats, in a continuous state of flux, can be
constantly enjoyed. Cockle Sand provides a rich feeding ground for a variety of
birds and the area is important for its abundance of eel grass, a favourite food of
the Brent goose. In Lympstone, keeping north along the metalled road, walkers
round a corner leading to the inlet to be confronted with a charming range of seaside
cottages and the delightful Peters Tower. The station is but a short walk up the
diminutive Strand.

BOAT TRIPS
Stuart Line River Cruises Exmouth (01395 222144/07968 586750; www.stuartlinecruises.co.uk).
A wide-ranging selection of river and sea cruises, fishing trips and private charter. All-weather, all
year round sailings in fully covered, heated boats. Bar and toilets. Telephone for further details or
collect brochure from TIC.

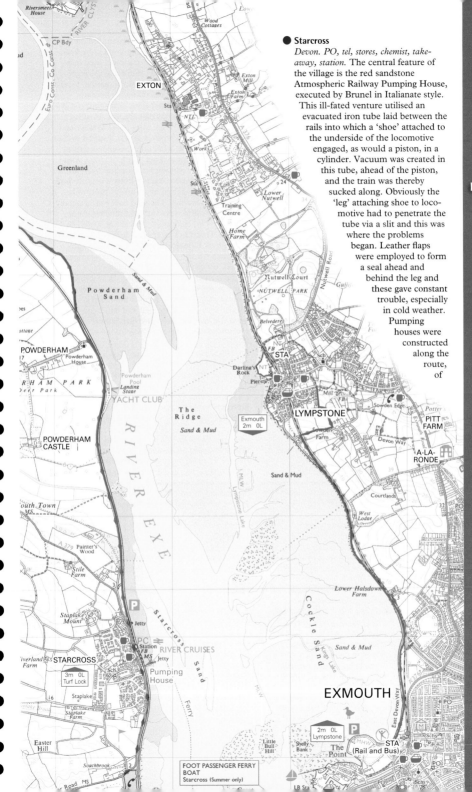

● **Starcross**

Devon. PO, tel, stores, chemist, take-away, station. The central feature of the village is the red sandstone Atmospheric Railway Pumping House, executed by Brunel in Italianate style. This ill-fated venture utilised an evacuated iron tube laid between the rails into which a 'shoe' attached to the underside of the locomotive engaged, as would a piston, in a cylinder. Vacuum was created in this tube, ahead of the piston, and the train was thereby sucked along. Obviously the 'leg' attaching shoe to loco-motive had to penetrate the tube via a slit and this was where the problems began. Leather flaps were employed to form a seal ahead and behind the leg and these gave constant trouble, especially in cold weather. Pumping houses were constructed along the route, of which this one in Starcross is a fine example. Today both railway and road dominate the village whose picturesque cottages are strung along the line of the estuary.

Starcross Ferry Starcross, Dawlish (01626 862452). Operates *Apr–Oct* from the pier beside the Atmospheric Railway Pumping House. *First crossing 10.00 and thence hourly, on the hour. Last crossing 17.00 Apr–May and 17.45 Jun–Oct.* Cycles carried. Charge. (*See* Exmouth for return crossing details.)

● **Kenton**

Devon. PO, tel, stores, garage. Set a little way off from the estuary, the village provides the access point for Powderham Castle, where there is also a farm shop (01626 891883). It is a pretty village, especially the streets behind the main road, with a striking Perpendicular church. The ashlar tower is 120ft high; there are elaborate porches and carvings, and the mullions are in Beer stone. In contrast, the remaining stonework is red sandstone, much patched with grey and white. The pulpit is 15th-C and there is considerable Victorian restoration. Opposite stands a charming row of late 19th-C almshouses.

Powderham Castle Kenton, Dawlish (01626 890243; www.powderham.co.uk). Medieval castle with beautiful gardens and grounds, miniature steam railway, children's secret garden, picnic area. Restaurant and plant centre. Castle and grounds *open Apr–Oct daily (except Sat) 10.00–17.30. Last guided tour 17.00.* Charge.

● **Exminster**

Devon. PO, tel, stores, garage. Again a little way from the navigation. The old village centre is now almost totally submerged in prolific dormitory housing for Exeter. To the east of the A379, on the track that leads from the Ship Canal to the southern end of the village, is a nice example of a Brunel–designed station house, built in 1848 for the South Devon Railway. Characteristic of his Italianate style, the building is two-storey with stuccoed elevations, Venetian windows, twin gables and prominent chimneys.

● **Exmouth**

Devon. All services. Exmouth probably first attracted attention when the Danes landed in 1001; the town became of consequence by the beginning of 13th C, by which time a castle had been built to guard the entrance to its sheltered harbour. During the Civil War it was alternately held by Parliamentarians and Royalists, finally falling to the former in March 1646. After a lengthy period of decline, the benefit of its balmy sea air, together with the sheltering hills to the east, was finally recognised and Exmouth became a celebrated seaside resort in Victorian times. The town developed in an irregular pattern with fine Georgian housing on Beacon Hill overlooking the sea and later building occupying the flat ground, at the base of the Beacon and facing the estuary. Further change was initiated by the Hon. Mark Rolle, during the second half of the 19th C, in an attempt to capitalise on the town's popularity – in its heyday it vied with Torquay in its importance as a seaside destination – but this has produced little of architectural

importance. The docks were constructed on the south west point in 1867 and proved to be financially unsuccessful. Notwithstanding, they were rebuilt in 1882 and today, somewhat incongruously, have been developed into a marina, totally encased with flamboyant, upmarket housing.

À la Ronde NT. Summer Lane, Exmouth (01395 265514; www.nationaltrust.org.uk). 16-sided cottage built in 1798 by Miss Jane Parmiter and her cousin, Mary Parmiter. It was inspired by San Vitale in Ravenna, which they visited as part of their ten year Grand Tour. Built of stone, with lozenge-shaped windows, the central hall – from which rooms radiate – is top-lit by a lantern roof. The gallery is reached by a narrow, grotto-like, shell-lined staircase. The tiled roof was originally thatched. Coffee, teas and light lunches. Shop. *Open Apr–Oct, daily except Fri and Sat, 11.00–17.30.* Charge. Timed tickets operate during busy periods.

Bicton Park Botanical Gardens East Budleigh, Exmouth (01395 568465; www.bictongardens. co.uk). 60 acres of beautiful gardens, a magnificent 19th-C palm house, an arboretum and a house of shells. An indoor exhibition hall packed with nostalgic delights for all ages. Miniature train, nature trail and children's play areas. Restaurant, shop and plant centre. *Open summer 10.00–18.00 and winter 10.00–17.00. Closed Xmas day.* Charge.

Knobblies Bike Hire 107 Exeter Road, Exmouth (01395 270182). Adult, children and toddler cycle hire. Repairs and spares. Good advice on local cycle routes. *Open Mon–Sat 09.00–17.00 and Sun during summer.*

Starcross Ferry Starcross, Dawlish (01626 862452). Operates *Apr–Oct on the half hour* from Exmouth Docks. *First crossing 10.30; last crossing 17.30 Apr–May and 18.15 Jun–Oct.* Cycles carried. Charge.

World of Country Life Sandy Bay, Exmouth (01395 274533; www.worldofcountrylife.co.uk). Hall of transport, exhibition hall, pets centre and children's play areas, falconry centre, adventure playground, quad bikes.

Tourist Information Centre Alexandra Terrace, Exmouth (01395 222299; www.exmouth-guide. co.uk).

● **Lympstone**

Devon. PO, tel, stores, station. A charming village set out around the inlet. Winding, narrow cobbled streets, little more than passages, tightly flanked by irregular rows of cottages, rambling down to the water. The village is best approached on foot or by train.

Peters Tower Lympstone. Delightful red and yellow brick-built clock tower, with a short spire, erected in 1885 by W.H. Peters in memory of his wife. The clock was designed to face seawards to tell the fishermen the time of the tides. There are two stone limekilns nearby.

● **Exton**

Devon. Tel, station. Just a few houses, sandwiched between the river and main road, lining the estuary and with splendid views. The Royal Marines training camp, complete with its own railway station, lies a little way to the south. The excellent pub is well worth a visit, justifying a break in the train journey!

Pubs and Restaurants

Galleon Inn The Strand, Starcross, Dawlish (01626 890412). Reputedly the ghost of a child can be heard bouncing a ball along the landing, whilst bottles are knocked off shelves in the bar by a more mature, female spirit. Food (V) *L and E (except Mon and Tue in winter)*. Real ale. Children and dogs welcome. Patio garden. *Monthly* live bands and regular karaoke. B & B.

Courtenay Arms The Strand, Starcross, Dawlish (01626 890426). Imposing village pub beside the Pumping House. Food (V) available *L and E*; inexpensive bar meals and *Sunday* roasts. Real ales. Children welcome. Beer garden. Pool table.

Atmospheric Railway Inn The Strand, Starcross, Dawlish (01626 890335). A striking inn sign, although somewhat strangely depicting a train hauled by a steam locomotive. Bar food (V) and real ales. Pub games. Patio seating.

Dolphin Inn Fore Street, Kenton, Dawlish (01626 891371). Something of the Tardis about this establishment – its diminutive appearance from the outside belies the never ending, rambling array of bars and eating spaces inside. Excellent selection of home-made bar snacks and meals (V) served *L and E (not Sun E or Mon L)* and a carvery operates on *Wed and Sun L*. Real ales and a pleasant ambience, enhanced by two old kitchen ranges that are lit throughout the winter months. Children welcome, beer garden.

Devon Arms Fore Street, Kenton, Dawlish (01626 890213; devon.arms@gateway.net.uk). Large village local dispensing real ale and home-cooked pub food (V) *daily L and E*. Children and dogs welcome. Garden and children's play area. B & B.

Rodean Restaurant The Triangle, Kenton, Dawlish (01626 890195). Attractive, village-centre restaurant serving a tasty range of British cuisine, prepared from local produce. À la carte and table d'hôte menus (V) available *L and E*. Telephone for opening times out of season.

Turf Locks Exminster, Exeter (01392 833128). Only accessible by boat, bike or on foot, this establishment enjoys a unique position in the Exe estuary at the entrance to the Ship Canal. Real ales and food (V) served *L and E*. *Summer* barbecues in the large lockside/estuary garden. B & B. Camping. *Open Mar–Oct only and open all day Jun–Aug*.

Swan's Nest Station Road, Exminster, Exeter (01392 832371; www.swans-nest.co.uk). Elton John's 1941 Wurlitzer occupies pride of place in this large pub-cum-restaurant with an extensive menu (V) serving traditional English food *L and E (not Boxing Day)*. Carvery, salad bar and live music at *weekends*. Real ales and a large selection of country wines. Children welcome. Garden.

Royal Oak Main Road, Exminster, Exeter (01392 832332). Traditional village local offering real ales and food (V) *E*. Children and dogs welcome. Skittle alley, darts and pool. Quiz *last Fri of month*. Beer garden.

Stowey Arms Main Road, Exminster, Exeter (01392 824216). Comfortable establishment created from a terrace of three cottages, originally belonging to the Stowey Estate. Traditional English à la carte menu (V) *L and E*. Real ales. Children and dogs welcome. Live music *alternate Fri nights*. Garden.

Beach Hotel Victoria Road, Exmouth (01395 272090). Overlooking the harbour and the estuary. Real ales and food (V) available *L and E*. No children. Outside patio seating. Live bands at *weekends*.

York Inn Imperial Road, Exmouth (01395 222488). Basic boozer opposite the bus and railway stations, offering real ales and bar snacks. No children. Large screen TV. Live bands *Fri*; karaoke *Sun and Mon*.

Strand Inn 1 The Parade, Exmouth (01395 263649). A long, low establishment with wooden panelling and floors and a friendly, local trade. Food (V) available *L*. Children's menus, 'meal deals' and a *Sunday* roast. Real ales. Children and dogs welcome. Karaoke *Tue*.

Powder Monkey 2–2A The Parade, Exmouth (01395 280090). A Wetherspoon pub dispensing an ambitious range of real ales, including at least one from local breweries. Food (V) available *all day until 22.00 (21.30 Sun)*. Patio seating.

Globe Inn The Strand, Lympstone, Exmouth (01395 263166). This pub offers open fires and a warm welcome from the singing landlord. A previous landlady fell down the stairs to her death, and is reputed to be still in residence. A reputation for excellent food (V), majoring on fresh, locally caught fish served *L and E*, together with real ales. *Sunday* roasts. Traditional fish & chips *Thur E*. Children and dogs welcome. Quiz *Tue* and music *Sat*. Outside seating.

Swan Inn The Strand, Lympstone, Exmouth (01395 270403). Traditional, friendly village local serving home-cooked bar food (V) *L and E*. Real ales. Children and dogs welcome; patio seating and regular *summer* barbecues.

Redwing Inn Church Road, Lympstone, Exmouth (01395 222156). Friendly village local serving real ale and real cider. Home-made food (V) *L and E* and an à la carte restaurant menu (*not Sun E*). Pétanque court and garden. Children and dogs welcome. Quiz *Mon*. Jazz on *Tue E* and live bands *on Fri*.

Puffing Billy Inn Station Road, Exton, Exeter (01392 877888). Comfortably furnished in a very modern style, this establishment majors on its wide diversity of food described as 'Pacific Rim meets Eastern and European'. À la carte meals (V) and snacks *L and E, daily*. Real ales. Children welcome; dogs only in the large garden. Jazz *Fri nights*.

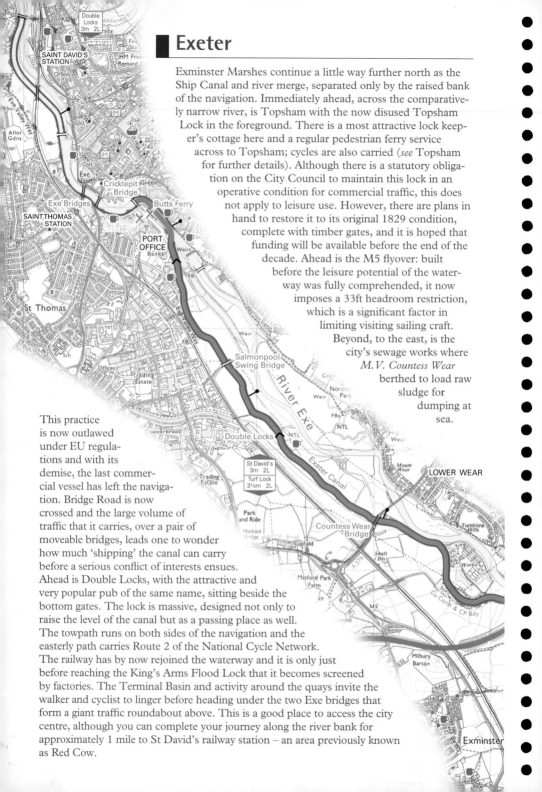

Exeter

Exminster Marshes continue a little way further north as the Ship Canal and river merge, separated only by the raised bank of the navigation. Immediately ahead, across the comparatively narrow river, is Topsham with the now disused Topsham Lock in the foreground. There is a most attractive lock keeper's cottage here and a regular pedestrian ferry service across to Topsham; cycles are also carried (*see* Topsham for further details). Although there is a statutory obligation on the City Council to maintain this lock in an operative condition for commercial traffic, this does not apply to leisure use. However, there are plans in hand to restore it to its original 1829 condition, complete with timber gates, and it is hoped that funding will be available before the end of the decade. Ahead is the M5 flyover: built before the leisure potential of the waterway was fully comprehended, it now imposes a 33ft headroom restriction, which is a significant factor in limiting visiting sailing craft. Beyond, to the east, is the city's sewage works where *M.V. Countess Wear* berthed to load raw sludge for dumping at sea.

This practice is now outlawed under EU regulations and with its demise, the last commercial vessel has left the navigation. Bridge Road is now crossed and the large volume of traffic that it carries, over a pair of moveable bridges, leads one to wonder how much 'shipping' the canal can carry before a serious conflict of interests ensues. Ahead is Double Locks, with the attractive and very popular pub of the same name, sitting beside the bottom gates. The lock is massive, designed not only to raise the level of the canal but as a passing place as well. The towpath runs on both sides of the navigation and the easterly path carries Route 2 of the National Cycle Network. The railway has by now rejoined the waterway and it is only just before reaching the King's Arms Flood Lock that it becomes screened by factories. The Terminal Basin and activity around the quays invite the walker and cyclist to linger before heading under the two Exe bridges that form a giant traffic roundabout above. This is a good place to access the city centre, although you can complete your journey along the river bank for approximately 1 mile to St David's railway station – an area previously known as Red Cow.

● **Topsham**

Devon. All services. Delightfully unspoilt, it is not hard to imagine the Topsham of 500 years ago when, as a port and centre for ship building, it was more important than Exeter. Its unique architectural heritage, with shops and housing dating from as early as the 14th C, can be enjoyed on foot. Take a stroll along The Strand to view some exquisite examples of 17th- and 18th-C merchant housing, with their characteristic Dutch gables. The nearby Goat Walk is equally charming; with its tiny beach it has been a walking and meeting place over many centuries. In spite of the bustle brought on by the tourist season, the locals remain tolerant, friendly and hospitable. There is a heated, open-air pool and a small museum.

Topsham Ferry Topsham, Exeter (01395 268001). Plying between Topsham Lock on the Ship Canal and the town carrying pedestrians and cyclists. Operating *Apr–Sep daily except Tue and Oct–Mar Sat, Sun and B Hols.*

● **Exeter**

Devon. All services. Early records for the city mention the construction of a fort, between AD55 and AD60, as headquarters for the 2nd Augustan Legion and located at the centre of the present city, overlooking the lowest possible crossing of the Exe. It was surrounded by a timber and earth rampart and a ditch; the foundation was exposed during an excavation in 1971, but was subsequently covered over again. The burgeoning Roman town took over much of the plan area of the fortress and spread beyond to be enclosed by a stone wall in the 2nd C. This is the basis of the present city wall which has been extensively rebuilt over the years. Urban life continued to flourish through the following centuries, with the withdrawal of the Roman garrison and the building of a monastery at which St Boniface was educated in the 7th C. The present High Street follows the line of the Roman main road and the four main medieval gates are sited on Roman gateways. Exeter was occupied by the Danes in AD877 when the chief religious establishment was St Mary Major, which survived in its Victorian form, in the cathedral

close, into the 1970s. The city became a See in 1050 and the Norman cathedral was built in the 12th C; later to be much remodelled in medieval times. From the 15th C onwards, Exeter was the chief cloth marketing town in the south west and by the 17th C had become one of the richest cities in England. It was a significant port, although imports greatly outweighed exports and it was prey to serious and sustained competition from Topsham, downstream on the Exe estuary. However, the eventual confirmation of its customs rights over the entire estuary during the 17th C, together with the relative success of the canal, restored much of its prosperity and resulted in the construction of the delightful Custom House and development of the City Quays. Over the 19th C the population almost trebled, aided by the appearance of the railway in 1844. Some 130 years later, the arrival of the M5 was a further improvement in the city's communication links with the rest of the country and a variety of light industries thrive. Exeter lost much of its rich architectural heritage during the pernicious bombings of the 1942 air raids and this has been replaced, in varying degrees, by insensitive redevelopment dating from the 1950s.

Barnfield Theatre Barnfield Road, Exeter (01392 271808). Mix of amateur and professional theatre, dance and music. Coffee, snacks and bar.

Devon Holiday Line (0870 6085531; www. devon4allseasons.co.uk). Source of walking and cycling leaflet referred to under Walking & Cycling. Also bookings for a range of accommodation in the area, from hotels to camping barns.

Devon Wildlife Trust Shirehampton House, 35–37 St David's Hill, Exeter (01392 279244; devonwt@cix.co.uk). The Trust cares for some 40 nature reserves around the county, totalling more than 3,000 acres in all. Most are *open to the public at all times*. The Old Sludge Beds lie between the Ship Canal and the Exe, just upstream from the M5 flyover, and are maintained as an area of reed bed which is home to a wide variety of wetland birds. There are two further reserves within reach of Exmouth.

Exeter Cathedral Cathedral Close, Exeter. Although completed in the 14th C by Bishop Grandisson, the two Norman transept towers date from the building's foundation. It was extensively remodelled by Bishop Bronescombe in the 13th C and the pepperpot roofs replaced the traditional Norman pyramids during further work in the 15th C.

> **BOAT TRIPS**
> *Southern Comfort* and *White Heather* sailing from Exeter Quay to Double Locks, *daily, Easter–Oct.* Telephone (07831) 108319 for further details.

There is much original glass in the late 14thC east window and Sir Gilbert Scott's canopied choir stalls incorporate the oldest set of misericords that survive complete; they were carved 1260–80. The bishop's throne, carved from oak in 1312, is quite exquisite.

Exeter City Museum & Art Gallery Queen Street, Exeter (01392 665858; www.exeter.gov.uk). A wealth of interesting items in a Victorian treasure house. Exhibitions include world cultures, local history and archaeology, exotic birds and butterflies, glassware and West Country silver, clocks and watches. Temporary visiting art exhibitions alongside a rotating permanent collection. Workshops and activities for children and adults throughout the year. Shop and licensed café.

Exeter Picture House Bartholomew Street West, Exeter (01392 435522; www.picturehouse-cinemas.co.uk). Award winning, purpose-built, two-screen cinema showing the best in contemporary film. Bar, coffee and tea.

Killerton House Broadclyst, Exeter (01392 881345; www.nationaltrust.org.uk). Elegant 18th-C house containing treasures from the renowned Killerton dress collection, revealing the secrets of a woman's wardrobe in days gone by. Large hillside garden, Victorian rock garden, ice house and woodland walks. Gift shop, plant centre and licensed restaurant. *Open Mar–Oct 11.00–17.00. House closed Tue and also Mon in Mar and Oct. Open daily throughout Aug. Garden open daily throughout year.* Charge. 7 miles north of Exeter.

Northcott Theatre University Campus, Exeter (01392 493493; www.northcott-theatre.co.uk). Venue for professional visiting theatre companies and the theatre's resident company. Backstage tours, theatre talks and visiting musicians. Restaurant serving tea, coffee and light meals. Licensed bar.

Phoenix Arts Centre Bradninch Place, Gandy Street, Exeter (01392 667080; www.exeterphoenix.org.uk). High calibre, eclectic mix of varied material on offer in a newly refurbished venue. Galleries, workshops and courses. Excellent café and bar. Worth a visit just to see the automaton phoenix in action as the hour strikes.

Exeter Quay Striking example of an inland port that has developed over the ages to reflect the city's prosperity, founded on the production of serge cloth. Today it is given over solely to leisure but this does nothing to detract from the wealth and diversity of the buildings, some dating back to the late 17th C. The Custom House, completed in 1681, was designed by Richard Allen and enabled Exeter to re-establish its dominance as a port over its long-time rival, Topsham, situated downstream in the tidal estuary. The building is brick-fronted, with two storeys and five bays and white painted stone quoins. The stairhall, together with some of the downstairs rooms, have superb plasterwork ceilings and the staircase incorporates bulbous, urn-shaped balusters. The warehouses north of the Custom House date from a similar period; cut into the cliffs, they provided a bonded stores. The two five-storey warehouses fronting the cliffs date from 1835, and the open fish market is also 19th-C. It incorporated a King's Beam, used for weighing dutiable goods. There are also two further warehouses nearby, built in the late 19th C, and used for storing wine. Further west, Cricklepit Mill (which gives its name to the nearby pedestrian bridge) dates from the end of the 17th C and encloses a large waterwheel. It was variously used for fulling, grist production and malting. On the other side of the water, set beside the basin constructed by James Green in 1830, is a large warehouse from the same period. The Quay House Interpretation Centre displays models, artefacts and pictures relating to the historic dock area, together with an audio-visual history of Exeter.

Rail Travel (Tickets 0870 900 2320; www.wessextrains.co.uk). As part of the refranchising process, local services in the area (covering both sides of the estuary) are now run by Wessex Trains. On the east side of the Exe services run from both Exeter St David's and Exeter Central, having originated in Barnstaple. The run north is well worthwhile as an extension to activities around the estuary. On the west side of the Exe stopping services depart from both Exeter stations (many also stop at Exeter St Thomas) and may have originated from Bristol or South Wales. A few are from Exmouth. For timetables, telephone 0870 900 2318. For cyclists, advanced bookings are essential on some services, usually the long distance routes. Telephone 0870 900 2318 to receive a copy of the *Cycling by Train* leaflet. RailRover tickets are available for either 3 days (any 3 days in 7) or 8 days (any 8 days in 15) and represent excellent value for off-peak travel.

Saddles & Paddles The Quay, Exeter (01392 424241; www.saddlepaddle.co.uk). Bike and canoe hire on the quayside. Sales, spares and repairs. Canoeing group nights out.

WALKING & CYCLING

There are two valuable leaflets produced by Devon County Council entitled *Making Tracks – Cycle Routes in Devon* and *Making Tracks – Walking Trails in Devon*. The first features over 70 cycle routes while the second covers over 700 miles of walks. *See* Devon Holiday Line amongst the Exeter attractions on page 47 for further details. Exeter City Council's Countryside Service publish a series of walks leaflets under the heading *Countryside Walks in Exeter*. Telephone (01392) 265890/265337 or visit www.exeter.gov.uk. They also manage the Riverside Valley Park which extends for 7 miles through the City forming part of a major wildlife highway linking Exmoor to the sea. This offers additional walking and cycling opportunities and is supported by further leaflets. *See also* Walking & Cycling on page 41.

Pubs and Restaurants

Double Locks Hotel Canal Banks, Marsh Barton, Exeter (01392 256947). A popular family pub overlooking the canal and serving food (V) *all day* together with a selection of real ales. Dogs welcome. Lockside seating. Open fires and regular music nights.

Welcome Inn The Quay, Exeter. Beside King's Arms Lock. Gas lighting and erratic opening hours. A very traditional local serving real ales.

Bar Venezia Piazza Terracina, Quayside, Exeter (01392 423688). Ristorante and café bar in a new development beside the quay. Traditional Italian menu (V); pizzas and Italian-style snacks *L and E*. Hot and cold drinks. Children welcome. Quayside seating. Regular music nights. *Open Tue–Thur 10.00–15.00 and 18.00–23.00, Fri–Sun 10.00–23.00. Closed Mon.*

Port Royal The Quay, Exeter (01392 272360). Reputed to be the longest pub in Exeter, its low ceilings serve only to substantiate this claim. It incorporates the old boathouse and serves an à la carte menu and bar snacks (V) *L and E*, together with real ales. Children and dogs welcome. Non smoking area. Quiz *Thur*. Patio seating and barbecues in *summer. Closed Mon in winter and open all day in summer.*

Prospect Inn The Quay, Exeter (01392 273152). Set in an attractive old building with exposed beams, panelled walls and multi-level seating areas, this establishment is *open all day in summer*, serving traditional English pub food (V) *daily*, together with real ales. Children welcome. Beer garden. Regular music nights.

Waterfront 5–9 Southern Warehouse, Quayside, Exeter (01392 210590). Occupying the bottom floor of a converted warehouse with vaulted brick ceilings, this establishment serves real ale and pizzas and snacks *L and E, daily*. Children's menu. Quayside seating.

Malthouse 7 Haven Road, Haven Bank, Exeter (01392 490555). Old riverside malthouse, tastefully restored with exposed brickwork and lots of beams. Alongside a range of old malting paraphernalia it serves real ales and food (V) *all day*. Fun Factory and soft toy area – a child's paradise.

Mill on the Exe Bonhay Road, Exeter (01392 214464; www.millontheexe.co.uk). Converted paper mill, closed for 60 years and now re-opened to serve real ales and an extensive international selection of food (V) in atmospheric surroundings. Children welcome. Gourmet nights *Fri*. Upstairs river balcony overlooking the weir and downstairs garden contribute towards making this a unique building.

Imperial New North Road, Exeter (01392 434050; www.jdwetherspoon.co.uk). This 'pub' makes use of all the downstairs rooms in a Georgian country house which is now a grade II listed structure. It includes a stunning orangery, the roof supported on cast-iron bow trusses and possibly originally built by Brunel on a site at Streatham Hall. Popular with the nearby university, it dispenses an ever changing array of real ales and a range of snacks and light meals (V) *L and E*. Garden.

Great Western Hotel St David's Station Approach, Exeter (01392 274039; www.greatwesternhotel.co.uk). A great draw for real ale connoisseurs, this unlikely venue dispenses an enormous selection of cask beer. Good food (V) available at the bar and in the restaurant *L and E*. B & B.

Jolly Porter St David's Hill, Exeter (01392 254848). Bar food (V) all day and real ales served in an atmospheric, panelled bar. Selection of wines by the glass in this popular local.

Artful Dodger Red Cow Village, Cowley Bridge Road, Exeter (01392 274754). Alcoves separated by stained glass panels make this a cosy pub dispensing real ales and bar meals (V) *all day*. Darts, pool, jenga.

Red Cow Red Cow Village, Cowley Bridge Road, Exeter (01392 490963). Log fires, bar snacks (V) and real ales available in this drinkers establishment. Pool.

Steam Packet The Quay, Topsham, Exeter (01392 875085). Friendly local with a landlord born and bred in the town. Traditional home-made pub grub (V) available *L*, tea and coffee served *all day*. Real ales. Children welcome if eating. Dogs welcome. Quiz *every other week*. B & B.

Lighter Inn The Quay, Topsham, Exeter (01392 875439). Once the custom house, now dispensing real ales and an appetising selection of food (V) *L and E*, with the emphasis on locally caught fish. Children's room and non-smoking area. Quayside seating. Quiz *alternate Thur*.

Galley Restaurant 41 Fore Street, Topsham (01392 876078; www.galleyrestaurant.co.uk). Wherever possible only local and organic produce is used in the preparation of a range of appetising food (V) served *L and E* in this charmingly located restaurant. Accommodation is also available in twin or double cabins. Telephone 07956 976413/396765 for further details.

Bridge Inn Bridge Hill, Topsham, Exeter (01392 873862; www.cheffers.co.uk). From the east side of the railway station, follow the road south east down the hill. Your walk will be well rewarded by real ales and bar snacks in this 15th-C inn beside the river. Free from all machines, the pub has been in the same family for over 100 years, and is popular with locals and visitors alike. Outside seating *in summer*, open fires *in winter*.

KENNET & AVON CANAL

MAXIMUM DIMENSIONS

Avonmouth to Bristol Harbour
Length: 325'
Beam: 50'
Draught: 18'
Air Draught: 90'

Bristol Harbour to Hanham Lock
Length: 80'
Beam: 18'
Draught: 6' 3"
Air Draught: 10' 3"

DOCK MASTER
0117 927 3633

Hanham Lock to Bath
Length: 75'
Beam: 16'
Headroom: 8' 9"

Bath to Newbury
Length: 70'
Beam: 13' 2"
Headroom: 8'
or
Length: 72'
Beam: 7'
Headroom: 7'

Newbury to Reading
Length: 70'
Beam: 14'
Headroom: 8'

MANAGER
01380 722859
enquiries.KandA@britishwaterways.co.uk

MILEAGE
AVONMOUTH entrance to Severn Estuary to:
Bristol Docks: 7¾ miles
HANHAM Lock (start of tidal section): 14¼ miles
Bath, junction with River Avon: 25½ miles
Dundas Aqueduct: 30¾ miles
Bradford-on-Avon: 35¼ miles
Devizes Top Lock: 47¼ miles
Pewsey Wharf: 59¼ miles
Crofton Top Lock: 65¾ miles
Hungerford: 73¼ miles
Kintbury: 76¼ miles
Newbury Lock: 82¼ miles
Aldermaston Wharf: 90¾ miles
Tyle Mill Lock: 92¾ miles
READING: 100¾ miles

Locks: 104

The Kennet & Avon Canal is one of the most splendid lengths of artificial waterway in Britain, a fitting memorial to the canal age as a whole. It is a broad canal, cutting across southern England from Reading to Bristol (shown in this guide from Avonmouth to Reading). Its generous dimensions and handsome architecture blend well with the rolling downs and open plains that it passes through, and are a good reminder of the instinctive feeling for scale that characterised most 18th- and early 19th-C civil engineering.

The canal was built in three sections. The first two were river navigations, the Kennet from Reading to Newbury, and the Avon from Bath to Bristol, both being canalised. Among early 18th-C river navigations the Kennet was one of the most ambitious, owing to the steep fall of the river. Between Reading and Newbury 20 locks were necessary in almost as many miles, as the difference in level is 138ft. John Hore was the engineer for the Kennet Navigation, which was built between 1718 and 1723 and included 11 miles of new cut. Subsequently Hore was in charge of the Bristol Avon Navigation, carried out between 1725 and 1727. These river navigations were interesting in many ways, often because of the varied nature of the country they passed through. The steep-sided Avon Gorge meant that a fast-flowing river had to be brought under control. Elsewhere the engineering was unusual: for example the turf-sided locks on the Kennet, now partially replaced with brick structures. For the third stage, a canal from Newbury to Bath was authorised in 1794. Rennie was appointed engineer, and after a long struggle the canal was opened in 1810, completing a through route from London to Bristol. The canal is 57 miles long, and included 79 broad locks, a summit level at Savernake 452ft above sea level and one short tunnel, also at Savernake. Rennie was both engineer and architect, anticipating the role played by Brunel in the creation of the Great Western Railway; in some ways his architecture is the more noteworthy aspect of his work. The architectural quality of the whole canal is exceptional, from the straightforward stone bridges to the magnificent neo-classical aqueducts at Avoncliffe and Limpley Stoke. Rennie's solution to the anticipated water supply problems on the top pound was to build a 4312yd tunnel, thereby providing a reservoir 15 miles long. The company called in William Jessop to offer a second – and hopefully cheaper solution – and it was he who suggested a shorter tunnel in conjunction with a steam pumping engine. This resulted in a saving of £41,000 and a completion date two years earlier. In some places the canal bed was built over porous rock, and so leaked constantly, necessitating further regular pumping.

Nevertheless, the canal as a whole was a striking achievement. West of Devizes the waterway descends Caen Hill in a straight flight of 16 locks. In total 29 locks are navigated within 2 miles of Devizes. The many swing bridges were designed to run on ball bearings, one of the first applications of the principle. The bold entry of the canal into Bath, a sweeping descent round the south of the city, is a firm expression of the belief that major engineering works should contribute to the landscape, whether urban or rural, instead of imposing themselves upon it as so often happens nowadays.

Later the Kennet & Avon Canal Company took over the two river navigations, thus gaining control of the whole through route. However traffic was never as heavy as the promoters had expected, and so the canal declined steadily throughout the 19th C. It suffered from early railway competition as the Great Western Railway duplicated its route, and was eventually bought by that railway company. Maintenance standards slipped, and this, combined with a rapidly declining traffic, meant that navigation was difficult in places by the end of World War I. The last regular traffic left the canal in the 1930s, but still it remained open, and the last through passage was made in 1951 by *nb Queen*, with the West Country artist P. Ballance on board. Subsequently the canal was closed, and for a long time its future was in jeopardy. However, great interest in the canal had resulted in the formation of a Canal Association shortly after World War II, to fight for restoration. In 1962 the Kennet & Avon Canal Trust was formed out of the Association, and practical steps towards restoration were under way. Using volunteers to raise funds from all sources, and with steadily increasing inputs from BW, the trust has catalysed the reopening of the entire navigation as a through route from Reading to Bristol. This achievement was commemorated on 8 August 1990, with HM The Queen navigating through Lock 43, at the summit of the Caen Hill flight, which now bears her name.

NAVIGATIONAL NOTES

1 Do not navigate in tidal waters without charts, tide tables, anchor, and all the other essential safety equipment. Ensure that your craft is suitable and well maintained. Seek expert advice if in any doubt. Inland waterways craft do navigate the Severn Estuary to Sharpness (and vice versa) but this is a foolish practice without suitable weather conditions and the services of a river pilot. For further details about pilotage telephone Amalgamated Gloucester Pilots on 07774 226143. *Safety Guidance for Small Boat Passage of Severn Estuary* is available free from www.glaxesterharbourtrustees.org.uk or by sending a large SAE to: The Harbourmaster, Sharpness Port Authority, Severnside House, Berkeley, Glos. GL13 9UD. See also *Nicholson Guide to the Waterways 2*.
2 Note that most insurance policies covering inland craft do not include cover for tidal waters for which there are often special requirements to be met and usually an additional charge. Contact your insurance company before planning your trip below Hanham Lock.
3 Bristol City Council publish the comprehensive *Bristol Harbour Information for Boat Owners,* available free by telephoning the Dock Master on 0117 927 3633. This covers everything from locking procedures into the floating harbour through to details relating to exiting the feeder canal at Nether Lock. There is also information relating to use of the Floating Harbour and its environs.

Avonmouth

The Severn Estuary, with its two dramatic road crossings, must be well known to all who travel the motorway system into Wales and the West Country. Equally well known is its extreme range of tides – giving rise to the Severn Bore – which in the world record books come second only to the Bay of Fundy, sandwiched between Nova Scotia and New Brunswick. The inland boater is, therefore, only likely to venture along the River Avon between Bristol and Avonmouth and thence out onto the Severn when making passage north to Sharpness on the Gloucester & Sharpness Canal (or of course, in reverse). This provides a means, for the intrepid navigator, to access the non-tidal river beyond Gloucester, avoiding a lengthy easterly detour. It is not something that will be undertaken lightly as the Navigational Notes make only too clear. For every boater who passes under the elevated section of the M5 at Avonmouth there will, no doubt, be hundreds of thousands of walkers and cyclists anxious to enjoy the beauties of the Avon Gorge from a slightly less exciting (though equally dramatic) vantage point. From Pill, on the south bank of the river, there is a combined cycleway and pedestrian path running the 5 miles to Bristol's Floating Harbour, so-called to differentiate it from its predecessor, a series of mud berths along the old course of The Avon through the city. On the north bank, the busy A4 heads for the city accompanied for some of the way by the Severn Beach railway line which terminates close to the Second Severn Crossing. Running through Pill and close companion to the cycleway is another, newly re-opened, freight line connecting Bristol to the docks at Portishead. Beyond Pill the river bends north, around a steep promontory as the gorge begins to close in from both sides. Initially the sides are rocky and free from trees and walkers and cyclists alike have uninterrupted views across the river to Shirehampton Park on the north bank. Then the river curls round to head in an almost southerly direction past a disused quarry and the old Roman settlement of Abona. Soon the bare rock becomes cloaked by the dense foliage of Leigh Woods. Further quarries are followed by The Avon Gorge Nature Reserve and then path and river head for the graceful Clifton Suspension Bridge.

WALKING & CYCLING

Bristol is the home of Sustrans whose vision spawned the National Cycle Network, and it would be very surprising indeed if the cyclist was not well catered for in this area. The Pill Riverside Path runs from the Harbour, along Cumberland Road to follow the river through to Pill. There is also a linking route into Leigh Woods and to Ashton. Further west the cycleway crosses the river by way of the M5 bridge and connects (at both ends) with the Avon Cycleway; an 85-mile signposted route along a mixture of traffic-free paths and quiet lanes around Bristol. A leaflet entitled *CycleCity – Bristol Cycling Map* is available (charge) by telephoning Sustrans (0117 929 0888; www.sustrans.org.uk). Leaflets covering local cycle routes are also obtainable from Bristol City Council (0117 922 2000). The routes mentioned are, of course, available to both walker and cyclist alike. On the north bank of the river, in Shirehampton Park, there are excellent walks, offering spectacular open views to the south, along the river and beyond.

Easton-in-Gordano

Somerset. Tel, garage. Largely a dormitory village for Bristol running into, and indistinguishable from, its neighbour, Pill. The western end, around the Kings Arms, is the more interesting part.

Pill

Somerset. PO, tel, stores, chemist, garage. A continuation of Easton-in-Gordano, only with some shops. Beyond the Railway Inn there are views across the River Avon.

Avonmouth Dock

In the 19th C, with the construction of increasingly larger ships such as the *SS Great Britain* in 1843, it was recognised that there was a need for an expansion of the deep-water docking facilities in the Port of Bristol. The more far-sighted realised that in order to compete with other large British ports (with their own seaboard) a new facility had to be built at the mouth of the Avon and not as an extension to the City Docks. Whilst this radical concept amounted to heresy in the eyes of many prosperous Bristol merchants, the construction of Avonmouth Dock was commenced in 1868 and completed in 1877.

Portishead Dock

This was opened in 1879, covering an area of 76 acres, largely to make up for the deficiencies in size and lock capacity of Avonmouth Dock on the other side of the river mouth. Again absorbed by Bristol Docks Committee in 1884 to make one unified port, it too soon proved itself woefully inadequate in the face of rapidly increasing shipping tonnage.

Royal Edward Dock

Opened by Edward VII in 1908 and interconnected with Avonmouth Dock, the Royal Edward Dock had an entrance lock measuring 875' x 100' thereby allowing the revitalised dock complex the chance again to become competitive.

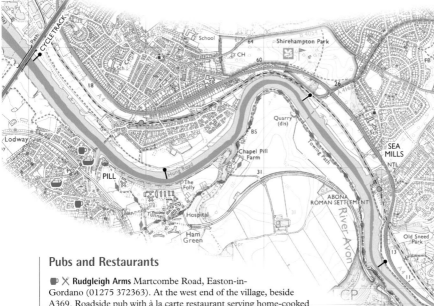

Pubs and Restaurants

🍴 ✕ **Rudgleigh Arms** Martcombe Road, Easton-in-Gordano (01275 372363). At the west end of the village, beside A369. Roadside pub with à la carte restaurant serving home-cooked food (V) *L and E* in both bar and restaurant. Real ales and *Sunday* roasts. Children and dogs welcome. Garden.

🍴 **Kings Arms** 12 St Georges Hill, Easton-in-Gordano (01275 372208). At the west end of the village. Cheerful, village local serving real ales and traditional home-cooked pub food (V) *L and E*. Children welcome. Beer garden and skittle alley.

🍴 **Railway Inn** Monmouth Road, Pill (01275 372107). Beside the railway line, near the start of the Avon Path. Real ale and bar snacks *L*. Patio garden and skittle alley.

Also try **Anchor Inn** Ham Green, Pill (01275 372253) and **Star Inn** Bank Place, Pill (01275 374926).

🍴 ✕ **George Inn** Manor Road, Abbotsleigh, Bristol (01275 372467). On A369 south of Leigh Wood. A friendly, welcoming pub serving home-made food (V) *L and E (all day Sun)* in both bar and à la carte restaurant. Also an excellent range of real ales available. Children welcome, as are dogs, in the large garden.

Bristol

River and cycleway now pass under the spectacular shadow of the Clifton Suspension Bridge, poised some 230ft above. This 700ft-long crossing into the elevated Clifton district of Bristol is breathtaking in both its concept and execution. Designed by Brunel, when he was only 23, it was not in fact completed until 1864, nearly five years after his death. Half a mile eastwards the navigation reaches the Entrance Lock and divides. The northerly channel leads into the Floating Harbour through the Entrance Lock, Cumberland Basin and Junction Lock while the river skirts round to the south, along

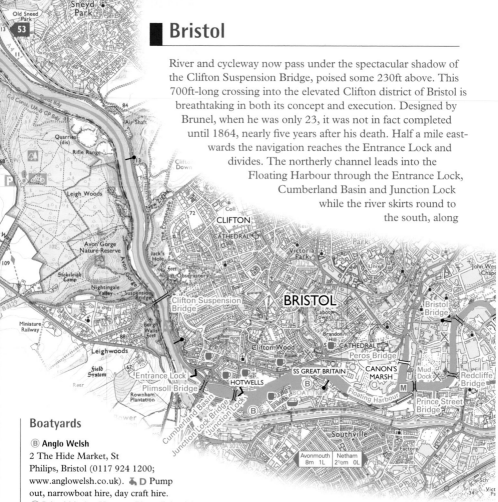

Avonmouth	Netham
8m 1L	2½m 0L

Boatyards

Ⓑ **Anglo Welsh**
2 The Hide Market, St Philips, Bristol (0117 924 1200; www.anglowelsh.co.uk). ♿ D Pump out, narrowboat hire, day craft hire.

Ⓑ **Bristol Marina** Hanover Place, Bristol (0117 926 5730; info@bristolmarina.co.uk). 🚿 🚻 ♿ D Pump out, electric boat recharging, overnight mooring, long-term mooring, winter storage, slipway, boat repairs, boat building and fitting out, wet dock, DIY facilities, telephone, toilets, showers, laundrette. *Emergency call out.*

Ⓑ **Force 4 Chandlery** Albion Dockyard, Hanover Place, Bristol (0117 926 8396). Chandlery, books and charts.

Ⓑ **Underfall Boatyard** Cumberland Road, Bristol (0117 954 0272). Winter storage, slipway, boat building, facilities for large vessels to 180 tonnes, all boatyard trades available on site.

BOAT TRIPS

Bristol Ferry Boat Co (0117 927 3416; www.bristolferryboat.co.uk). The company operates their distinctive yellow and blue round-trip waterbus services on the historic harbour *every day from Apr–Sep and at weekends throughout the winter.* A selection of boats, each with an individual character, plying the harbour. Also available for private charter *throughout the year.*

Bristol Packet Boat (0117 926 8157; www.bristolpacket.co.uk). Regular public sailings to include cruises around the harbour and trips up and down the River Avon. Telephone for further details.

Waverley Excursions (0141 243 2224; www.waverleyexcursions.co.uk). Waverley and Balmoral operate an exciting and varied selection of trips departing from a host of locations up and down the Bristol Channel. Telephone for a timetable covering the *May–Oct* cruising season.

an artificial cut constructed in 1804 when the harbour was built. There is a pleasing combination of old and new quays – some dating back to the 13th C – and a contrasting selection of bridges all adding variety to what is now an entirely leisure-orientated dock complex. In the main harbour, before Redcliffe Bascule Bridge is reached, the navigation passes the 'Mud Dock', which dates from 1625 and provided a soft mud berth for shipping when the quays were still subject to the tidal fluctuations of the two rivers. It is now the site of a café and cycle hire centre. Turning through a right-angled bend, the waterway now makes a beeline for Netham Lock (0117 977 6590) in concert with a busy main road along its south bank. On the apex of the bend is the site of Totterdown Basin and Old Totterdown Lock, which once provided an access into the tidal Avon. This has now become a wildlife area. Also at this point, the Avon Walkway crosses over Marsh Lane Bridge and for most of the way to Nether Lock follows the river. Meanwhile the feeder canal leads the navigation past a series of factories, some with attractively landscaped grounds, to be finally reunited with the river which curls away through the cities' suburbs.

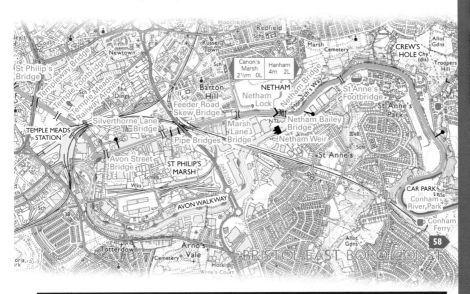

NAVIGATIONAL NOTES

1 Mooring – aim to moor either at recognised points in the Floating Harbour or on the feeder canal as set out in the *Bristol Harbour Information for Boat Owners* guide as there is no suitable overnight mooring between Netham and Hanham Locks. Also consult the guide for all facilities and their availability within the harbour complex.
2 Below Hanham Lock the river comes under the jurisdiction of Bristol City Council to whom a licence fee is payable. Visitors may purchase a licence – the cost of which is based on length of stay and length of craft – from the lock keeper at Netham Lock or from the Harbour Office (0117 903 1484; www.bristol-city.gov.uk) Underfall Yard, Cumberland Road, Bristol – located at the western end of the Floating Harbour.
3 Visitor moorings are available in the Floating Harbour and are allocated by the Harbour Master (0117 903 1484; city_docks@bristol-city.gov.uk).
4 To contact bridge operators for a bridge swing within the Floating Harbour telephone 0117 929 9338 or the Harbour Master as above.
5 When navigating under Redcliffe Bridge do not use east and west arches. For Bristol Bridge use centre of arches and do not use east arch.

● Bristol

Bristol. Daily markets. All services. Bristol grew up on the confluence of the Rivers Avon and Frome and was one of two cities prominent at the end of the Saxon period; the other being Norwich. It was probably established in the late 10th C beside a bridge over the Avon from which it derived the name Bridge-Stow: the place of the bridge. It developed on an easily defended site between the Avon and its tributary, the River Frome and initially built up trading links with South Wales and Ireland. By the 14th C Bristol had outgrown the small Saxon burgh of its origins and additional walls were built to enclose the newly populated areas to the south of the Avon. However, still left outside the walls were the church of St Mary Redcliffe, the Monastery of St Augustine, as well as three major friaries. The monastery and cathedral were by now one and the same. As a port Bristol was dominant along the coasts of the Severn Estuary and its local trade extended from Ireland to the Midlands where goods were transhipped into barges at Bewdley. That Bristol prospered as a port throughout the medieval period is somewhat surprising, given its location up the severely tidal River Avon and its unsatisfactory mud berthing arrangements. Yet it went on to dominate a burgeoning world trade as is witnessed by its rich legacy of Renaissance buildings – from brick classical merchants' town houses to country houses and suburban villas – and to embark on the Industrial Revolution second only to Liverpool as Britain's major transatlantic port. As a pivotal part of the slave trade, Bristol imported tobacco, timber, rum, cotton and sugar and together with its human cargoes, exported finished cotton goods, glass, brassware and soap. Its decline as a port, in the face of increasingly successful competition from Liverpool, lay as much in the Lancashire port's advantageous relationship to the expanding canal network, as to Bristol's position up a difficult tidal river in the face of the increasing size of 19th-C shipping. Today Bristol has an immense water-bound leisure facility in place of its once proud docks; home to wealth of activity, maritime and otherwise. As a contemporary city, its prosperity is founded upon a range of financial institutions from insurance to banking; on the aerospace industry and on high technology electronic research and production.

Bristol Cathedral College Green, Bristol (0117 926 4879). Major example of a 'hall' church, one of the finest in the world; the nave, choir and aisles are all of the same height. Founded in the middle of the 12th C as the Abbey of St Augustine, the Chapter House and Abbey Gatehouse clearly remain to be seen. In 1539 the Abbey was closed and the unfinished nave demolished. However in 1868 the architect G. E. Street drew up plans to complete the nave founded on the original pillar bases. Book shop and coffee shop.

Bristol Industrial Museum Princes Wharf, Wapping Road, Bristol (0117 925 1470; www. bristol-city.gov.uk/museums). Exhibits illustrating Bristol's rich industrial heritage. Family weekends offer the opportunity to get afloat on one of the museum's working boats; ride on a harbourside steam train; see a steam crane in action or try your hand at printing. *Open Apr–Oct, Sat–Wed 10.00–17.00, Nov–Mar, Sat–Sun 10.00–17.00.*

Bristol Zoo Gardens Clifton, Bristol (0117 973 8951; www.bristolzoo.org.uk). They breed endangered species, aim to raise awareness of the threat to a wide range of habitats, and support conservation projects worldwide. Restaurant, burger bar and covered picnic area. *Open daily 09.00–17.30 summer and 09.00–16.30 winter. Closed Xmas.* Charge. Buses 8 and 9 from city centre.

City Museum & Art Gallery Queen's Road, Bristol (0117 922 3571; www.bristol-city.gov.uk/museums). Temporary exhibitions, fascinating objects and artworks from all over the world. Family activities include 'fundays' on *first Sun of month* and workshops linked to displays. *Open daily 10.00–17.00.* Shop and licensed café serving a variety of meals and snacks.

Clifton Suspension Bridge Visitor Centre Bridge House, Sion Place, Bristol (0117 974 4664; www.clifton-suspension-bridge.org.uk). This potent symbol of the City of Bristol, from a design by I. K. Brunel, led a very chequered career from its inception in 1754 to final completion in 1864. The centre takes the visitor through all the ups and downs of the structure with the aid of models and interactive exhibitions. Photographic archive. *Open daily 10.00–17.00 summer, daily 11.00–16.00 (Sat–Sun closes 17.00) in winter.* Shop. Charge.

Floating Harbour Towards the end of the 18th C Bristol's importance as a port started to slip, largely on account of the large rise and fall in the tides and the difficulties encountered by ships berthing on the river mud, placing considerable stress on a vessel's hull. In 1802 William Jessop was invited to submit plans for a 'floating harbour'. Work began in 1804 and was completed some five years later. For a while the port thrived but, to a greater or lesser extent, was always handicapped by its position up the river. The last steamships used the docks in the 1950s. Today the harbour is primarily a focus for recreational activity.

Georgian House 7 Great George Street, Bristol (0117 921 1362; www. bristol-city.gov.uk/museums). An 18th-C West India merchant's house furnished in the style of the period and owned by John Piny, a sugar trader who owned both land and slaves in the Caribbean. Look out for 'living history days' when actors bring the house to life. *Open Sat–Wed, Apr–Oct 10.00–17.00.*

Imax Theatre Anchor Road, Harbourside, Bristol (08453 451235; www.at-bristol.org.uk). Cutting edge cinema technology combined with hands-on science centre and a multimedia mix to get you into the incredible history and variety of life on earth. *Open daily (except Xmas day) 10.00–18.00.* Charge.

St George's Bristol Great George Street, off Park Street, Bristol (0117 923 0359; www.stgeorgesbristol.co.uk). Music to suit all tastes in marvellously acoustic surroundings. Bar and gallery in beautifully restored crypt area.

St Mary Redcliffe Redcliffe Parade West, Bristol (0117 929 1487). Described by Elizabeth I as 'The fairest, goodliest and most famous Parish Church in England'. Coffee and light lunches served *Mon–Thur*.

SS Great Britain Great Western Dockyard, Gas Ferry Road, Bristol (0117 926 0680; www.ss-great-britain.com). Sea travel took a great leap forward when the famous Victorian engineer Isambard Kingdom Brunel applied his skills to the construction of an iron, steam-driven passenger ship capable of maintaining a schedule on voyages to America and the antipodes. *Open daily 10.00–17.30 Apr–Oct and 10.00–16.30 Nov–Mar.* Gift and coffee shops. Charge.

Watershed 1 Canon's Road, Harbourside, Bristol (0117 925 3845; www.watershed.co.uk). Bristol's arts centre with a wide mix of entertainment that is well up to expectation. Café/bar.

Tourist Information Centre Wildscreen Walk, Harbourside, Bristol (0117 926 0767; www. visitbristol.co.uk).

WALKING & CYCLING

The Avon Walkway-cum-Cycleway can be seen as the spinal route following the River from Pill to Bath and thence to Limpley Stoke and beyond. As such it forms the basis for a series of superb expeditions which can be linked into the extensive collection of routes radiating out from the Bristol City centre, accessed from the Floating Harbour, just north of St Augustines Reach. This also provides a direct link to the Bristol & Bath Railway Path which in turn interconnects with the Avon Cycleway – *see* previous notes for further details. Any permutation can provide circular routes with widely contrasting scenery. Many combinations are both flat and traffic-free. Cycle West, a charity that promotes cycling throughout the former Avon area, can be contacted for a range of free maps and detailed route advice (0117 922 4483; cyclewest@wpsd.demon.co.uk or voicemail 0117 936 5993). Bicycles are available for hire from: Bristol Bicycle Hire Cumberland Road, Bristol (0117 966 5069); Mud Dock Cycleworks, The Grove, Bristol (0117 9292151; www.mud-dock.com); Blackboy Cycles, Blackboy Hill, Bristol (0117 973 1420).

Pubs and Restaurants

There are a wide range of bars, cafés, clubs and eating houses thronging the Floating Harbour.

🍺 **Adam & Eve** 7 Hope Chapel Hill, Hotwells, Bristol (0117 9291508). Atmospheric, comfortable and welcoming pub. Real ale. Large portions of inexpensive food (V) *L and E*.

🍺 **Merchants Arms** Merchants Road, Hotwells, Bristol (0117 904 0037). Friendly traditional local with wood panelling and boarded floors. Real ale. Bar snacks *L and E*. Children welcome. No smoking area. Quiz *alternate Mon*. Live folk music *Tue*.

🍺 **Pump House** Merchants Road, Hotwells, Bristol (0117 927 9557). Old pumping station supplying water to the docks, turned chapel, turned slaughterhouse. Real ales. Wide ranging menu (V), available all day *Easter–Xmas (L and E in winter)*. Carvery *Sun 12.00–15.00*. Children welcome. Dockside patio seating. Quiz *Mon*.

🍺 ✕ **Spring Gardens** 188 Hotwells Road, Hotwells, Bristol (0117 927 7112). Atmospheric bar-cum-bistro serving appetising, upmarket food (V) *L and E* (bar snacks *L*; no food *Sat L*). Real ales. Children and dogs welcome. Outside patio and veranda seating. Quiz *Sun* and jazz *alternate Wed*.

🍺 **Bag O'Nails** 141 St George's Road, Hotwells, Bristol (0117 940 6776; www.bagonails.org.uk). Wood-panelled bar, glass portholes in the floor, gas lighting and an ever-changing range of unusual real ales make this small pub a gem.

🍺 ✕ **Arnolfini Café Bar** 16 Narrow Quay, St Augustine's Reach, Bristol (0117 929 9191; www.arnolfini.demon.co.uk). Situated within the well-known art gallery. Superb quality and value food (V) served *all day* in comfortably relaxed surroundings. Everyone welcome. Real ale. Quayside location.

✕ **Severnshed** The Grove, Harbourside, Bristol (0117 925 1212). A versatile establishment with a wealth of food, drinks and entertainment all corralled within a 'hoverbar'. Tasty café food (V) available *12.00–midnight*; a more substantial restaurant menu (V) available *12.00–16.00 and 18.30–22.30*; cocktails and drinks *12.00–01.00*. Live music events *throughout the year*.

✕ **Belgo** Old Granary Building, Queen Charlotte Street, Bristol (0117 905 8000; www.belgo-restaurants.com). Belgian food (V) served *L and E* in a strikingly handsome warehouse building. Excellent deals on food for *weekday L and early E*. Children welcome and can be fed free with an adult who is eating.

🍺 ✕ **Beese's Tea Gardens** Conham Ferry, Eastwood Road, Bristol (0117 977 7412). Waterside café set in the wooded Avon Valley serving buffet food (V), teas and barbecues. Mooring, large garden, children welcome. *Open Easter–Oct Wed–Fri 19.00–21.30 (approx) and Sat–Sun 12.00–21.30 (approx)*.

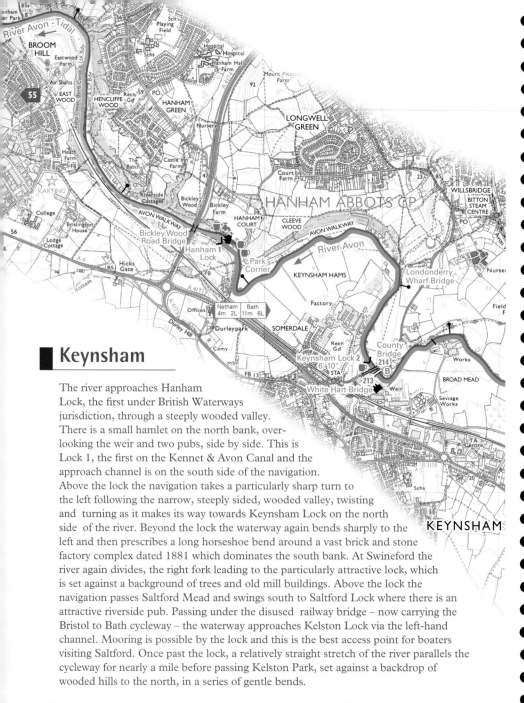

Keynsham

The river approaches Hanham
Lock, the first under British Waterways
jurisdiction, through a steeply wooded valley.
There is a small hamlet on the north bank, overlooking the weir and two pubs, side by side. This is
Lock 1, the first on the Kennet & Avon Canal and the
approach channel is on the south side of the navigation.
Above the lock the navigation takes a particularly sharp turn to
the left following the narrow, steeply sided, wooded valley, twisting
and turning as it makes its way towards Keynsham Lock on the north
side of the river. Beyond the lock the waterway again bends sharply to the
left and then prescribes a long horseshoe bend around a vast brick and stone
factory complex dated 1881 which dominates the south bank. At Swineford the
river again divides, the right fork leading to the particularly attractive lock, which
is set against a background of trees and old mill buildings. Above the lock the
navigation passes Saltford Mead and swings south to Saltford Lock where there is an
attractive riverside pub. Passing under the disued railway bridge – now carrying the
Bristol to Bath cycleway – the waterway approaches Kelston Lock via the left-hand
channel. Mooring is possible by the lock and this is the best access point for boaters
visiting Saltford. Once past the lock, a relatively straight stretch of the river parallels the
cycleway for nearly a mile before passing Kelston Park, set against a backdrop of
wooded hills to the north, in a series of gentle bends.

● **Keynsham**
Somerset. All services. Keynsham has grown
steadily along the Bristol road, and so is now a
vast shapeless suburb. However, the centre still

retains a feeling of independence, and has many
traces of Keynsham's past.
● **Bitton**
Somerset. PO, tel, stores, garage. Although a main

road village, Bitton's heart survives intact south of the road. Here is a fine group formed by the church, the grange and the 18th-C vicarage, all built around the churchyard. The church has a long Saxon nave with Norman details, a 14th-C chancel, and a magnificently decorative late 14th-C tower.

Avon Valley Railway Bitton Station, Bath Road, Bitton, Bristol (0117 932 5538; www.avonvalleyrailway.co.uk). Short length of preserved steam railway operating a limited service *in the summer and on some other occasions.* Telephone the talking timetable for further details (0117 932 7296). Cream teas, snacks and light refreshments.

● **Swineford**
Somerset. Tel, farm shop. Although bisected by the A431, the settlement by the river is still attractive. The old mill buildings constructed in 1840 overlook the long weir. There is a farm shop next to the pub, *open daily 08.00–18.00 except Wed and Sun 14.00–18.00.*

People and Planet Swineford Mill, Swineford (0117 932 3505). An attractive shop and tea garden promoting products from the Third World. Open *Wed–Sat 10.30–17.00.* Gifts, foods, jewellery, textiles, books, clothes and environmentally friendly products. Home-made teas and light lunches. Mooring for patrons.

● **Saltford**
Somerset. PO, tel, stores, garage. Although Saltford has been developed as a large-scale dormitory suburb, the older parts by the river are still pretty and secluded.

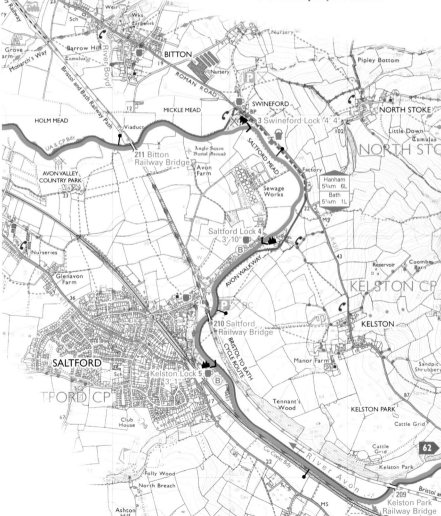

Kennet & Avon Canal

Keynsham

NAVIGATIONAL NOTES

1 The River Avon is usually only tidal to Hanham, however high spring tides can reach as far as Keynsham Lock.
2 Upstream craft should give way to downstream craft on fast-flowing sections of the river.
3 Downstream craft should approach the bend at Keynsham with caution and sound their horn to warn craft leaving Portavon Marina of their approach. Approach the lock cut entrance with care as it can be obscured by trees.
4 Visitor moorings are very limited on the river below Bath so boaters should plan their itinerary accordingly.
5 Bath Locks are padlocked when the river is in spate so at times of high water levels boaters should not embark on a journey upstream without first ensuring that they can leave the navigation for the safe haven of the canal.
6 See also Navigational Note 1 on page 51.

Pubs and Restaurants

🍺 ✕ **Chequers** Hanham (0117 967 4242). Comfortable, well appointed, riverside pub serving real ales. Food (V) available *all day* in bar and in restaurant *L and E*. Children welcome. Riverside garden. Moorings for patrons.

🍺 **Old Lock and Weir** Hanham (0117 967 3793). Riverside pub serving real ales and food (V) *L and E (not Sun and Mon E)*. Booking advisable *Fri, Sat and Sun E*. Barbecues *in summer*. Overnight moorings available for boaters eating at the pub. *Aug B Hol* beer festival.

🍺 **Lock Keeper** Keynsham Lock (0117 986 2383). Unpredictable flood waters forced many a crew to stay the night at the Lock Keeper. Real ales and food (V) available *all day*. Children and dogs welcome. Garden.

🍺 **White Hart** Bitton (0117 932 2231). Real ales and bar food (V) *L and E (except Sun E)*. Garden, children welcome. Regular *summer* barbecues.

🍺 ✕ **Swan** Swineford (0117 932 3101). Near Swineford Lock. 200-year-old stone-built cottage pub. Real ales on offer, drawn from the 'wood'. Home-cooked food (V) available *L and E (except Sun E)*. Children welcome if dining *before 21.00*. Garden.

🍺 ✕ **Jolly Sailor** Saltford (01225 873002). By Saltford Lock. A popular pub dating back to 1727. Real ale and guest ales. Food in bar and gazebo restaurant *L and E*. Barbecues *weekends during the summer*. Children welcome.

🍺 **Bird in Hand** Saltford (01225 873335). A beautifully kept village local offering locally brewed real ales and superb country views. Good food (V) *L and E*. Large conservatory, garden and terrace. Children welcome. Family room.

🍺 ✕ **Riverside Inn** Saltford (01225 873862). Next to Kelston Lock. Smart bar and restaurant overlooking the river. Real ale. Food (V) available *all day* in the bar and *E* in the candlelit, à la carte restaurant. Live entertainment *Fri and Sat E*. Children welcome. Outside seating and family room.

WALKING & CYCLING
Between Hanham and Bath walkers and cyclists may find it easier to make use of the cycleway along the old railway track which can be accessed at either Bitton Steam Centre or west of Swineford Lock. The Bristol to Bath cycleway is part of an extensive, interconnecting network of cycle paths around the Avon area, many of which are traffic free. A section of the railway path is used by the Avon Cycleway, an 85-mile signposted route using a network of quiet lanes around Bristol. Further details are available from Bristol City Council (0117 922 2000).

Boatyards

ⓑ **Port Avon Marina** Bitton Road, Keynsham. (0117 986 1626). 🚿 🚽 ♿ D Gas, overnight mooring, long-term mooring, winter storage, slipway, crane, chandlery, books, maps and gifts, boat sales and repairs, engine sales and repairs (including outboards), toilets, showers.

ⓑ **Bristol Boats** Mead Lane, Saltford (01225 872032). Near Saltford Lock. Gas, long-term mooring, slipway, gantry, boat sales and repairs, outboard engine sales and repairs, chandlery, toilets. *Closed Sun.*

ⓑ 🍺 ✕ **Saltford Marina** The Shallows, Saltford (01225 872226). Beside Kelston Lock. 🚿 ♿ D Overnight mooring. Restaurant and bar.

▌Bath

The river, on passing Kelston Park, prepares to leave its wide, wandering course and the pastures flanking both banks in favour of the urban sprawl of Bath. It soon passes under the elegant single stone arch of New Bridge carrying the A4 and again ducks through another disused railway bridge, now the Bristol to Bath cycleway. The main line from London to South Wales closely follows the south bank, vanishing at one point into a tunnel. Soon the River Avon approaches the industrial suburbs of Bath and enters a wooded section. Ahead is Weston Lock and the lock cut is the northern channel. Beyond the lock the navigation meanders into the city in long, gentle curves flanked by roads, the railway and areas of light industry. There are several footbridges across the river and the cycleway makes two further crossings. There are good moorings east of Churchill Road bridges, convenient for a supermarket. The canal joins the Avon immediately below Bath Bottom Lock No 7 in the middle of the industrial quarter of the city. The railway station is opposite the junction of canal and river and the fine Georgian city surrounds the unnavigable river to the north and east. The junction (and moorings to the north) are the best points of access for Bath as a whole. The Widcombe flight of six locks lifts the waterway swiftly above the city allowing magnificent views in all directions. There was once a seventh lock in the flight but locks 8 and 9 were merged as part of a road building scheme, making one new lock with a fall of over 19ft. This now vies with Tuel Deep Lock, on the Rochdale Canal, for deepest lock on the navigable waterways system. Above the flight the navigation enters a cutting and passes through an ornamental tunnel that carries housing and Cleveland House, the old canal company's headquarters. Beyond the tunnel another cutting carries the waterway past two pretty cast iron bridges, both dated 1800 and houses seem almost to hang out over the water. There is another tunnel with fine Adamesque portals as the canal leaves the confines of Sydney Gardens and passes the last of the Georgian buildings lining its banks. On the south bank there are gardens running down to the water which accompany the canal into Bath and there is a useful range of shops to the west of bridge 188. The navigation makes a magnificent exit from the city, cut into the hill, sweeping round to the south to join the river as they begin to follow the same route towards Bathampton. There are extensive views across Bath and from this point it is possible to pick out many of the features of the city; the Georgian terraces can be seen spread out over the far side of the valley. The railway is now accompanied by the new stretch of the A4 whose traffic drones continuously. The canal continues on a straight course, closely flanked by the railway, which is in a cutting below and then passes through Bathampton, on a low embankment above the school and church. Following the course of the River Avon the waterway swings sharply to the south, towards Bathford church on the opposite side of the valley, leaving behind the groups of houses that heralded the suburbs of Bath.

WALKING & CYCLING

The towpath is in excellent condition throughout its entire length to Reading, although eastern sections bordering the river navigation can become very overgrown in the height of the summer. It is a very popular long distance route for walkers and cyclists alike and the latter are asked to exercise care and to give way to people on foot. The Bristol & Bath Railway Path and the riverside walk give direct, safe access into the centre of Bath. East of Bath the National Cycle Network Route 4 follows the towpath to Devizes.

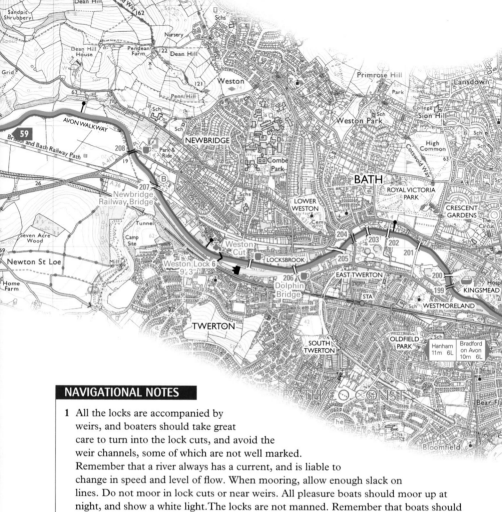

NAVIGATIONAL NOTES

1. All the locks are accompanied by weirs, and boaters should take great care to turn into the lock cuts, and avoid the weir channels, some of which are not well marked. Remember that a river always has a current, and is liable to change in speed and level of flow. When mooring, allow enough slack on lines. Do not moor in lock cuts or near weirs. All pleasure boats should moor up at night, and show a white light. The locks are not manned. Remember that boats should always be held by ropes while the locks are being operated, as there is a strong flow in these large locks.

2. Do not moor in the Widcombe Lock flight as the levels of intermediate pounds are subject to considerable fluctuations.

3. See also Navigational Notes on page 60.

BOAT TRIPS

Bath Boating Station Forester Road, Bathwick, Bath (01225 466407). A unique surviving Victorian boating station with tea gardens and a licensed restaurant. Traditional boats; skiffs, punts and canoes, for hire by the hour or the day. Free instruction for those new to punting. *Open Apr–Sep, daily 10.00–18.00* for boating. Restaurant *open L, also E and teas in summer.*

Bath Narrowboats Sydney Wharf, Bath (01225 447276). *John Rennie* 60-seater restaurant boat available for private charter. On-board catering with a wide selection of menus.

Pride of Bath North Parade Bridge, Bath (01225 333769). Large, 120-passenger cruise boat available for charter. Bar, servery, dance floor. Also public lunch and afternoon tea cruises. Telephone for further details.

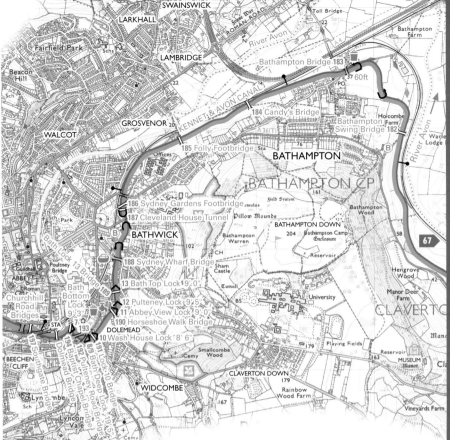

● **Bath**

Somerset. All services. Bath was first developed by the Romans as a spa town and resort because of its natural warm springs. They started the trend of bathing and taking the waters which survives today. There are extensive Roman remains to be seen in the city, not least the baths themselves. The city grew further during the medieval period, when it was a centre of the wool trade; the fine abbey dates from this time. But the true splendour of Bath is the 18th-C development, when the city grew as a resort and watering place that was frequented by all levels of English society, from royalty downwards. Despite heavy bombing in World War II, Bath is still a magnificent memorial to the 18th C and Neo-classicism generally. The terraces that adorn the steep northern slope of the Avon valley contain some of the best Georgian architecture in Britain. Much of the city was designed by John Wood the Younger, who was responsible for the great sweeping Royal Crescent. Other architects included Thomas Baldwin, who built the Guildhall, 1766–75, and the Pump Room, 1789–99, and Robert Adam, whose Pulteney

Bridge carries terraces of shops across the Avon. Bath is best seen on foot, for its glories and riches are far too numerous to list. Visitors should not fail to try the waters, which gush continuously from a fountain outside the Pump Room.

Bath Abbey Set in an attractive piazza, the abbey is a pleasingly uniform Perpendicular building, founded in 1499. Twin towers crown the west front, decorated with carved angels ascending and descending ladders. Inside, the abbey is justly famous for its fan vaulting, which covers the whole roof of the building but is not all of the same date. Inside also is a wealth of memorials of all periods, an interesting indication of the vast range of people who, over the ages, have come to die in Bath.

Holburne Museum and Crafts Study Centre
Great Pulteney Street, Bath (01225 4666690; www. bath.ac.uk). Housed in an 18th-C Palladian building that was designed as part of the Sydney pleasure gardens, it contains collections of silver, ceramics, 18th-C paintings and furniture, 20th-C art and craft work. Teahouse. *Open mid Feb–mid Dec Mon–Sat 11.00–17.00 and Sun 14.30–17.30. Charge.*

Jane Austen Centre 40 Gay Street, Bath (01225 443000; www.janeausten.co.uk). Enjoy the pleasure of Bath as Jane Austen knew it. A Georgian town house in the heart of the city where the visitor can find out more about the importance of Bath in her life and work. *Open daily Mon–Sat 10.00–17.30 and Sun 10.30–17.30.* Charge. Also walking tours of Jane Austen's Bath, *daily Apr–Sep and weekends Oct–Mar, commencing 13.30* from Abbey Churchyard. Charge.

Museum of Costume Assembly Rooms, Bath (01225 477000; www.museumofcostume.co.uk). Display of fashion from the 17th C to the present day; one of the largest collections of costume in the world. *Open daily 10.00–17.00.* Charge.

Postal Museum 8 Broad Street, Bath (01225 460333; www.bathpostalmuseum.org.uk). The place from which the first postage stamp was sent on 2 May 1840. The history of the postal service and the development of the written word. *Open Mon–Sat 11.00–17.00, Sun 14.00–17.00.* Charge.

Roman Baths Museum Stall Street, Bath (01225 477000; www.romanbaths.co.uk). The great bath buildings with their dependent temple were the centre of Roman Bath. Much of these survive, incorporated into the 18th-C Pump Room. The museum, attached to the bath buildings, contains finds excavated from the site. *Open all year, daily Apr–Sep 09.00–18.00 and Oct–Mar 09.30–17.00.* Charge.

1 Royal Crescent Bath (01225 428126). The first house of this magnificent crescent built by John Wood the Younger between 1767–74. Complete with original furniture and fittings. *Open Feb–Oct 10.30–17.00 and Nov 10.30–16.00. Closed Mon and G Fri. Open B Hols.* Charge.

Thermae Bath Spa Hot Bath Street, Bath (01225 780308; www.thermaebathspa.com). Recently restored, these five historic buildings plus a contemporary addition by Nicholas Grimshaw & Partners allow all-year bathing in natural thermal waters. Full range of spa treatments and complementary therapies, plus views from a roof-top pool! *Open daily 09.00–22.00 (last entry 20.00). Closed Xmas Day, New Years Eve and New Years Day.* Charge. Shop, visitor centre, restaurant. Disabled access.

Victoria Art Gallery Bridge Street, Bath (01225 477000; www.victoriagal.org.uk). Collection of 18th-C and modern paintings, prints and ceramics. Visiting exhibitions. Gallery shop and refreshments. *Open Tue–Fri 10.00–17.30, Sat 10.00–17.00 and Sun 14.00–17.00. Closed B Hols.*

Tourist Information Centre Abbey Churchyard, Bath (01225 477000; www.visitbath.co.uk).

● **Bathampton**
Somerset. PO, tel, stores, garage. The centre of the village surrounds the canal and is still compact and undeveloped, but new housing around the edges has turned it into a suburb of Bath. The church is mostly 19th-C.

Pubs and Restaurants

Bath is well-endowed with distinguished restaurants, lively wine bars and excellent pubs. The following is a selection of pubs close to the canal.

🍺 ✕ **Appleton's at the Boatyard** Newbridge, Bath (01225 482584). Just west of New Bridge. Pub and restaurant beside the River Avon. Real ale. Food available *all day, every day.* Children welcome. Riverside garden and moorings for patrons.

🍺 **Dolphin** Locksbrook Road, Bath (01225 445048). On the Weston Cut. Real ales and bar meals (V) available *L and E* with separate menus for each. Garden and moorings. Children welcome. Darts, dominoes and crib. *Open all day.*

🍺 **Golden Fleece** 1–3 Avon Buildings, Lower Bristol Road, Bath (01225 429572). One-bar local 50yds south of the river, serving a selection of real ales. Traditional pub games.

🍺 ✕ **Bathampton Mill** Mill Lane, Bathampton (01225 469758). 400yds north of Bathampton Bridge. Food (V) and real ales available at the bar *all day* and in the restaurant *L and E Mon–Fri and all day Sat and Sun.* Garden with play area and attractive riverside terrace.

🍺 **George Inn** Bathampton, Bath (01225 425079). Family pub with canalside garden and children's play area. Real ales. Extensive and enticing range of freshly prepared food (V) available in the bar *L and E. Open all day Sat and Sun in summer.*

Boatyards

Ⓑ **Bath Marina** Brass Mill Lane, Bath (01225 424301). Long-term mooring. Under new management so facilities may change. Telephone for details.

Ⓑ **Bath Narrowboats** Sydney Wharf, Bath (01225 447276; www.bath-narrowboats.co.uk).

🚽 ⚒ D Pump out, narrowboat hire, day boat hire, gas, engine sales, boat repairs, chandlery, books, maps, gifts. *Emergency call out.*

Ⓑ **Digger's Yard** Warminster Road, Bath (07790 872705). 🚽 🚽 ⚒ D Overnight mooring, winter storage, DIY facilities. Fresh produce.

Claverton

Open country continues, allowing views across the valley to Bathford church and Warleigh Manor. The navigation follows the contours of the land as it leaves Bath, maintaining the level of the nine mile pound that runs from Bath Top Lock to Bradford. The waterway approaches a thickly wooded stretch passing Claverton to the west. Although the village flanks the canal it is all but hidden by the folds of the land. Access is easy and both the village and Claverton Manor are worth a visit. Claverton Pumping Station houses a water-powered pump which lifts water from the Avon to feed the canal. The pump has been restored by the Kennet and Avon Canal Trust, with help from engineering students from Bath University. Now a side-cutting takes the canal towards Dundas Aqueduct preceded by the turnover bridge and a basin complete with a small wharf and crane standing over the water. Here is the junction with The Somerset Coal Canal which, until its closure in 1904, ran south from the Kennet & Avon Canal towards Paulton. At the wharf the waterway turns suddenly onto the aqueduct – perhaps the best-known feature of the Kennet & Avon Canal – which carries it across the railway and the Avon valley to the east side. Passing the village of Limpley Stoke, scattered over the valley side, the navigation runs through thick woods clinging to steep banks until the countryside again opens out on the approach to Avoncliff Aqueduct.

Boatyards

ⓑ **Bath & Dundas Canal Co**. Brassknocker Basin, Monkton Combe (01225 722292; www.bathcanal.com). At the end of the Somersetshire Coal Canal, where boats up to 60ft can turn, BUT do not bring your boat in without first walking along the main road to the office to check if space is available. ⚓ D E pump out – *24hrs notice required*, gas, narrowboat hire, day-hire craft (including canoes), long-term mooring, slipway, dry dock, books and maps, boat sales and repairs, outboard engine sales and repairs, dry dock, wet dock, books, gifts and maps, cycle hire, historical display of Somerset Coal Canal, telephone, café, toilets, B & B. *24hr emergency call out* on 07748 654202. Provisions are available at the garage above Dundas Wharf.

● **Claverton**
Somerset. Tel. Although devoid of all facilities, Claverton is well worth a visit. It is a manorial village of stone houses, surrounding the 17th-C farm, and in early days was clearly dependent upon Claverton Manor. The main road misses the village, increasing the peace and seclusion.
The American Museum in Britain Claverton Manor, Bath (01225 460503; www.americanmuseum.org). The manor was built in 1820 by Sir Jeffry Wyatville in the Greek revival style. It now houses a museum of American decorative arts from the late 17th C to the mid 19th C. Teas. *Open Apr–Oct, 14.00–17.00. Closed Mon except during Aug and B Hols.* Charge.
Claverton Pumping Station Ferry Lane, Claverton. Enquiries on (0117) 986 7536. The waterwheel pump at Claverton is the only one of its kind on British canals. Designed by John Rennie, the pump was built to feed the 9 mile Bradford–Bath pound, and started operating in 1813. The two undershot breast wheels, each 15ft in diameter and 11ft wide, then powered the pumping machinery until a major breakdown in 1952 prompted its closure, and replacement by a temporary diesel pump. The original machinery has now been restored, and pumping weekends are organised. New electric pumps now do the day-to-day work, raising water from the Avon 47ft below. The Pumping Station is run by the Kennet & Avon Canal Trust volunteers. *Open Easter–Oct, Sun 10.30–16.30.* Pumps fully working *on fourth Sun in month.* Partial disabled access and picnic area. Charge.
● **Limpley Stoke**
Wilts. PO, tel, stores. Built on the side of the valley overlooking the river, Limpley Stoke is a quiet village, a residential outpost of Bath. The little church includes work of all periods, from

Norman to the 20th C: inside is a collection of carved coffin lids.

Dundas Aqueduct Built in 1804, this three-arch classical stone aqueduct is justifiably one of the most well-known features of the canal, and stands as a fitting monument to the architectural and engineering skill of John Rennie. It is necessary to leave the canal and walk down into the valley below to appreciate the beauty of the aqueduct, and to see it in the context of the narrow Avon valley into which it fits so well. The aqueduct was named in honour of the first chairman of the Kennet and Avon Canal Company and is widely regarded as Rennie's finest architectural work. Urgent repair work had to be carried out in the early 1980s involving relining the structure with reinforced concrete.

Somersetshire Coal Canal Opened in 1805, this narrow canal was sponsored by the Somerset Coal owners, who wanted a more efficient means of moving their coal to Bath, Bristol and the rest of England. Originally surveyed by Rennie in 1793, the canal was to run from Limpley Stoke to Paulton, with a branch to Radstock. There were steep gradients to overcome at Midford and Combe Hay, and these plagued the canal throughout its life. The Radstock Arm was never completed and tramroads were built over the difficult stretches. The main line was completed throughout, but not before some remarkable solutions to the problems of the Combe Hay gradient had been tried out. First there was Robert Weldon's caisson lock; a watertight caisson, large enough to hold a narrowboat and crew, was pulled up and down an 88ft-deep water-filled cistern by means of a rack and pinion. This terrifying device was soon replaced by an inclined plane, which in turn was replaced by a conventional flight of locks. Once open, the canal carried a large tonnage of coal throughout the 19th C: it served 30 collieries more directly than the railway. However, by the end of the century the inevitable competition was taking away the traffic, which finally stopped in 1898. The canal was officially abandoned in 1904. The first 1/4 mile has now been restored and is used by a boatyard, and for moorings. A stop lock at the entrance restricts its use to craft of 7ft beam only.

● **Freshford**
Somerset. PO, tel, station. Although not on the canal, Freshford is well worth the 1/2 mile walk south from Limpley Stoke. It is a particularly attractive village, set on the side of the steep hill that flanks the confluence of the rivers Avon and Frome. At the top of the hill is the church, and terraces of handsome stone houses fall away in both directions, filling the valley below, and crowding the narrow streets. At the bottom of the hill is the river, crossed by the medieval bridge. The hills around were a rich source of Bath stone, limestone and fuller's earth and in the early 19th C the village was involved with the production of broad cloth in its extensive factory. Ruins of an old hermitage and friary, possibly connected with Hinton Abbey, were excavated locally, as were the remains of a Roman encampment.

Pubs and Restaurants

● ✕ **Viaduct Hotel** Brassknocker Hill, Monkton Combe (01225 723187). Real ale. Food (V) available in bar and restaurant *L and E, daily.* Children welcome. Large garden. B & B.

✕ � **Angelfish Café/Restaurant** Brassknocker Basin, Monkton Combe (01225 723483). Generous portions of appetising, home-made food served in an attractive setting with a distinctly continental feel. Tea, coffee, home-made cakes, filled baguettes and crêpes, hot meals (V), drinks and ice creams. Family orientated. Café *open daily all year 10.00–18.00 (10.00–17.00 in winter).* À la carte restaurant *open Fri and Sat E from 19.30 and on other evenings* for functions and pre-booked groups (minimum 20). Regular events. Booking advisable for restaurant.

✕ ♱ **Nightingale's** Limpley Stoke (01225 723150). An attractive restaurant in the centre of the village specialising in regional Italian cuisine *Tue–Sat E 19.00–22.00.* Non-smoking. Booking advisable.

● **Rose and Crown** Limpley Stoke (01225 722237). Village pub serving real ale and food (V) *L and E Mon–Fri and all day Sat and Sun.* Children welcome. Garden.

● ✕ **Hop Pole** Limpley Stoke (01225 723134). Moor at Limpley Stoke Bridge, walk down to the railway bridge and turn left to find this popular traditional oak-panelled pub, featured in the film 'Remains of the Day'. The building is at least 400 years old, originally the monks' wine lodge – it is now famous for its Hop Pole pies. Real ale. Extensive bar and à la carte menu (V) and wine list *L and E daily.* Children welcome in designated areas, as are dogs. Old English country garden.

✕ **Fordside Tea Garden** Limpley Stoke (01225 722115). 100yds south of Limpley Stoke Bridge. Attractive private garden and tearoom, accessed through a hole in the hedge, serving tea, coffee, snacks, home-made cakes and refreshments. *Open weekends and most weekdays 11.00–18.00.* Large parties please give prior notice.

● **The Inn** Freshford (01225 722250). It is well worth the walk to this splendid, traditional pub overlooking the river. Real ales. Bar meals (V) available *every day.* À la carte menu *L and E, daily.* Garden. Children welcome.

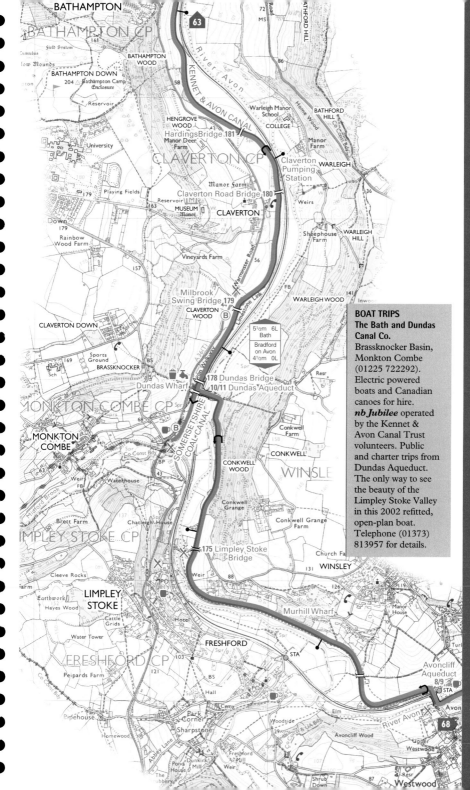

BOAT TRIPS
The Bath and Dundas Canal Co.
Brassknocker Basin, Monkton Combe (01225 722292). Electric powered boats and Canadian canoes for hire. *nb Jubilee* operated by the Kennet & Avon Canal Trust volunteers. Public and charter trips from Dundas Aqueduct. The only way to see the beauty of the Limpley Stoke Valley in this 2002 refitted, open-plan boat. Telephone (01373) 813957 for details.

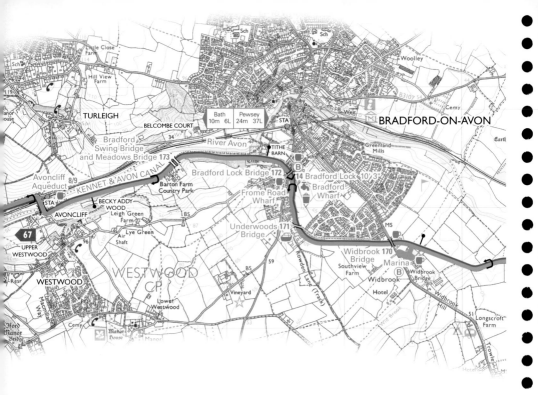

Bradford on Avon

At the aqueduct the towpath crosses under the canal to the north side and the thick woods give the canal user a feeling of total seclusion. Avoncliff makes a worthwhile stop with its tearoom (*open daily in summer 10.00–17.30*) and pub overlooking the river and the elegant stone arches (recently restored) of Rennie's fine aqueduct. Towards Bradford, the Avon rushes along beside the towpath and beyond it the railway appears and disappears among the trees on the far side of the valley, whilst the waterway pursues its more sedate course. Cyclists appear with great frequency since this is part of the Wiltshire Cycleway route. The town is approached through beautiful woods leading to the Tithe Barn, beyond which there are fine views of Bradford spread out above the river. Above the lock and Bradford Basin, the navigation skirts an extensive residential area and is set slightly below the surrounding area, burrowing out towards open country-side again. River and canal make their separate departures from the town to converge again with the canal high above in a side cutting, initially shielded by trees. Then fine views northwards open out over the Avon valley as the waterway crosses first the River Biss, followed by the railway on two, splendid stone aqueducts. The classical arch over the river is particularly handsome; it is necessary to walk down the side of the embankment to see it properly. To the west of Hilperton, the canal passes the grounds of Wyke House, whose Jacobean-style towers stand among the trees. Passing the boatyard and large marina basin the navigation curves around Hilperton; although the main part of the village is a mile to the south. There is a convenient pub, post office and stores by the road bridge. Beyond, the countryside opens out into the wide Avon valley as the canal makes a beeline for Devizes and the Caen Hill Lock Flight.

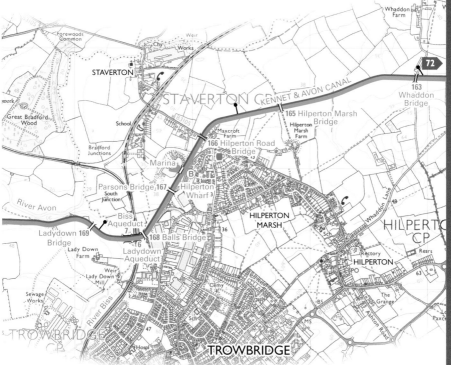

WALKING & CYCLING
BW publish a Discovery trail for Bradford on Avon obtainable from their Devizes office (01380 722859; enquiries.kanda@britishwaterways.co.uk) or the TIC. Bradford is an excellent place for the cyclist to access the towpath with level rides towards Bath and bikes for hire.

Boatyards

ⓑ **Lock Inn Cottage** Frome Road, Bradford on Avon (01225 867187). Day boat hire for groups and individuals in electric launches. Canoe and cycle hire. Café.

ⓑ **Sally Boats** Bradford on Avon Marina (01225 864923; www.sallyboats.ltd.uk). Narrowboat hire, dry dock, DIY facilities, chandlery.

ⓑ **Bradford on Avon Marina** Trowbridge Road, Bradford on Avon (01225 864562). 🚽 🔌 D Pump out, gas, overnight mooring, long-term mooring, narrowboat hire, slipway, boat sales, DIY facilities, dry dock, toilets, showers.

ⓑ **Wessex Narrowboats** Wessex Wharf,

Hilperton Marina, Trowbridge (01225 769847; www.wessexboats.co.uk). 🔌 E Gas, overnight mooring, long-term mooring, winter storage, hoist (2 tonne), narrowboat hire, day hire craft, boat and engine sales, boat and engine repairs, boat building and fitting out, dry dock, DIY facilities, wet dock, gifts, books and maps. *24 hr emergency call out.*

ⓑ **Hilperton Marina** Staverton Marina, The Slipway, Trowbridge (01225 765243). 🚽 🚽 🔌 D Pump out, gas, overnight mooring, long-term mooring, winter storage, chandlery, books, maps, boat sales, DIY facilities, solid fuel, toilets.

BOAT TRIPS

Barbara Mclellan 53-seat widebeam boat operated by Kennet & Avon Canal Trust Volunteers
from Bradford Lock. 1½ hour public trips *Easter–Oct.* Disabled access by lift. Private charter with
facilities for meals available. Telephone (01225) 782080 for details.

Avoncliff

Wilts. Station. A hamlet clustered in the woods
beside the canal. Originally it was a centre of
weaving, and many traces of the old industry can
be seen: weavers' cottages, and the old mills on
the Avon, which falls noisily over a weir at this
point. At one time the mills were used for flock-
ing, a process which involved the breaking up of
old woollen material to make stuffing for mattresses and chairs. The hamlet is dominated by
Rennie's aqueduct, built in 1804 to take the
canal across the valley to the north side. A
classical stone structure, it suffered from casual
repair work and patching in brick when owned by
the Great Western Railways, due mainly to the
inferior nature of the stone from which it was
constructed. Thankfully it has recently undergone an extensive and highly skilled restoration.

Bradford on Avon

Wilts. PO, tel, stores, garage, bank, station. Set in
the steeply wooded Avon valley, Bradford is one
of the beauty spots of Wiltshire, and one of the
highlights of the canal. Rather like a miniature
Bath, the town is composed of fine stone terraces
rising sharply away from the river, which cuts
through the centre of the town. Until the 19th C
it was a prosperous centre for weaving, but a
depression killed the industry and drove most
of the workers away. At the time that the canal
was built Bradford had no less than 30 water-
powered cloth factories and some of these
buildings still survive. Bradford is rich in
architectural treasures from the Saxon period to
the 19th C, while the abundance of fine 18th-C
houses make the exploration of the town a
positive pleasure. The centre is very compact,
and so the walk down the hill from the canal
wharf lays most of it open to inspection,
including the town bridge, Holy Trinity Church,
the Victorian town hall and the fine Gothic
Revival factory that dominates the riverside.
There is also a swimming pool near the canal.

Bradford Upper Wharf The canal wharf is
particularly attractive. There is a small dock with
some of the original buildings still standing,
plenty of mooring space, and an old canal pub
beside the lock. The lock here was built to raise
the canal to the same level as the Wilts and Berks
Canal which joins the canal at Semington.

Kennet & Avon Canal Trust Bradford Lock,
Bradford on Avon (01225 868683). Canal shop
and exhibition, range of canal books, souvenirs,
gifts and light refreshments. Picnic area. *Open
daily Easter–Oct 10.00–16.00.*

Great Tithe Barn Bradford on Avon (01225
865797). Standing below the canal embankment,
this great stone building is one of the finest tithe
barns in England. It was built in the 14th C by
the Abbess of Shaftesbury. Its cathedral-like
structure (168ft long) is broken by two porches,
with massive doors that open to reveal the
beamed roof. The barn is part of Barton Farm,
a medieval farm which was part of the monastic
estate of Shaftesbury Abbey. The Granary
and Cow Byres now house craft shops and
galleries.

Holy Trinity Church Basically a 12th-C building
with additions dating over the next three centuries.
Inside are some medieval wall paintings, and fine
18th-C monuments. Many of the names that
appear relate to the woollen industry.

Lock Inn Cottage 48 Frome Road, Bradford on
Avon (01225 868068). Canalside café serving
death-defying boatmen's breakfasts, light
lunches and cream teas. *Open all year, including
Sun and B Hols, 08.45–18.00.* Also restaurant –
see under Pubs and Restaurants. Canoe and
electric launch hire. Bicycle sales, repairs and
hire. All hire bikes can be used in conjunction
with trailers for children, trailer bikes and child
seats. Also tandems. Every permutation catered
for! *Open all year, daily 09.00–18.00 (except
Xmas Day).* For hire details telephone (01225)
867187.

Saxon Church of St Lawrence Founded in AD705,
this tiny church was enlarged in the 10th C.
Since then it has survived essentially unchanged,
having been at various times a school, a cottage
and a slaughterhouse. The true origins and
purpose of the building were only rediscovered
in the 19th C, and so it remains one of the best-
preserved Saxon churches in England.

Town Bridge The nine-arched bridge is unusual in
having a chapel in the middle, one of only four
still surviving in Britain. Parts of the bridge,
including the chapel, are medieval, but much
dates from a 17th-C rebuilding. During the 17th
and 18th C the chapel fell out of use, and was

turned into a small prison, serving as the town lock up.

Westwood Manor One mile south west of Bradford. This 15th-C stone manor house contains original Jacobean plaster and woodwork, although much was lost when the manor became a farm in the 18th C. Skilful restoration by the National Trust has returned the manor to its former glory. *Open Apr–Sep, Sun, Tue and Wed 14.00–17.00.* Charge.

Tourist Information Centre 34 Silver Street, Bradford on Avon (01225 865797; www.bradfordonavontown.com).

● **Staverton**
Wilts. Tel. The village lies to the north of the

canal, spreading down to the bank of the Avon. A small isolated part of the Avon is navigable here, and is used by a few pleasure boats. In the village are terraces of weavers' cottages, a sign of what was once the staple trade of the area.

● **Hilperton**
Wilts. PO, tel, stores (open Mon–Sat 07.00– 21.00 and Sun 08.00–20.00), garage. A scattered village that stretches away from the settlement by the canal wharf. Wyke House stands to the west of the village. This very ornate Jacobean mansion was in fact built in 1865, a replica of the original house. House *not open to the public.*

Pubs and Restaurants

🍽 **Cross Guns** Avoncliff Aqueduct (01225 862335; www.crossguns.freeserve.com). One of the most attractive pubs on the navigation with its low ceilings, stone walls and flagged floors. The terraced gardens are busy in summer with people enjoying this beautiful setting in a wooded valley. Real ales including their own brew. Good selection of imaginative, well-priced home-made food *L and E.* Children welcome. Booking advisable. B & B.

✕♀ **Lock Inn Cottage** Frome Road, Bradford on Avon (01225 868068). A unique establishment whose proprietors openly admit to scant portion control; welcome (amongst others) 'kids, cats and dogs, muddy boots, scaffolders, bankers, plumbers (when they turn up) and old age travellers', whilst justifiably claiming to be 'suppliers of happiness and laughter'. Excellent, appetising and inexpensive food for all the family, served in the café *daily 08.45–18.00,* and a tantalising restaurant menu available *Thur–Sat, 18.30 'till late.* Only moaners and unruly parents are banned!

🍽 **Canal Tavern** Lower Wharf, Bradford on Avon (01225 867426). It was outside the back door of this friendly pub that the first sod for the commencement of the canal was cut. The pub continues to benefit from its trade with an attractive terrace overlooking the navigation. Real ale. Home-made food (V) *L and E.* Barbecues and music in the garden *in summer.* Children welcome. Moorings for patrons.

✕ **Curry Inn** Bradford on Avon (01225

866424). Across the road from the Canal Tavern. Tandoori restaurant and takeaway. *Open Mon–Sat 18.00–23.00 also Fri–Sat 12.00–14.00.*

🍽 **Barge Inn** Bradford Wharf (01225 863403). Comfortable one-bar pub. Good choice of real ale and wine list. Attractive eating area, decorated with canalware, where food is served *Mon–Sat L and E and Sun 12.00–15.00.* Children welcome. Canalside garden. Moorings for patrons. B & B.

🍽 **Mill House** The Marina, Bradford on Avon (01225862004). Overlooking the marina this establishment serves real ales and food (V) *L and E.* Children's play area. Garden and patio. Barbecues on *summer weekends.*

🍽 **Beehive** Widbrook Bridge, Bradford on Avon (01225 863620). Unadulterated local serving real ales and food (V) *L and E (not Sun E or Tue L).* Open fires, a garden and pub games. Children welcome in the garden. Barbecues *weekends during summer.*

🍽✕ **Old Bear Inn** Staverton (01225 782487). 1/3 mile north west of Hilperton Bridge. Nicely kept 300-year-old inn. Real ales. Extensive menu (V) available in the bar and restaurant *L and E.* Children welcome. Garden.

🍽 **Kings Arms** Hilperton Wharf (01225 755168). A pub serving real ale and bar food (V) *L and E (not Sun E).* Children welcome. Garden with play area.

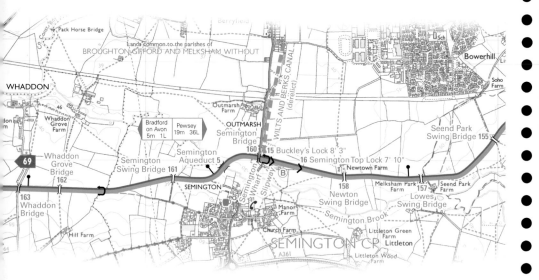

Seend Cleeve

The two Semington Locks continue the ascent towards Devizes with an attractive lock house by Lock 15. Just before the lock the canal is crossed by the A350; this is the best access point for Semington. A close examination of the north bank, just after the bridge, will reveal a bricked-up side bridge; this marks the site of the junction with the long abandoned Wiltshire & Berkshire Canal which used to go to Abingdon. The navigation continues its easterly course, maintaining a fairly straight line through open country before reaching the five Seend Locks. Beside the third lock there is a pub and a lane leading to Seend Cleeve village, although the best access is from bridge 152 below Seend Top Lock. The hills to the south climb steeply up to the village of Seend and to the north flat pasture land stretches away as the canal, passing two swing bridges, turns through Sells Green in a low cutting that hides most of the village.

Boatyards

ⓑ **Tranquil Boats** Lock House, Semington, Trowbridge (01380 870654). Electric day boat for hire, covered dry dock, slipway, DIY facilities, trailboat storage.
ⓑ **Scotts Wharf** Sells Green, Trowbridge (01380 828200). Immediately to the west of Sells Green Bridge 149, on the off-side. Day boat hire.

● **Semington**
Wilts. PO, tel, stores (open until 21.00 daily), garage. Despite the main road, Semington is a pretty village. There are several large, handsome houses with fine gardens, some dating from the 18th C. The little stone church, crowned with a bellcote, is at the end of a lane to the west of the village.
● **The Wiltshire & Berkshire Canal**
Opened in 1810, the canal wound in a meander-

ing course for 51 miles between Semington on the Kennet & Avon Canal and Abingdon on the River Thames. A branch was opened in 1819 from Swindon to connect with Latton on the Thames & Severn Canal. Although the carriage of Somerset coal was the inspiration for the canal, its eventual role was agricultural. Profits were never high, partly because the wandering line of the canal and its 45 locks made travel very slow, and so it suffered early from railway competition.

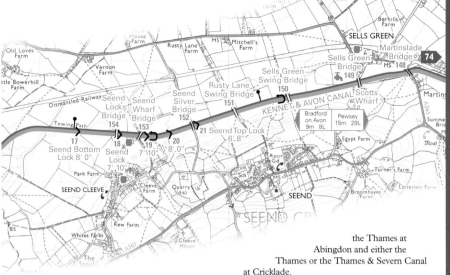

the Thames at Abingdon and either the Thames or the Thames & Severn Canal at Cricklade.

By the 1870s, moves were afoot to close the canal, and, despite various efforts to give it a new lease of life, the situation had become hopeless by the turn of the century. Traffic finally stopped in 1906, and the canal was formally abandoned in 1914. In 1977 the Wilts & Berks Canal Amenity Group was formed with the aim of preserving both the main line of the canal and the northern branch to Latton. Twenty years later its avowed aim is to restore the waterway to form a navigable link between the K & A,

● **Seend Cleeve**
Wilts. Tel. An agricultural village built on the steep slopes of the hills that overlook the canal.

● **Seend**
Wilts. PO, tel, stores, garage. Although the main road cuts the village in half, Seend is still attractive. Elegant 18th-C houses flank the road, and conceal the lane that leads to the battlemented Perpendicular church.

● **Sells Green**
Wilts. Tel, garage. A scattered main road village, the houses doing their best to hide from the traffic behind decorative gardens.

Pubs and Restaurants

💬 ✗ **Somerset Arms** Semington (01380 870067). About ¼ mile south of Semington Bridge. A traditional, old village pub, more than 400 years old, serving real ales and meals (V) in the bar and restaurant *L and E, daily*. Children welcome. Garden.

💬 **Brewery Inn** Seend Cleeve (01380 828463). 200yds south of Lock 19. A genuine, unadulterated village local. Real ales and traditional ciders. Bar snacks available *L* and meals *Fri and Sat E (no food Sun)*. Children and dogs welcome. Large garden with children's play area. Traditional pub games and a selection of board games.

💬 ✗ **Barge Inn** Seend (01380 828230). By Lock 19. An extensive and extremely popular pub occupying the former wharf house and stables, dating back to 1805. The house was once the home of the Wiltshire Giant, Fred Kempster, who reached the inconvenient height of 8ft 2ins. An interesting collection of

canalware adorns the walls. Real ales. Meals (V) in the bar and restaurant *L and E, daily*. Children welcome. Canalside garden. Occasional barbecues *in summer*.

💬 ✗ **Bell Inn** Seend (01380 828338). ½ mile south of Lock 21. An exciting conversion of an old brewhouse once patronised by Cromwell and his troops when they breakfasted here on their way to attack Devizes Castle in 1645. Traditional values and service. Real ales. Food (V) in bar and restaurant *L and E*. *Booking advisable at weekends (no food Mon E except B Hols)*. Children welcome. Outside terrace with panoramic views over Salisbury Plain.

💬 **Three Magpies** Sells Green (01380 828389). 200yds south of Sells Green Bridge. A comfortable pub, with converted stables housing the restaurant. Real ale. Imaginative menu (V) available *L and E*. Garden. Barbecues *Sun in summer*. Children's play area and camping.

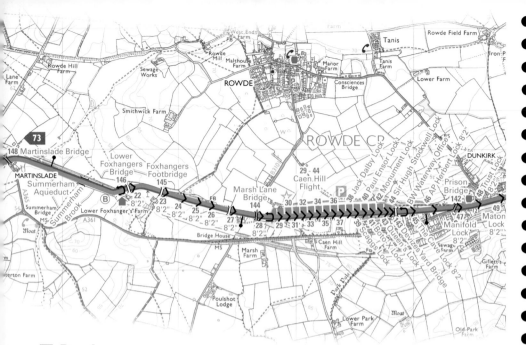

Devizes

At Lower Foxhangers the waterway swings left, under the turnover bridge, and enters Lock 22, the first of 7 locks with conventional pounds that precede the Caen Hill Flight proper. Immediately beyond Marsh Lane Bridge, carrying the B3101 to Rowde, the 16-lock Caen Hill section begins; wide lock follows wide lock up the hill, each with an enormous side pound. These were designed to hold sufficient water while permitting the locks to be close together to follow the slope. The scale of the whole flight is most impressive. The towpath is in very good condition and the whole area is obviously used for recreation by visitors and the people of Devizes alike. To the south the busy A361 accompanies the canal up the hill but it is out of sight for most of the way. Above Lock 44 the remaining locks are spaced out and finish at the generous stone bridge, with its separate towpath arch, that leads the navigation into Devizes Wharf, where the Kennet & Avon Canal Trust has a museum and shop in a converted warehouse. 29 locks have been negotiated in just 2^{1}/4 miles. The wharf is also the home of a theatre and trip boat operation. The waterway now enters a long, wooded cutting, spanned by several very elegant large stone bridges (some listed as ancient monuments) all of which offer easy access to the town. Houses appear, their gardens overlooking the cutting and running down to the water's edge. Soon the navigation passes the marina and moves out into the more remote landscape of the Wiltshire Wolds.

NAVIGATIONAL NOTES

Operating times for the Caen Hill Flight (locks 29-44) are: *Apr–Oct 08.00–14.00 (clear locks by 16.30) and Nov–Mar 08.00–13.00 (clear locks by 15.30).*

BOAT TRIPS

White Horse Boats 8 Southgate Close, Devizes (01380 728504/07976 162223; www.whitehorseboats.co.uk). Trips on *nb Kenavon Venture* from Devizes Wharf *Easter–Sep, Sun 14.00; Jul, Aug and B Hols (except G Fri) Sat afternoons.* Please telephone to confirm. Also available for private charter.

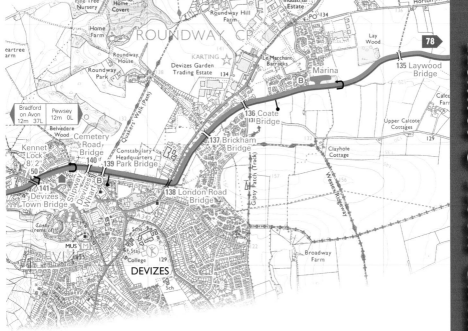

78

WALKING & CYCLING

The Kennet & Avon Canal Partnership publish a Discovery Trail to the area around the Caen Hill Lock Flight obtainable from BW (01380 722859) or Devizes TIC. The National Cycle Network route 4 joins the towpath at Devizes before heading west to South Wales via Bath.

Pubs and Restaurants

There are many good pubs and restaurants in Devizes. The following are simply a convenient selection.

George & Dragon High Street, Rowde, near Devizes (01380 723053). This pub is held in high esteem for its award winning food (V), all freshly cooked to order, served *L and E (not Sun and Mon)*. Fresh fish is a speciality. Real ales. Traditional pub games, no intrusive electronic machines and open fires. Children welcome *before 21.00* and dogs are allowed in the bar. Cottage-style garden and camping. Booking essential.

Caen Hill Tearooms (01380 724880). Beside Lock 44. Ice creams, tea, coffee and home-made cakes. *Open Easter–Sep, daily 12.00–18.00.*

Black Horse Devizes (01380 723930). By Lock 48, on the Caen Hill section. Well placed to refresh those exhausted by the locks. Real ale and food (V) *L and E (not Sun in winter)*. Canalside garden. Darts, skittles and pool.

Lamb 20 St John's Street, Devizes (01380 725426). Old-fashioned local drinking house dispensing real ale. Traditional pub games and enclosed yard. No children; dogs welcome. Solos and duos night *first and third Wed in month*.

Hare & Hounds Hare & Hounds Street, Devizes (01380 723231). A range of real ales served in traditional pub surroundings together with food (V) *L (not Sun)*. Garden, open fires and pub games.

British Lion 9 Estcourt Street, Devizes (01380 720665). Traditional, good value, down-to-earth local, attracting a mix of customers of all ages who appreciate real ale and cider and good conversation. *Open all day.*

White Bear Monday Market Street, Devizes (01380 722583). Real ale served in a popular, town local together with bar meals (V) *L*. Open fires. B & B.

Wharfside Restaurant The Wharf, Devizes (01380 726051). Farmhouse cooking (V) in a canalside restaurant *open daily 09.00–16.00 in summer and 09.00–15.00 in winter*. Also morning coffee, afternoon teas and home-made snacks.

Boatyards

Ⓑ **Devizes Narrowboat Boatbuilders** Foxhanger Wharf, Rowde, Devizes (01380 828848). Boat building, boat repairs and refits, boat fitting out.

Ⓑ **Foxhanger Wharf** Lower Foxhangers, Devizes (01380 828254). ⛽ ⚓ Gas, narrowboat hire, long-term moorings, toilets, showers, telephone, camping, B & B, self-catering holidays.

Ⓑ **BW Waterway Office** Bath Road, Devizes (01380 722859). Self-operated pump out.

Ⓑ **Wharfside Chandlery** Couch Lane, Devizes (01380 725007/723250). Extensive range of chandlery, waterproofs and marine paint. *Limited winter opening – please telephone for details.*

Ⓑ **White Horse Boats** 8 Southgate Close, Pans Lane, Devizes (01380 728504 or 07976 162223; www.whitehorseboats.co.uk). Hire boats – short and long-term – and boat building.

Ⓑ **Devizes Marina** Horton Avenue, Devizes (01380 725300; www.devizesmarina.atfreeweb. com). ⛽ ⚓ D Pump out, gas, overnight mooring, long-term mooring, slipway, boat sales and repairs, engine sales and repairs, engine hoist (1 ton), boat painting, boat building and fitting out, dry dock, wet dock, DIY facilities, solid fuel, chandlery, books, maps and gifts, solid fuel, toilets. *24hr emergency call out.*

● **Devizes**
Wilts. PO, tel, stores, garage, bank, cinema. Despite the effects of traffic, Devizes still retains the atmosphere of an old country market town. Originally the town grew up around the castle, but as this lost its significance the large market-place became the focal point. In the early 19th C Devizes held the largest corn market in the west of England and was also a centre for the selling of hops, cattle, horses and cloth, there being many manufacturers of wool and silk in the area. The lower floor of the town hall was the site of the cheese market. Handsome 18th-C buildings now command the square, while the market cross records the sad story of Ruth Pierce. Elsewhere there are timbered buildings from the 16th C. The two fine churches, one built for the castle and the other for the parish, tend to dominate the town, and hold it well together. Only the mount and related earthworks survive of the original Norman castle; the present building is an extravagant Victorian folly. The town's own brewery, Wadworth, in Northgate Street, fills the air with the aroma of malt and hops. Wadworth still deliver their beer around the town by horse and dray.

Battle of Roundway Down, 13 July 1643 Devizes was held by a Royalist army that had already tested the Roundhead forces, who were tired, dispirited and short of supplies after their defeat at Lansdown Hill, near Bath. A Royalist cavalry charge took the Roundheads by surprise, and most of the confused and battle-weary Roundheads were killed or captured. The battlefield, off the A361 north east of Devizes, is still largely intact, and can easily be explored on foot. Mock battles are re-enacted here.

Devizes to Westminster Canoe Race The toughest and longest canoe race in the world takes place *every Easter.* The course, from Park Road Bridge, Devizes, to County Hall Steps, Westminster, includes 54 miles of the Kennet & Avon, and 71 miles of the Thames, the last 17 of which are tidal. There are 77 locks. The race grew from a back-ground of local rivalry in Pewsey and Devizes to find the quickest way to the sea by boat; in 1948

the target was 100 hours. In 1950 the first regular annual race over the course took place; three years later the junior class was introduced. Anyone may enter the race, but they would have difficulty in beating the highly trained army and navy teams from Britain and Europe.

Devizes Museum 41 Long Street (01380 727369; www.wiltshireheritage.org.uk). One of the finest prehistoric collections in Europe including finds from the Neolithic, Bronze and Iron Age sites in Wiltshire, the most famous being the Stourhead collection of relics excavated from burial mounds on Salisbury Plain. There are also Roman exhibits. *Open Mon–Sat 10.00–17.00. Closed Sun and B Hols.* Charge.

Devizes Visitor Centre Cromwell House, Market Square (01380 729408; www.kennet.gov.uk). This is home to an interactive exhibition introducing visitors to the medieval origins of the town. Tourist information and gift shop. *Open Mon–Sat 09.30–16.30/17.00.* Free.

Kennet & Avon Canal Trust The Wharf, Devizes (01380 721279; www.katrust.org). The Trust's Headquarters with an award winning museum tracing the history of the canal by interactive video and exhibitions. Small charge. Meeting room and well-stocked shop with large selection of canal books, souvenirs, maps and videos. Canal Information Centre *open daily Feb–Dec 10.00–17.00 (16.00 in winter).*

St John's Church Built by Bishop Roger of Sarum, who was also responsible for the castle, this 12th-C church with its massive crossing tower is still largely original. There are 15th-C and 19th-C additions, but they do not affect the Norman feeling of the whole.

St Mary's Church Dating from the same time as St John's, this church was more extensively rebuilt in the 15th C; plenty of Norman work still survives, however.

Wharf Theatre The Wharf, Devizes (01380 725944).

Traveline (0870 6082608).

Tourist Information Centre (01380 729408; www.kennet.gov.uk). See entry under Visitor Centre for details of opening times.

All Cannings

At Horton Bridge, where there is a convenient canalside pub, the waterway leaves another short cutting and the tower of Bishop Canning church comes into view, half hidden by trees: a footpath from the swing bridge is the quickest way into the village. The rolling hills climb fairly steeply to the north, while the pasture falls away to the south. Beyond Horton, the lock-free pound now extends eastwards all the way to Wootton Rivers. Following the contour of the land, it swings in a series of wide arcs past All Cannings, curling around the Knoll, a major feature of the landscape to the north. Several villages are near the navigation, all visible and easily accessible from the many bridges but none actually approach the waterside. Their interests lie rather in the rich agricultural lands that flank the canal. The waterway continues to meander through the open countryside, roughly following a contour line to maintain its level. Its progress is marked by a series of shallow cuttings and low embankments. The navigation passes the delightfully named Honey Street with its pub and boatyard. Beyond the village, to the north, can be seen the white horse cut into the hill in 1812, a copy of the one at Cherhill. Approaching Woodborough Hill, the tower of Alton Priors church comes into view as the long pound continues eastwards. To the south the land falls away while to the north the hills take on an almost sculptural quality as evidence of ancient terracing can be seen.

Honey Street (see page 78)

● **Bishops Cannings**
Wilts. Tel, stores. Apart from one or two old cottages, the main feature of this village is the very grand church. This cruciform building, with its central tower and spire, is almost entirely Early English in style; its magnificence is unexpected in so small a village. Traces of the earlier Norman building survive. Inside is a 17th-C penitential seat, surmounted by a giant hand painted on the wall with suitable inscriptions about sin and death.

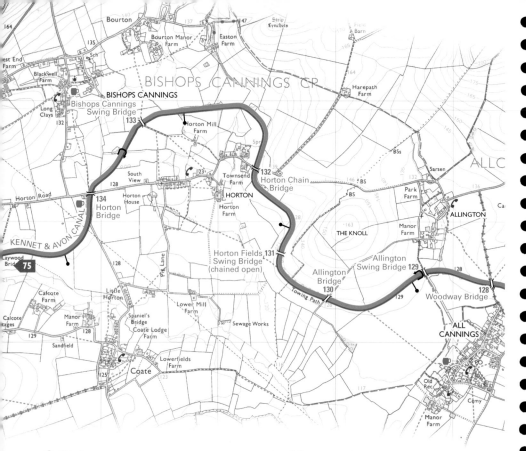

● **Allington**
Wilts. Tel. A small agricultural village with picturesque cottages scattered around a Victorian church. East of the village is All Cannings Cross, a large Iron Age settlement.

● **All Cannings**
Wilts. PO, tel, stores open Mon–Sat 08.00–18.00, Sun 09.30–12.00. An attractive village built around a square, with houses of all periods. To the south there is a large green, overlooked by the church with its tall central tower. Although the church is mainly 14th-C, its most interesting feature is the ornamental High Victorian chancel, added in 1867.

● **Stanton St Bernard**
Wilts. Tel. Built in a curve of the hills, the village has one main street, flanked by pretty gardens. The best building is the 19th-C manor, which incorporates relics of an earlier house. The battlemented church is Victorian.

● **Alton Priors**
Wilts. Tel. Approached along a footpath from Alton Barnes churchyard, the isolated church is the best feature of this scattered hamlet. This pretty Perpendicular building with its wide, well-lit nave contains a most interesting monument: a big box tomb is surmounted with a large engraved Dutch brass plate, dated 1590, rich in extravagant symbolism. To the east of the village the Ridgeway runs southwards towards Salisbury; this Bronze Age drover's road swings north east along the downs for 50 miles, finally joining the Thames valley at Streatley.

● **Alton Barnes**
Wilts. Tel, stores. The village runs along the road northwards from Honey Street. The best part is clustered around the church. Fine farm buildings and an 18th-C rectory are half hidden among the trees. The church is essentially Anglo Saxon, but has been heavily restored; everything is in miniature, the tiny gallery, pulpit and pews emphasising the compact scale of the whole building.

● **Honey Street**
Wilts. A traditional canalside village, complete with sawmills, incorporating some new development and, arguably, one of the most attractively landscaped and charming on the waterways.

Boatyards

Ⓑ **Gibson Boat Services** Old Builders Wharf, Honey Street (01672 851232). 🚽 ♨ D E Pump out, gas, overnight mooring, solid fuel, boat surveys, toilet.

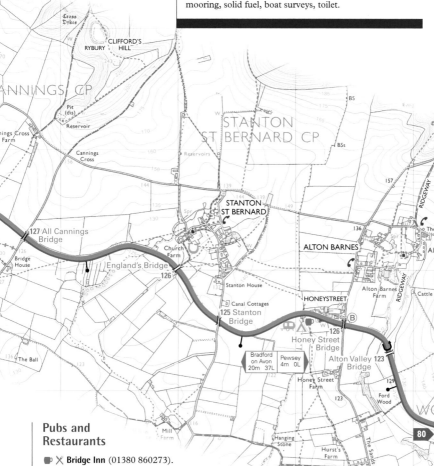

Pubs and Restaurants

🍺 ✕ **Bridge Inn** (01380 860273). At Horton Bridge. Attractively refurbished pub with mellow brick interior. Real ale. Food (V) available in the bar and restaurant *L and E daily*. Barbecues *in summer*. Children welcome. Disabled facilities. Garden.

🍺 **Crown Inn** Bishops Cannings (01380 860218). A friendly village pub, serving real ale. Food (V) available *L and E (except Sun in winter)*. Children welcome. Large garden with crazy golf and swings.

🍺 **Kings Arms** All Cannings (01380 860328). 1/4 mile south of Woodway Bridge. Comfortable and charming village pub, serving real ale, and good value, home-made bar food (V) *L and E (not Mon E)* together with a warm welcome. Darts, pool, dominoes and crib. Children welcome *until 21.00*. Large garden with spectacular views over the Vale of Pewsey. Dogs on leads welcome.

🍺 **Barge Inn** Honey Street, Pewsey (01672 851705). An imposing canalside pub which was once a slaughterhouse, a bakehouse, a brewery and a grocers. Real ale and food (V) served *L and E. Open all day, every day May–Sep and all day Sat and Sun Oct–Apr.* Children welcome. Canalside beer garden. International crop circle centre. Music *most Sat eves.* Temporary moorings. Camping, toilets and showers.

80

Pewsey

The canal skirts Woodborough Hill giving views to the south over open countryside to the village of Woodborough itself. The equally dominant Pickled Hill now fills the north bank, giving a good view of the field terracing that is a relic of Celtic and medieval cultivation. Further east, the waterway passes through the elaborately decorated Lady's Bridge and enters the tranquil, wooded Wide Water. In 1793 this stretch was owned by Lady Susannah Wroughton who objected to the canal cutting through her land. She was appeased by £500, the building of a highly ornate bridge (dated 1808 and attributed

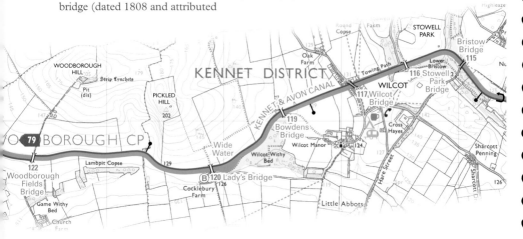

to Rennie) and the landscaping of the marshy area around it. Beyond, a straight stretch leads to the first cottages of Wilcot; the rest of the village is to the south. Woods lead the waterway past Stowell Park, whose landscaped grounds extend to the north. The house, built early in the 19th-C, can be seen clearly from the canal. Closer to the navigation is a selection of delightful estate cottages built in the picturesque style. A miniature suspension bridge, the only surviving example of its kind, carries a private footpath from the park across the canal which now approaches Pewsey Wharf in a low, wooded cutting. The waterway passes well outside the town which fills the Vale to the south. Pewsey Wharf is 1 mile from the town centre and so has developed as a separate canalside settlement, with a pub, cottages and warehouse buildings. To the north, hills descend to the water's edge and to the south the land opens out, giving fine views over the Vale of Pewsey. The 15-mile-long pound continues east, now accompanied by the railway, passing New Mill – a small hamlet to the south of the canal – where there is still evidence of a small wharf.

- **Wilcot**
  Wilts. Tel. A pretty village scattered round the green; there are several thatched houses, and a converted village school with a prominent bell. Parts of the church date from the 12th C, but it was mostly rebuilt in 1876 after a fire. An important event in the village is the annual carnival dating back to 1898. Lasting for two weeks it *commences on the third Sat in Sep* – drawing large crowds – and there is at least one event every evening thereafter.
- **Pewsey**
  Wilts. PO, tel, stores, garage, bank, station. The little town is set compactly in the Vale of Pewsey. At its centre is a fine statue of King Alfred, erected in 1911, from where all the roads radiate. There is the usual mixture of buildings; but while many are attractive, none are noteworthy. The church is mostly 13th- and 15th-C, but parts of the nave are late Norman: the altar rails were made from timbers of the *San Josef*, captured by Nelson in 1797. The immaculate railway station harks back to the former days of GWR supremacy and is a joy to patronise.

Kennet & Avon Canal

Pewsey

82

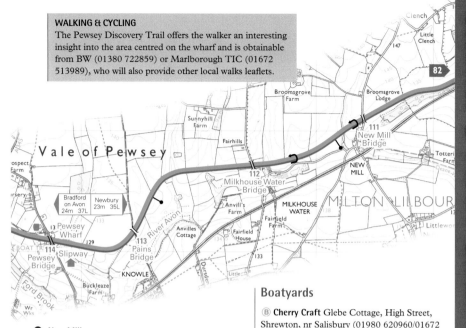

WALKING & CYCLING
The Pewsey Discovery Trail offers the walker an interesting insight into the area centred on the wharf and is obtainable from BW (01380 722859) or Marlborough TIC (01672 513989), who will also provide other local walks leaflets.

● **New Mill**
Wilts. Tel. A pretty hamlet scattered below the canal. The mill that gave it its name is now a house, with a fine garden.

Pubs and Restaurants

● **Golden Swan** Wilcot (01672 562289). A one-handed ghost is said to haunt this pub, which stands beyond the green at the far end of the village. A very affable landlord and friendly locals, together with real ale and home-made bar meals (V) *L and E (except Sun E and Mon L and E)*. Bar billiards, darts and crib. Families welcome. Random folk nights. Two cricket teams are based at the pub as well as a rugby team. Camping and B & B.

● **Coopers Arms** Ball Road, Pewsey (01672 562495). Characterful thatched pub, tucked away up a side street. Real ale and cider. Food (V) available *E and weekends*. Outside seating, open fires in winter. Pub games, children's room. Dogs welcome. Live bands *Fri eves*. Camping.

● **Greyhound** North Street, Pewsey (01672 562439). Lively, welcoming pub serving real ale. Children welcome. Garden and tree house. Crib, darts, pool, cards and children's games. Night club *Fri and Sat 22.00–01.00. Open all day*. The very active Pewsey Vale Railway Society (not totally unconnected with the delightful, local station!) meet here on *first Wed in the month at 20.00*.

● **The Crown** Wilcot Road, Pewsey (01672 562653). Real ale together with inexpensive,

home-made bar meals (V) served *L and E (no food L in winter)*. Children welcome. Garden and play area. Darts, dominoes, pool and cards.

✕ **Waterfront** Pewsey Wharf, Marlborough Road, Pewsey (01672 564020). Canalside café, beer garden and steak house. *Open 08.00–20.00 in summer and 09.00–16.00 in winter. Closed Mon.* Everything from snacks (V) to steaks. Children and dogs welcome. Wharfside seating area. Also gas, long-term mooring, cruiser day hire, canoe hire.

● **Royal Oak** North Street, Pewsey (01672 563426). In the town centre – a family pub with a warm welcome. Real ale and an appetising range of inexpensive, home-made food (V) available *L and E (not Mon L)*. Garden and children's play area. Darts, pool, crib and dominoes. *Winter* events. B & B.

● ✕ **French Horn** Pewsey (01672 562443; www.french-horn-pewsey.co.uk). Just north of Pewsey Wharf, on the A345. A friendly pub, newly refurbished, serving real ale together with bar snacks and main meals (V) *L and E, daily*. Interesting à la carte menu (specialising in fresh fish) available in the bar and restaurant. The emphasis is very much on family eating. Garden. *Sun* quiz nights *during winter*.

Boatyards

Ⓑ **Cherry Craft** Glebe Cottage, High Street, Shrewton, nr Salisbury (01980 620960/01672 564924/mobile: 07710 299417). Beside Ladies Bridge 120. Narrowboat hire, long-term mooring.

Burbage Wharf

The charming, predominantly thatched, village of Wootton Rivers lies beside the eponymous bottom lock, stretching away to the north. The third lock is in the middle of Brimslade Farm, whose attractive tile-hung buildings date from the 17th C; while Wootton Top Lock sits beside a pretty cottage and garden. Above, the short summit pound leads the waterway through pasture and arable land and, as the ground rises steeply on both banks, it prepares itself for the short Bruce Tunnel. Immediately before the high brick bridge, carrying the A346, lies Burbage Wharf; several of the original brick canal buildings still stand, attractively converted to domestic use, and a restored wooden wharf crane hangs, a little insecurely, beside the water. Woods line the approach to the tunnel's western portal, hiding the railway, which is on the south bank before crossing over the tunnel. To the north are the extensive parklands of Tottenham House and Savernake Forest itself. The towpath, passing under the railway, climbs over the top of the tunnel and descends steeply to the navigation, still secluded in a deep, wooded cutting.

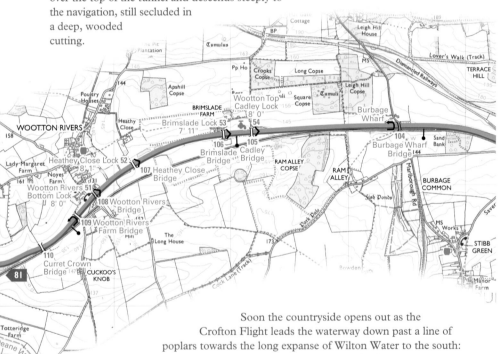

Soon the countryside opens out as the Crofton Flight leads the waterway down past a line of poplars towards the long expanse of Wilton Water to the south: a dammed valley fed by springs, from which the Crofton pumps draw some of their supply. The engine house stands on a rise above the canal, its iron-bound chimney making its purpose unmistakable. Beyond outlying hills and a wooded section, the navigation descends towards Great Bedwyn, passing the church at the final lock before the wharf and village are reached.

NAVIGATIONAL NOTES

No moorings permitted in the Crofton Flight. Visitors to the pumping station should moor at the bottom.

● **Wootton Rivers**
Wilts. Tel. A particularly pretty village composed almost entirely of timber-framed, thatched houses, climbing gently up the hill away from the waterway. The church has an unusual clock, its face having letters in place of numbers. Inside, its mechanism is equally eccentric, being assembled from a bizarre collection of cast-off agricultural implements.

● **Crofton**
Wilts. The scattered village is dominated by the brick pumping station with its separate chimney. It houses two 19th-C steam engines, one built in 1812 by Boulton and Watt, the oldest original working beam engine in the world still performing its original duties, the other in 1845 by Harvey's of Hayle, Cornwall. Both have been

restored, and are steamed on several weekends in the year. The pumping station, engines and canal shop are open for viewing *Easter–Oct, daily 10.30–17.00.* For details of steaming weekends – which are *approximately once a month Easter–Aug* – telephone (01672) 870300.

Bruce Tunnel Named in honour of Thomas Bruce, Earl of Ailesbury. 502yds with the remains of the chains on the walls, which were used to pull boats through.

● **Wilton**
Wilts. Tel. A compact village at the southern end of Wilton Water, with a pretty duck pond in the centre.

Wilton Windmill Wilton (01672 870427). 1 mile south of the canal, along the footpath at Lock 60. *Open Easter–Sep, Sun 14.00–17.00.*

Pubs and Restaurants

🍽 ✕ **Royal Oak** Wootton Rivers (01672 810322; www.wiltshire-pubs.com). North of the canal.
A very attractive 16th-C pub in the main street, serving real ale and a good choice of wines.
Very extensive range of home-cooked meals (V), prepared with fresh local ingredients,
available *L and E, daily.* Children welcome, as are dogs on a lead.
Patio. Darts, dominoes, pool and board games.
B & B. Open all day Sat and Sun.

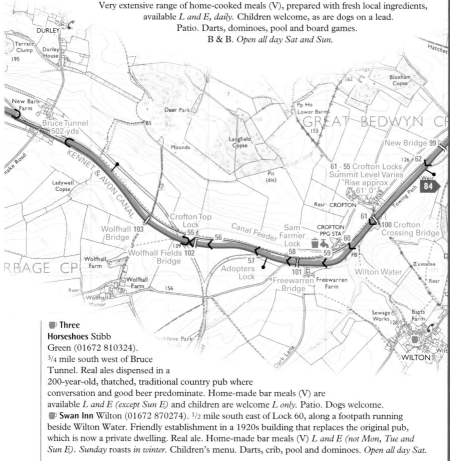

🍺 **Three**
Horseshoes Stibb
Green (01672 810324).
³/4 mile south west of Bruce
Tunnel. Real ales dispensed in a
200-year-old, thatched, traditional country pub where
conversation and good beer predominate. Home-made bar meals (V) are
available *L and E (except Sun E)* and children are welcome *L only.* Patio. Dogs welcome.
🍺 **Swan Inn** Wilton (01672 870274). ¹/2 mile south east of Lock 60, along a footpath running
beside Wilton Water. Friendly establishment in a 1920s building that replaces the original pub,
which is now a private dwelling. Real ale. Home-made bar meals (V) *L and E (not Mon, Tue and
Sun E). Sunday* roasts *in winter.* Children's menu. Darts, crib, pool and dominoes. *Open all day Sat.*

Froxfield

Great Bedwyn is ranged over the hillside to the north of the waterway, newer houses spilling downwards towards the canal and railway station. The navigation leaves the village, accompanied by the infant River Dunn and approaches Little Bedwyn in a shallow side-cutting. To the north is a hill fort, overlooking ridges that break up the farmland. The village is cut in half by the navigation and the railway. In the centre the lock continues the descent towards Hungerford. The spire of the village church is a prominent feature as is the Berks and Wilts main railway line that keeps constant companionship with the

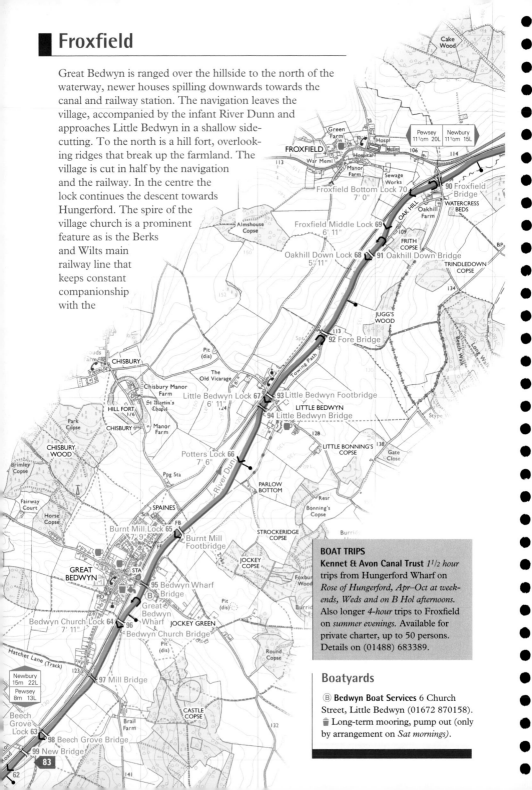

Pewsey 11½m 20L   Newbury 11½m 15L

FROXFIELD

Green Farm
War Meml
Manor Farm
Sewage Works
Hospital
106   114

Froxfield Bottom Lock 70
7' 0"

90 Froxfield Bridge
WATERCRESS BEDS

OAK HILL
Oakhill Farm

Almshouse Copse

Froxfield Middle Lock 69
6' 11"

109
FRITH COPSE

Oakhill Down Lock 68
5' 11"

91 Oakhill Down Bridge
TRINDLEDOWN COPSE

134

JUGG'S WOOD

113   92 Fore Bridge

Long Walk   Beech Walk

CHISBURY

Pit (dis)

The Old Vicarage

Chisbury Manor Farm
St Martin's Chapel
HILL FORT 176

Little Bedwyn Lock 67
6' 11"

93 Little Bedwyn Footbridge

LITTLE BEDWYN

94 Little Bedwyn Bridge

Stype

Park Copse

CHISBURY   Manor Farm

128

LITTLE BONNING'S COPSE

138
Gate Close

CHISBURY WOOD

Potters Lock 66
7' 6"

Brimley Copse

Ppg Sta

PARLOW BOTTOM

Resr

Bonning's Copse

Fairway Court

Horse Copse

SPAINES
Sch

Burnt Mill Lock 65
7' 9"

FB

Burnt Mill Footbridge

STROCKERIDGE COPSE

Burrie

JOCKEY COPSE

Foxbur Wood

GREAT BEDWYN
STA

95 Bedwyn Wharf Bridge
Great Bedwyn Wharf

Pit (dis)

JOCKEY GREEN

Burrie

PO

Bedwyn Church Lock 64
7' 11"

96
Bedwyn Church Bridge

Pit (dis)

Round Copse

Hatchet Lane (Track)

123

97 Mill Bridge

Newbury 15m 22L
Pewsey 8m 13L

CASTLE COPSE

132

Beech Grove Lock 63

Brail Farm

98 Beech Grove Bridge

99 New Bridge

83

62   141

BOAT TRIPS

Kennet & Avon Canal Trust *1½ hour* trips from Hungerford Wharf on *Rose of Hungerford*, Apr–Oct at weekends, Weds and on B Hol afternoons. Also longer *4-hour* trips to Froxfield on *summer evenings*. Available for private charter, up to 50 persons. Details on (01488) 683389.

Boatyards

Ⓑ **Bedwyn Boat Services** 6 Church Street, Little Bedwyn (01672 870158). 🛏 Long-term mooring, pump out (only by arrangement on *Sat mornings*).

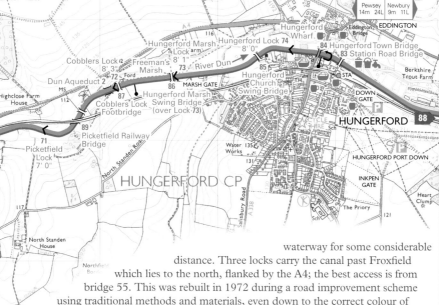

waterway for some considerable distance. Three locks carry the canal past Froxfield which lies to the north, flanked by the A4; the best access is from bridge 55. This was rebuilt in 1972 during a road improvement scheme using traditional methods and materials, even down to the correct colour of brick. To the west of the River Dunn Aqueduct the railway crosses the waterway and remains on the south bank through Hungerford. The roar of the frequent high speed trains to and from the West Country is the only interruption to the natural peace and solitude of the canal. Crossing a tree-lined embankment, beside the river, the navigation approaches the common land of Hungerford Marsh via Cobblers Lock. Water meadows and pasture, rich in buttercups, meet the water, which seems to form more of a river than a canal. On the outskirts of the town the 19th-C church is passed to the south as the waterway descends to the old wharf, flanked by an original stone warehouse. The handsome bridge gives easy access to the centre of the town set out along a wide, main street. Beyond, the waterway once again strikes off through open meadows, closely paralleled by the clear, sparkling waters of the River Kennet.

NAVIGATIONAL NOTES

1 Hungerford Marsh Swing Bridge is over Hungerford Marsh Lock. Boats over 30ft long (approx) will have to swing it clear before using the lock.
2 In spite of its benign appearance the River Kennet can make a considerable impact on the navigation when in spate. In such conditions the boater should consider carefully his own capabilities and those of his craft before proceeding east beyond Hungerford (or west beyond Reading). Hazards to be particularly aware of are: **a)** Strong pulls at the top of all draw-off weirs – look out for signs. **b)** Powerful side currents at the bottom of locks and lock cuts. **c)** Speed of craft downstream necessitated by need to maintain steerage in fast currents. **d)** Craft heading upstream, often obscured by the many blind bends on the navigation. **e)** Difficulty setting down and picking up crew at locks and moveable bridges – plan all such manoeuvres well ahead.
3 Many of the winding holes marked between Hungerford and Reading are at points where the river and lock cuts diverge and therefore should NOT be used to turn a boat when the river is flowing strongly as they lead directly to weirs.
4 Top paddles between Hungerford and Reading are a mixture of ground and gate paddles. The gate paddles can be particularly fierce, especially in the deeper locks. Moor your boat well back in the lock chamber and open gate paddles with great care.

● **Great Bedwyn**
Wilts. PO, tel, stores, station. The main street climbs gently away from the canal and the railway. It is wide, with generous grass verges; attractive houses of all periods line the street. At the top are the pubs. The large church, with its well-balanced crossing tower, is mostly 12th- and 13th-C; inside are some interesting monuments. The road running westwards to the church passes the Bedwyn Stone Museum, an amazing establishment (*see below*).

Bedwyn Stone Museum A collection of stone work of all types, not without humour, showing the work of seven generations of stonemasons. There are statues, tombstones, casts, even the fossilised footprint of a dinosaur. *Open daily.*

● **Little Bedwyn**
Wilts. Tel. Divided by the canal, the village falls into two distinct parts. North is the estate village, pretty 19th-C terraces of patterned brick running eastwards to the church, half hidden among ancient yew trees. To the south is the older farming village, handsome 18th-C buildings climbing the hill away from the canal.

● **Froxfield**
Wilts. Tel. The village is ranged along the A4, which has obviously affected its development. The main feature of the village is the Somerset Hospital, a range of almshouses founded by the Duchess of Somerset in 1694, extended in 1775 and again in 1813. Facing onto the road, the hospital is built round a courtyard, which is entered by a Gothic-style gateway, part of the 1813 extension.

Littlecote 1½ miles north of Froxfield. A Tudor building of the 16th C. Littlecote is the most important brick mansion in Wiltshire with its notable Great Hall, Armoury and Long Gallery. The formal front overlooks the gardens that run down to the Kennet. Not open to the public.

● **Hungerford**
Berks. PO, tel, stores, garage, bank, station, laundrette. Hungerford is built along the A338, which runs through the town southwards from the junction with the A4. The pleasant 18th- and 19th-C buildings are set back from the road, giving the spacious feeling of a traditional market town. None of the buildings are remarkable, but many are individually pretty. Note the decorative ironwork of the house by the canal bridge. The manor was given to John of Gaunt in 1366, and any monarch passing through the town is given a red rose, the Lancastrian emblem, as a token rent.

Hocktide Ceremonies On the *second Tuesday after Easter*, 99 commoners (those living within the original borough who have the rights of the common and the fishing) are called to the town hall by the blowing of a horn. Two Tuttimen are appointed, who have to visit the houses of the commoners to collect a 'head penny' from the men and a kiss from the women: they give oranges in return. All new commoners are then shod by having a nail driven into their shoes. This ceremony dates from medieval times.

WALKING & CYCLING
Great Bedwyn is a good, central point to access the Ridgeway Walk.

Dunmill Lock, Hungerford (see page 88)

Pubs and Restaurants

Cross Keys Great Bedwyn (01672 870678; thecrosskeys@greatbedwyn.fsnet.co.uk). Friendly, 17th-C oak-beamed pub, run by ex-residential boaters. Real ales, log fires and home-cooked food (Mexican and (V) dishes a speciality) served *L and E (not Sun E)*; take-away pizza also available. Attractive pub garden; children and dogs welcome (though please contact landlord before bringing your dog). Jazz and blues *Sat night*; quiz *Wed*. Pub and children's games. B & B.

Three Tuns Great Bedwyn (01672 870280). Newly refurbished and in the hands of an enthusiastic retired TV actor-turned-chef, this cosy hostelry offers real ales and home-made food (V) *L and E (not Sun E)* in both the bar and candle-lit restaurant. The menu is varied and changes daily. Well-behaved children welcome. Garden.

Harrow Little Bedwyn (01672 870871; www.harrowinn.co.uk). Upmarket restaurant serving award winning food (V) and listed in serious eating guides. Outstanding wine list. The menu offers an enticing range of modern British cooking, served *Wed–Sun (not Sun E); L 12.00–14.00 and E 19.00–22.00*. Well-behaved children welcome. Dining terrace.

Pelican Froxfield (01488 682479). Country pub set in an area of outstanding natural beauty, two minute's walk from the canal. Real ales and food (V) available *L and E* with Scotch steaks and fresh fish a speciality. *Sun L* jazz sessions. Large country garden with lake and river. Children welcome. B & B.

Lamb Charnham St, Hungerford (01488 686390; dave@thelambinn.org.uk). North of canal. Old Georgian coaching house that now dispenses real ale and bar food (V) *L and E, daily*; à la carte *E* menu served in restaurant. *Sunday* roasts. *Monthly weekend* music nights. Garden. B & B.

Bear Charnham St, Hungerford (01488 682512; www.jarvishotels.co.uk). North of the canal. Chain hotel with 13th-C restaurant serving cordon bleu menu *L and E*. Also morning coffee, packed lunches, afternoon tea and bar meals (V) *L and E*. Brasserie serving fresh fish, meat and local game. Real ales. Visited by several illustrious visitors over the centuries – including Elizabeth I, Henry VIII and Samuel Pepys – this hotel has, today, a very relaxed atmosphere together with charming courtyard and riverside seating. Also an original Parliamentary clock used to time the mail coaches. Children and dogs welcome. B & B. *Open all day.*

John of Gaunt Hungerford (01488 683535). 16th-C pub north of the canal, serving real ale and bar meals (V) *L and E, daily*. Children and dogs welcome in this family oriented establishment. Walled patio. Dominoes and Jenga. B & B. *Open all day.*

Plume of Feathers Inn Hungerford (01488 682154). South of the canal. Real ale and an extensive and appetising range of home-made food (from the very experienced, West End chef/owner) (V) *L and E (not Sun E)*. This pub has recently been completely refurbished. Children welcome. Garden. *Open all day.*

Three Swans Hotel Hungerford (01488 682721). Resort hotel, south of the canal. Real ale together with restaurant meals *L and E, daily* and bar snacks (V) *L*. Afternoon tea. Children welcome. B & B. *Open all day.*

Railway Tavern Hungerford (01488 683100). 200yds south of Station Road Footbridge. Real ale together with inexpensive bar meals (V) available *all day Tue–Sun*. Garden, children welcome. Darts and pool. Live music on *Fri and Sat*. Entertainment *Sun*.

Downgate Down View 13 Park Street, Hungerford (01488 682708). 1/4 mile south east of Station Road Footbridge. Charming little pub overlooking the common. Real ales. Food available (V) *L and E (not Sun and Mon E)*. Children welcome. Garden, open fires *in winter* and traditional pub games.

CLOSE(ISH) ENCOUNTERS

Hungerford commoners, anxious to exercise their piscatorial rights (*see* Hocktide Ceremonies, opposite), should be grateful to have been spared the experience of one Alfred Burtoo. This 78-year-old fisherman, whilst casually casting into the nearby Basingstoke Canal one night, was disturbed by the arrival of two figures in green overalls, 4 feet tall, wearing helmets with smoked visors. After pausing for several seconds they beckoned him to follow them, which he did. 'I was curious,' explained Alfred, 'They showed no sign of hostility and at 78, what had I to lose?' He was led along the towpath to a large oval object – 40–50 feet wide – and upon ascending some steps found himself inside an octagonal room. Here he stood until a voice instructed him to stand under an amber light fixed to the cabin wall. He was asked his age and, after a further pause, the voice bade him depart, stating: 'You are too old and infirm (sic) for our purpose'.

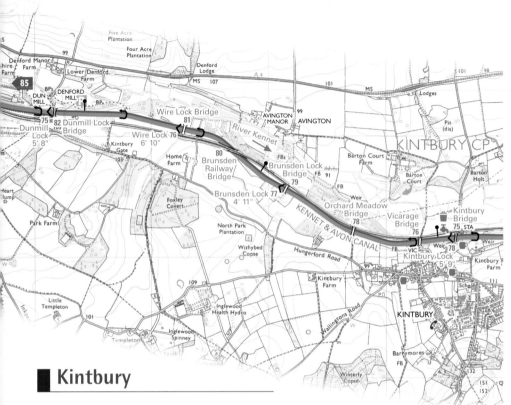

Kintbury

Pretty woods keep company with the waterway to the south as it
leaves Hungerford, while to the north river and canal run side by side through water
meadows, separated only by a narrow ridge carrying the towpath. As the diminutive
River Kennet accompanies the canal past Dunmill Lock, the towpath turns over to the
north bank. From the bridge there is a good view of Denford Mill. Locks 76 and 77
carry the navigation past Avington, with its Norman church visible among the trees.
The railway and the River Kennet are constantly present as the waterway heads
towards Kintbury through open countryside, passing the Victorian Gothic vicarage.
The canal enters the village beside the railway station and the Dundas Arms, which
overlooks the lock. The centre of Kintbury is up on the hill to the south of the lock.
Leaving the wharf, the navigation steadily descends the locks towards Newbury,
making this a particularly attractive stretch. Wooded, rolling hills flank the waterway
to the south as it passes through Drewett's, Copse and Hamstead Locks and into the
delightful landscape of Hamstead Park.

● **Avington**
Berks. The village is best approached along the
track that runs east from Wire Lock, although the
more adventurous can go directly across the
water meadows, crossing the Kennet on a small
footbridge. The little church is still wholly
Norman, and contains a variety of original work;
the chancel arch, the corbels and the font are
particularly interesting.

● **Kintbury**
Berks. PO, tel, stores, station. A quiet village with
attractive buildings by the canal, including a
watermill and canalside pub. The church is
originally 13th-C, but was restored in 1859;
the railway lends excitement, and noise, to the
situation.

NAVIGATIONAL NOTES

Allow for river current when winding and when approaching Copse Lock, especially after heavy rain.

Pubs and Restaurants

White Hart Hamstead Marshall (01488 658201). 1 mile south of Hamstead Lock – there is a footpath avoiding the road. For superb, classical Italian cuisine from the dedicated owner/chef and a warm welcome this pub is really worth the walk. Not cheap but excellent value for money. Food (V) available in both bar and restaurant *L and E, Mon–Sat*. Children catered for. Real ale. Log fires in a heavily beamed building, dating from 1684, where tenants once paid their annual dues to the estate. Friendly female ghost. Attractive B & B in converted stables.

Dundas Arms Kintbury (01488 658263/658559; www.dundasarms.com). The River Kennet and the canal flow on either side of this pub, which was named after the Lord Dundas who opened the canal in 1810. Real ale. Restaurant has interesting menu and good wine cellar. Food (V) available *L and E (except Sun L and E and Mon E)*. Children welcome. Canalside garden. B & B.

Prince of Wales Kintbury (01488 658269). 300yds south east of Kintbury Bridge. Rotating guest real ales in a traditional village local with a friendly, welcoming landlord. Inexpensive home-made bar food (V) served *L and E, daily*. Children welcome. Garden. Darts, pool and crib. Occasional quiz nights. *Open all day Sat.*

Blue Ball Kintbury (01488 608126). 500yds south of Kintbury Bridge. Friendly, village pub serving real ale and home-cooked food (V) *L and E (not Sun E)*. Large garden. Dogs on leads welcome. Children's menu. Darts and pool. *Open all day Sat and Sun.*

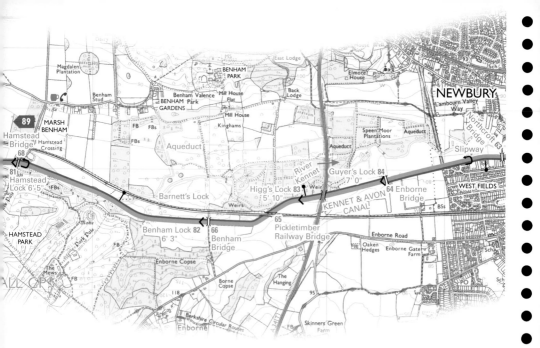

Newbury

West of Newbury the waterway again passes through extensive water meadows as the wooded hills open out to the south revealing a stretch of the controversial bypass. Above Newbury Lock is the delightful, quiet West Mills area, where rows of terraced houses face the navigation and there are extensive moorings. The river cuts right through the town and the town makes the most of it. Below the lock, where the channel gets narrower and faster, is a splendid stone balustraded bridge followed, after 500yds, by a park and an extensive wharf area opposite. This used to be the terminus of the Kennet Navigation from Reading, before the Kennet and Avon Canal Company extended it to link up with the Avon at Bath. There are plans to recreate a basin in this area. There is also a collection of old warehouses and a stone building used by the K & A Canal Trust as an information centre and shop. The waterway leaves Newbury Wharf under a handsome new road bridge.

NAVIGATIONAL NOTES

1 Below Newbury lock there are strong cross-flows from both sides of the navigation when the river levels are raised. Upstream boaters should prepare the lock ahead of the craft.
2 In times of fresh water there are strong flows in the narrow section below Newbury bridge and progress upstream can be very slow. Downstream craft should keep a very careful lookout.
3 All craft should keep to the right of the centre arch through the new Victoria Park Bridge.

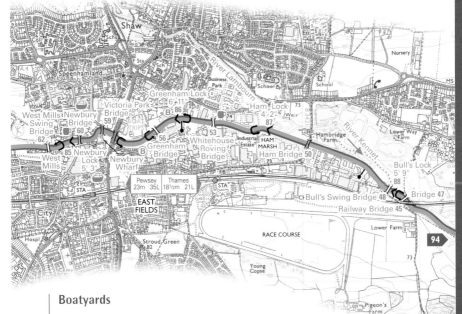

Boatyards

Ⓑ **Newbury Boat Co.** Greenham Lock Cottage, Newbury (01635 42884; newburyboatco@dial.pipex.com). 🚿 🚽 ⚓ D Pump out, gas, overnight mooring, long-term mooring, crane, books and maps, boat and engine repairs, dry dock, DIY facilities, toilet, telephone, gifts, solid fuel. The boatyard is divided between three sites: Greenham Island to the west; Ham Lock to the east; and the main office and workshop on the central site at Greenham Lock

Cottage. For the shop and basic services – diesel, pump out, etc – boaters should go to Greenham Island. Long-term moorings are located at all sites. All mooring enquiries to the office at Greenham Lock Cottage. For enquiries regarding services, the shop, etc. telephone (01635) 31672, and for engineering (01635) 37606.

● **Newbury**
Berks. All services. Newbury developed in the Middle Ages as a cloth town of considerable wealth, its stature indicated by the size of the church. Although the cloth trade has long vanished, the town has managed to retain much of its period charm. It is a busy shopping centre, and the shop fronts in the main streets have buried many 17th- and 18th-C houses. Elsewhere in the town the 18th C is well in evidence, especially in the West Mills area. There are fine almshouses, and a pretty ornamental stone bridge over the navigation. There are also signs of the agricultural importance of Newbury: the 19th-C Italianate Corn Exchange, for example (*see* below).
1st Battle of Newbury, 20 Sep 1643 Site of Wash Farm off A343. 1³/4 miles south of Guyer's Lock. The Royalists were defeated by the Parliamentarians in one of the bloodiest onslaughts of the Civil War. Guyer's and Higg's Locks are named after troop commanders in the battle.

2nd Battle of Newbury, 28 Oct 1644 Donnington Castle, Donnington. 1¹/2 miles north of Newbury Lock off the A34. The Royalists were in possession of Donnington Castle when the Parliamentarians attacked. Charles' army withdrew to Oxford, but a week later they returned and relieved the castle. There is a reconstruction model of the battle in Newbury Museum.
Corn Exchange Market Place, Newbury (01635 522733). Now sensitively restored, the Corn Exchange offers an extensive range of arts activities – film, theatre, dance, music, comedy and children's events. *Open Mon–Sat all year.*
District Museum The Wharf, Newbury (01635 30511). Originally built in 1626 as a cloth-weaving workshop to give employment to the poor, this is one of the most interesting buildings in Newbury. Adjoining is the corn store, once on the edge of the Kennet Wharf. The museum collection illustrates the prehistoric and Saxon history of the region, as well as the

medieval and modern. Also a natural history section with an excellent display of moths and butterflies. An audio-visual presentation tells the story of the Battle of Newbury and hot air ballooning. *Open Apr–Sep, Mon–Sat 10.00–17.00; Oct–Mar, Mon–Sat 10.00–16.00. Closed Wed all year except during school holidays.* Free.

The Stone Building, Kennet & Avon Canal Trust, The Wharf, Newbury (01635 522609). Canal shop and exhibition. Books, gifts, souvenirs, maps and information. Picnic area, tea, coffee, light refreshments. A place for a chat and the opportunity to find out more about the canal in Newbury. *Open Feb–Xmas, daily 10.00–16.00.*

Newbury Fair Northcroft Lane, Northcroft, Newbury. Leave canal at Kennet Bridge. Annual Michaelmas fair held since 1215, on the *Wed following 11 Oct.*

Newbury Buses (01635 567500). Network of local urban and rural services.

Newbury Racecourse Newbury (01635 40015). *Midweek and weekend racing.* Flat racing *Apr–Sep* and National Hunt Racing *Oct–Mar.* Charge.

Round Barrow Cemetery Wash Common, near the site of the 1st Battle of Newbury in 1643. Memorial stones to the victims surmount the two smaller mounds.

St Nicholas Church West Mills, Newbury. Borders the canal on the south bank. A large Perpendicular church, built c.1500 at the height of Newbury's prosperity as a wool town. Its 17th-C pulpit is most unusual.

St Nicholas School Enborne Road, Newbury. By Butterfield, 1859.

Watermill Theatre & Restaurant Bagnor, near Newbury (01635 46044/45834). Enterprising theatre, set in an idyllic location, staging a variety of drama, music and musicals, including world premieres. Also licensed restaurant serving snacks and meals *L* and *E*. Telephone for programme. Although 2¹/₂ miles north of the town this makes a rewarding walk or taxi ride.

Wyld Court Rainforest Hampstead Norreys, Thatcham, near Newbury (01635 200221/ 202444). The opportunity to experience the beauty of rainforest plant life under glass. Three climates featuring different plant species and rainforest creatures. *Open daily (except Xmas Day and Boxing Day) Mar–Oct 10.00–17.00 and Nov–Feb 10.00–16.30.* Charge. Bus (Newbury–Reading route) or taxi from Newbury.

Hamstead Park A very fine park bordered by the canal. There used to be a castle here and several interesting buildings adjoin the church on the side of the hill. There is an old watermill by the lock. The hamlet of Hamstead Marshall lies to the south, 1¹/₂ miles from Hamstead Lock.

Tourist Information Centre The Wharf, Newbury (01635 519562; www.westberks.gov.uk). Opening times as per the museum and on *Wed.*

BOAT TRIPS
Kennet Horse Boat Co. 32 West Mills, Newbury, Berks (01635 44154). Horse drawn and motor barge. *2 hour* public trips *mid Apr–Sep* on the motor barge *Avon* from Newbury Wharf. Also 1¹/₂ *hour* trips on the horse-drawn boat *Kennet Valley* operating from Kintbury. Tea, coffee, bar and catering facilities on board. Private charter. Telephone for further details. Booking essential.

West Mills, Newbury (see page 91)

Pubs and Restaurants

🍺 ✕ **Red House** Marsh Benham (01635 582017) About ¼ mile north east of Hamstead Lock. Charming pub-cum-restaurant in a thatched estate village near Benham Park. Once the local bakery it now dispenses ales. Expensive, though appetising menu by award winning chef, served in bar and restaurant (V) *L and E, daily.* Attractive conservatory and gardens.

🍺 **Snooty Fox** Cheap Street, Newbury (01635 47336). 50yds south of Newbury Bridge. Real ale and cider. Food (V) available *L, Mon–Sat.* No children.

🍺 **Catherine Wheel** 35 Cheap Street, Newbury (01635 47471). South of Newbury Bridge. A small, town pub offering real ale. *Open all day.*

🍺 **Lion** West Street (off Northbrook Street), Newbury (01635 528468). Alcoved areas in the bar and jazz memorabilia give this pub a cosy atmosphere set off by the wooden floor. Real ales together with food (V) *L, daily.* Outside seating in summer. Large-screen sports TV. Disabled access.

🍺 **Lock Stock & Barrel** 104 Northbrook Street, Newbury (01635 42730). Real ale served in a spacious, riverside pub with an attractive terrace. Food (V) available *all day from 11.00 daily (not after 17.00 Sun in winter).* Children welcome in garden only. Non-smoking area and disabled access. *Open all day.*

✕ **Bricklayers Arms** 137 Bartholomew Street, Newbury (01635 43254). 200yds south of Newbury Bridge. Pub kitchen establishment where the chef can be seen preparing the food behind the bar. Interesting range of snacks and meals (V) available *11.00–22.00.* Children welcome at the discretion of the manager. Outside patio seating.

🍺 **Old Waggon & Horses** Market Place, Newbury (01635 46368). 100yds east of Newbury Bridge. This comfortable pub has a pleasant terrace (with moorings) overlooking the river. Food (V) available *12.00–16.00, daily.* No children.

🍺 ✕ **White House** Riverside, Newbury (01635 42614). North east of Whitehouse Bridge. Real ale together with traditional, home-cooked pub food (V) *L and E, daily.* Children welcome. Karaoke *Sun* and disco/live bands *Fri and Sat.* Moorings and garden. *Open all day.*

🍺 **Hogshead** 1-3 Wharf Street, Newbury (01635 569895). Once the local auction rooms, this spacious pub still displays posters featuring its former trade. Real ale and cider, and large range of bottled beers. Food (V) available *daily 12.00–21.00 (until 20.00 Fri–Sun).* Open fires and disabled access. Small riverside terrace.

Cruising near Kintbury (see page 88)

Kennet & Avon Canal

Newbury

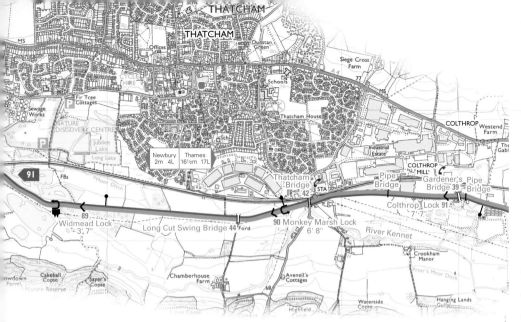

Thatcham

Beyond Bull's Lock and the railway bridge the canal now flows very straight through isolated water meadows towards Thatcham. The village itself is a mile to the north west but the station is conveniently close beside the navigation. This section of the waterway probably best serves to illustrate the wide variety of work jointly undertaken by a consortium made up of county and district councils, Manpower Services job creation programmes, British Waterways and the Kennet and Avon Canal Trust, who have been at the forefront of fund raising for more than 30 years. For example, Heale's Lock to the east and Bull's Lock to the west have both been rebuilt with consortium labour, while Widmead Lock has been reconstructed to a very high standard by outside contractors at a cost in excess of £385,000. The many swing bridges have either been totally rebuilt or, in some cases, replaced by a high-level structure: Colthrop Bridge being privately funded. Old Monkey Marsh Lock, one of only two remaining examples of a turf-sided lock, has been listed as an ancient monument by English Heritage. It is now restored with iron-piling to two feet above low water level, turf-lined banks sloping to the top of the lock, together with a timber framework to delineate the actual lock chamber when full. The lock should be left empty after use.

● **Thatcham**
Berks. All services. The main square of this rapidly expanding village, now almost a suburb of Newbury, is all but dominated by sprawling housing development. Set back from the A4, it manages to retain some peace which carries over into the nearby cluster of older buildings grouped at the east end of the pretty Victorian church and churchyard.
Nature Discovery Centre Muddy Lane, Lower Way, Thatcham (01635 874381; www.westberks. gov.uk [nature and environ- ment]). North of Widmead Lock. A centre for

the study of the unique lake and reed bed habi- tats of the area; rare moths and large Reed and Sedge Warbler populations. A multi-activity base where children (and adults) can make their own discoveries and the chance to get a bird's eye view of the world. Shop and café. *Open in term time Tue–Fri 11.00–17.00 Mar–Oct and 12.00–15.00 Nov–Feb (11.00–17.00 during school hols except Xmas); and weekends 12.00–17.00.* Seasonal adjustments – telephone for details.

● **Woolhampton**
Berks. PO, tel, stores, garage, station. A village on the A4 that owes its existence to the days of mail

coaches on the old Bath road. There is a good mixture of buildings in the main street, several pubs and hotels. Up on the hill to the north of the village are the Victorian church, the Georgian buildings of Woolhampton Park and Douai Abbey and School, the latter a fine group of 19th-C buildings with more recent additions.

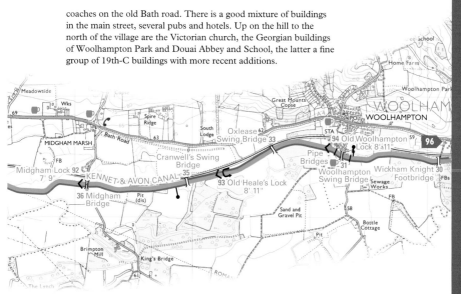

NAVIGATIONAL NOTES

1 **Woolhampton Lock** The current below the lock can cause problems, so take care! When approaching **upstream** set the lock before swinging the bridge, head into the current, turning into the lock at the last moment. When coming **downstream** swing the bridge before leaving the tail of the lock and aim straight for the skewed bridge. **Ensure that the bridge is fully open.**
2 There is a ledge on the south side of Widmead Lock.

Pubs and Restaurants

Crickets High Street, Thatcham (01635 862113). Real ales and bar food (V) *L (Tue–Sun)* are served in a pub that takes sport very seriously: three rugby teams, a cricket and a football team are all based at this establishment. For the more sedentary there are dominoes and crib. *Open all day.*

White Hart High Street, Thatcham. Old coaching inn, dating back more than 350 years. Real ales. Excellent home-cooked food (V) served *L and E (not Sat L or Sun E)*. Children welcome if eating. Patio. *Open all day Mon–Fri.*

Kings Head Thatcham (01635 862145). Real ales and bar meals (V) *L*. Garden and children's play area. Pool room. Darts, crib and dominoes. Music *Sun*. B & B. *Open all day Thur–Sat.*

Old Chequers Thatcham (01635 863312). Comfortable old pub, popular with young people, serving real ale and food (V) *12.00–*

18.30 Mon–Fri and Sat 12.00–14.30. No children. Outside seating. *Open all day.*

Angel Inn Bath Road, Woolhampton (0118 971 3307). An imposing ivy-clad building in the centre of the village. The pub serves real ale and food (V) *L and E (no food Sun)*. Quiz *last Sun in month*. *Open all day.*

Falmouth Arms Bath Road, Woolhampton (0118 971 3202). Bar meals (V) available *L and E (except Sun E)* together with *Sunday* roasts and real ale. Children welcome during eating hours and dogs welcome outside eating hours. Patio area. Live music or a disco *Fri*. Darts and pool. B & B.

Row Barge Station Road, Woolhampton (0118 971 2213). Popular canalside pub offering both restaurant and bar food (V) *L and E, daily*. Renowned for its wide range of well-kept real ales. Children and dogs welcome. Large garden. *Open all day Sat and Sun.*

Aldermaston

At Aldermaston Wharf there is a mechanically operated lift bridge carrying a busy road into the village. The navigation remains close to the railway and A4 which have both shared its course for many miles. The canal heads north east, constantly joining and rejoining the River Kennet. The moorings at Tyle Mill are administered, together with many others on this waterway, by BW; telephone (01380) 722859 for further details. Beyond Tyle Mill are a series of gravel pits, excavated since 1960, which offer an undisturbed habitat for all forms of wildlife. The nature reserves of Cumber Lake to the north and Woolwich Green Lake to the south can both be reached by a short walk from Sulhamstead Lock. A pleasant, tree-lined straight cut takes the navigation through wooded fields towards Sulhamstead. Further woods and pasture land lead to Theale Swing Bridge; the village is 3/4 mile to the north. Fortunately, since the completion of the M4, this bridge has reverted to carrying relatively infrequent road vehicles, so the passage of a boat no longer causes a major traffic hold-up.

Boatyards

Ⓑ **Froud's Bridge Marina** Froud's Lane, Aldermaston (0118 971 4508). 🛏 🚻 🔧 D Gas, pump out, overnight mooring, long-term mooring, winter storage, boat sales, toilets, showers, chandlery, books, maps, gifts, solid fuel.

Ⓑ **Reading Marine Co.** Aldermaston Wharf, Padworth, Reading (0118 971 3666; www.readingmarine.com). 🛏 🔧 D E Gas, pump out, narrowboat hire, overnight mooring, long-term mooring, crane, boat sales and repairs, engine sales and repairs, boat building and fitting out, books, maps and gifts, telephone, toilets, chandlery, solid fuel, RYA international helmsman's certificate courses. *Emergency call out.*

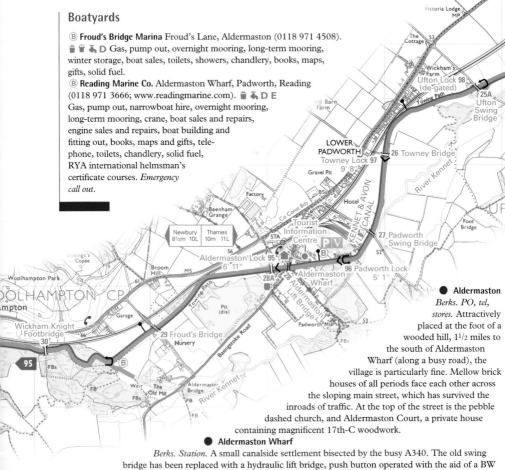

● **Aldermaston**
Berks. PO, tel, stores. Attractively placed at the foot of a wooded hill, 1¹/₂ miles to the south of Aldermaston Wharf (along a busy road), the village is particularly fine. Mellow brick houses of all periods face each other across the sloping main street, which has survived the inroads of traffic. At the top of the street is the pebble dashed church, and Aldermaston Court, a private house containing magnificent 17th-C woodwork.

● **Aldermaston Wharf**
Berks. Station. A small canalside settlement bisected by the busy A340. The old swing bridge has been replaced with a hydraulic lift bridge, push button operated with the aid of a BW key. It cost the local council £250,000 to build.

Visitor Centre, Kennet & Avon Canal Trust, Aldermaston Wharf, Padworth, Reading (0118 971 2868). Canal shop and exhibition. Books, gifts, souvenirs, maps and information. Picnic area, tea, coffee, light refreshments. *Open Apr–Oct, daily 10.00–16.00.*

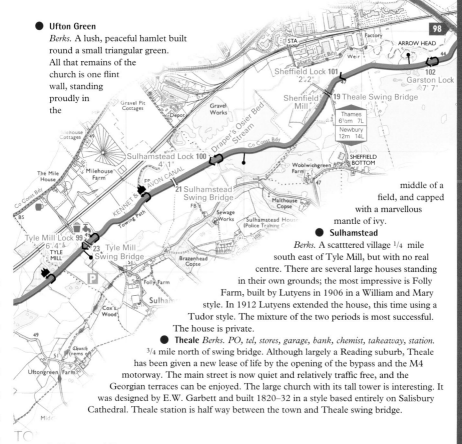

● **Ufton Green**
Berks. A lush, peaceful hamlet built round a small triangular green. All that remains of the church is one flint wall, standing proudly in the middle of a field, and capped with a marvellous mantle of ivy.

● **Sulhamstead**
Berks. A scatttered village ¼ mile south east of Tyle Mill, but with no real centre. There are several large houses standing in their own grounds; the most impressive is Folly Farm, built by Lutyens in 1906 in a William and Mary style. In 1912 Lutyens extended the house, this time using a Tudor style. The mixture of the two periods is most successful. The house is private.

● **Theale** *Berks. PO, tel, stores, garage, bank, chemist, takeaway, station.*
¾ mile north of swing bridge. Although largely a Reading suburb, Theale has been given a new lease of life by the opening of the bypass and the M4 motorway. The main street is now quiet and relatively traffic free, and the Georgian terraces can be enjoyed. The large church with its tall tower is interesting. It was designed by E.W. Garbett and built 1820–32 in a style based entirely on Salisbury Cathedral. Theale station is half way between the town and Theale swing bridge.

Pubs and Restaurants

● ✗ **Hind's Head** Aldermaston (0118 971 2194; aldermaston@hindshead.freeserve.co.uk). An imposing building which faces up the main street. Formerly the Congreve Arms, until it changed hands following the devastation of a great fire. The Hind's Head once brewed its own beer, selling at 2d a pint; real ales are still dispensed at the bar. Good food (V) available in both bar and attractive dining room *L and E, daily;* snacks available *during the afternoon.* Garden, children welcome. B & B.

● ✗ **Butt Inn** Aldermaston Wharf (0118 971 2129). 100yds walk from Aldermaston Lift Bridge. Family run pub serving real ales and excellent food (V) *L and E, daily. Sunday* roasts. Children and dogs welcome. Large garden. *Open all day Sun in summer.*

✗ ♈ **Spring Inn** Bath Road, Sulhamstead (0118 930 2307). ½ mile north of Tyle Mill. Unusual establishment serving a fish-based menu in comfortable, old world surroundings, *L and E.*

● **Crown Inn** Church Street, Theale (0118 932 3614). Real ale and bar food (V) available *L, Mon–Fri.* Children welcome. Garden. Darts, dominoes and pool. *Open all day.*

● **Red Lion** 5 Church Street, Theale (0118 930 2394). Real ales and inexpensive bar meals (V) served *L and E, daily (not Mon E).* Children welcome. Patio seating. Darts, skittle alley, dominoes, crib and shove ha'penny. *Open all day.*

● **Falcon** High Street, Theale (0118 930 2523). Old-fashioned 18th-C pub, sporting several friendly ghosts who appear to bar staff and customers alike from time to time. Real ales. Food (V) available *L and E.* Open fires and disabled access. Children and dogs welcome. Traditional pub games. Garden. *Open all day.*

● **Volunteer** Church Street, Theale (0118 930 2489). Large, single-room pub serving real ale and food (V) *L and E, daily.* Children welcome *until 19.00.* Garden. Traditional pub games.

Reading

The M4 motorway and the railway inevitably affect the peace and quiet of this section, although almost to the outskirts of Reading the gravel pits bring a degree of serenity. The Kennet winds through water meadows, the straight stretches marking the canal sections. Continuing east, the navigation passes Burghfield Bridge, a handsome stone arch. The river gradually approaches the town, descending Fobney Lock and passing through Fobney Meadow, before beginning to wriggle its way through the outskirts. At County Lock the navigation passes over a low weir which at times of fresh water can become quite ferocious. Rows of riverside cottages and a surprising variety of bridges decorate the Kennet in Reading, High Bridge being the most central access point. The river cuts across the middle of the town and so access to all facilities is easy. However, the waterway through Reading is narrow, shallow and fast flowing, being a river navigation; also there are several sharp blind bends (now reduced as a result of the Oracle Development, *see* page 100).

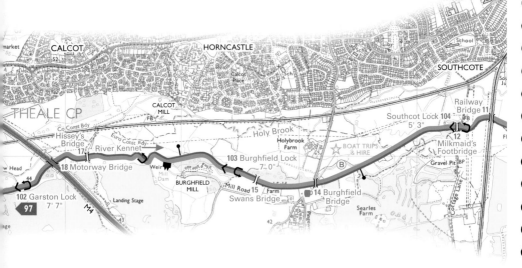

This section is controlled by traffic lights – boaters should not proceed until a green light is displayed. A variety of new developments complement the river's passage through this part of the town. The Kennet leads north east out of the centre of Reading, passing Blake's Lock (0118 957 2251), the only lock maintained by the Thames Conservancy that is not actually on the Thames. Soon the Kennet approaches its junction with the Thames which is marked by a gasometer and the main railway, which runs parallel with the south bank of the river.

Boatyards

There are currently no boatyards on the Kennet & Avon in Reading. For details of boatyards on the River Thames *see* page 136.
Ⓑ **Kennet Cruises** 14 Beech Lane, Earley, Reading (0118 987 1115, mobile 07831 326482). 🚿 🚽 ⛽ Pump out, narrowboat hire, day hire craft, overnight mooring, long-term mooring.

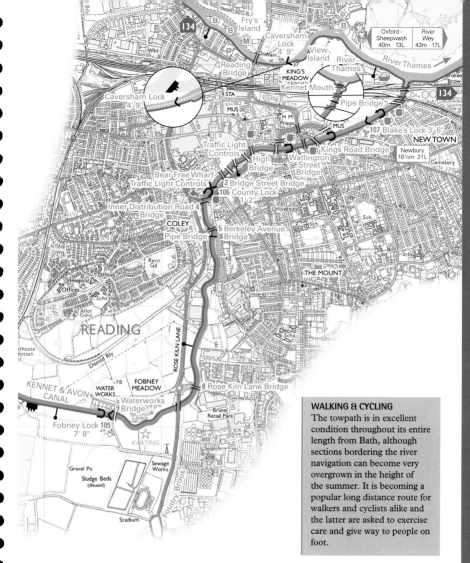

WALKING & CYCLING

The towpath is in excellent condition throughout its entire length from Bath, although sections bordering the river navigation can become very overgrown in the height of the summer. It is becoming a popular long distance route for walkers and cyclists alike and the latter are asked to exercise care and give way to people on foot.

NAVIGATIONAL NOTES

1 See Navigational notes on page 62 before heading west from Reading.
2 **Fobney Lock** – care should be taken when using the landing stage below the lock as a strong weir stream flows at right angles.
3 River Thames licences are obtainable from the Environment Agency (*see* page 102).
4 For up-to-date information on lock closures, the Thames winter works programme and flood conditions, telephone the EA Navigation Information Line on 0845 988 1188.

Ufton Swing Bridge, Aldermaston (see page 96)

BOAT TRIPS

Kennet Cruises operate *Sun* boat trips *Easter–mid Sep* from the Cunning Man, Burghfield Bridge to Garston and back. Also *Wed mid Jul–Aug* and special, longer cruises, during summer months. Telephone 0118 987 1115 for further details.

● **Reading**

Berks. All services. The town lies at the extremity of the Berkshire Downs and the Chiltern Hills, where the Thames becomes a major river. It is the Victorian architecture that makes this town interesting, as the university buildings are not to everyone's taste. Once the Oracle Development, in the centre of Reading, is completed, the towpath along the Kennet will be continuous from the Thames throughout the town.

Abbey Ruins Fragmentary remains of this 12th-C abbey built by Henry I lie on the edge of Forbury Park. The 13th-C gatehouse, altered by Scott in 1869, still stands.

Film Theatre PO Box 217, Palmer Building, Whiteknights, Reading (0118 986 8497). Imaginative programme of non-mainstream cinema, showing approximately four times a week. Visit Tourist Information for up-to-date details.

Gaol Forbury Road. Designed by Scott and Moffatt in 1842–4 in the Scottish Baronial style. Oscar Wilde wrote *De Profundis* while imprisoned here.

Reading Museum The Town Hall, Blagrave Street (0118 939 9800). Features *The Story of Reading*, tracing the town's development from a Saxon settlement on the River Kennet to the present day. Special features include a reconstructed section of the abbey and the Oracle gates entrance to the 17th-C workhouse. In the upper gallery is a full 230ft sweep of Britain's Bayeux Tapestry, Reading's faithful replica of the 11th-C original. *Open Tue–Sat 10.00–16.00 (19.00 Thur), Sun 11.00–16.00.* Free.

Museum of English Rural Life Royal History Centre, Whiteknights, University of Reading (0118 931 8660). All aspects of rural life in England as it was lived about 150 to 175 years ago, before the invention of the tractor. *Open Tue–Sat 10.00–13.00 and 14.00–16.30.* Small charge.

21 South Street The Hexagon, Queen's Walk, Reading (0118 950 4911). A wide-ranging programme of music (all types), workshops and drama in a lively arts centre which also incorporates: **Macdevitt's Bar** (0118 956 8155). *Open* for drinks and home-cooked food *Mon–Sat, L and E.* Disabled access.

Hexagon Queen's Walk, Reading (0118 896 6060). Mainstream theatre, pantomime, films, shows and art exhibitions.

Encore Café Bar *Open Mon–Sat 10.00–17.00 and 1¹/2 hours before evening shows.* Inexpensive, home-made food.

Reading Buses (0118 959 4000/0870 6082608). Information on urban and rural services.

Tourist Information Centre Church House, Chain Street, Reading (0118 956 6226; www.readingtourism.org.uk).

Pubs and Restaurants

✕ **Bridge Café** Burghfield, near Reading. Opposite the Cunning Man. *Open all day* for breakfast, snacks, meals and takeaways.

🍺 ✕ **Cunning Man** Burghfield Bridge, near Reading (0118 959 0771). Harvester pub with large canalside garden. Food (V) available *L and E, daily.* Family establishment where children are well catered for.

🍺 **Hook & Tackle** Parthia Close, Reading (0118 950 0830). South east of County Lock, beyond Inner Distribution Road (via pedestrian underpass). Situated below the noise from Reading's over-zealous flirtation with the motor car this pub offers sanctuary, together with a selection of real ales. Substantial portions of inexpensive, home-made food are available *L* as well as good value bar snacks. Children welcome *until 19.30.* Garden. Sport TV. Traditional pub games and quiz *Sun. Open all day.*

🍺 **Sweeney & Todd** 10 Castle Street (off St Mary's Butts), Reading (0118 958 6466). Something of a local institution – a pub integrated with a pie shop and dispensing real ale. Excellent, inexpensive food *L and E. Open all day, closed Sun.*

🍺 **Horn** St Mary's Butts, Reading (0118 957 4794). North of Bridge Street Bridge. Listed 16th-C timber-framed pub serving real ale together with home-made bar food (V) *L and E.* Patio, darts and crib. Children welcome. *Open all day.*

🍺 **Hop Leaf** 163–165 Southampton Street, Reading (0118 931 2330). Thriving town local, with brewhouse at the rear, serving a selection of their own real ales. Outside seating. Children's room and traditional pub games. *Open all day Fri, Sat and Sun. Weekdays from 16.00 and also 12.00–14.00 Thur.*

🍺 **Hobgoblin** 2 Broad Street, Reading (0118 950 8119). Constantly changing range of real ales including a selection from Wychwood. Real cider. No children. Non-smoking area. *Open all day, every day.* Outside seating. No mobile phones allowed.

3B's Café Bar Town Hall, Blagrave Street, Reading (0118 939 9803). Cosmopolitan establishment situated in the old town hall, with a leaning towards a younger clientele. Real ale. Food (V) *L and E.* No smoking *10.00–18.00.* Regular live music nights. *Closed all day Sun.*

🍺 **Retreat** 8 St John's Street, Reading (0118 957 1593). Real ale along with peace and quiet in this cosy pub. *Thur* evening sing-a-longs and traditional pub games. Children allowed at landlord's discretion.

🍺 **Fisherman's Cottage** Kennetside, Reading (0118 957 1553). Pretty 18th-C canalside pub, west of Blake's Lock. Real ale. Food (V) *L and E.* Children welcome. Garden with playhouse. Dogs welcome away from eating areas. Open fires. *Open all day Fri–Sat and Sun in summer.*

🍺 **Jolly Angler** Kennetside, Reading. East of Blake's Lock. There is a quaint façade to this pub which marks the last refreshment point before the Thames. This establishment has recently changed hands so visit to find out more!

RIVER THAMES

FROM INGLESHAM TO TEDDINGTON:

The Environment Agency
Thames Region
Kings Meadow House
Kings Meadow Road
Reading
Berks RG1 8DQ
0118 953 5525; waterways.enquiries
@environment-agency.gov.uk

Those on the river are urged to obtain a copy of **A User's Guide to the River Thames**, published by the Agency, which details all navigational requirements.

All vessels must be registered with the Agency *before* using the non-tidal river – apply to the Craft Registration Dept at the above address. Vessels joining the river for short periods from connecting waterways can obtain short period registration from Thames locks adjacent to those waterways.

Boats must be constructed and equipped in accordance with the Boat Safety Requirements.

Pollution If you notice any pollution, notify the relevant Navigation Office (below), a lock keeper, or telephone Freefone (0800) 807060. *Navigation Offices*:
Oxford: 01865 721271
Reading: 0118 953 5533
Maidenhead: 0118 953 5577
Shepperton: 01276 454900

Speed Limit The maximum is 5 mph, in practice about 3 mph (the same as a brisk walking pace), and slower if your wash may cause damage to the river bank or small craft.

BELOW TEDDINGTON:

Port of London Authority
Bakers' Hall
7 Harp Lane
London EC3R 6LB
0207 743 7900; www.portoflondon.co.uk

The Port of London Authority (PLA) issues *The Pleasure Users Guide* obtainable free from the office above.

All river users are governed by the Port of London River Bye-laws, a copy of which can be obtained from (charge):

The Chief Harbour Master
London River House
Royal Pier Road
Gravesend
Kent DA12 2BG
01474 560311

All river movements on the tidal section of the river covered by this guide are under the control of **Woolwich Radio** who can be contacted by telephone on 0208 855 0315 and VHF channel 14.

All vessels over 20 metres must carry VHF radio and boat owners are reminded that they should hold an appropriate licence to operate such equipment.

MAXIMUM DIMENSIONS
Below Oxford
Length: 120'
Beam: 17' 9"

Above Oxford
Length: 109' 10"
Beam: 14' 8"

MILEAGES:
INGLESHAM Junction with the Thames & Severn Canal to:
Lechlade: 1/2 mile
Newbridge: 17 1/2 miles
Kings Lock *Junction with Duke's Cut, Oxford Canal*: 27 1/2 miles
Oxford *Junction with Oxford Canal (Isis Lock)*: 30 1/2 miles
Abingdon Lock: 39 1/2 miles
Wallingford Bridge: 53 1/2 miles
Reading *Junction with Kennet & Avon Canal*: 70 1/2 miles
Marlow Lock: 87 1/2 miles
Windsor Bridge: 100 1/2 miles
Shepperton *Junction with River Wey*: 114 miles
Teddington Lock: 125 1/2 miles
Brentford *Junction with Grand Union Canal*: 130 1/2 miles
Limehouse Basin *Junction with Regent's Canal and River Lee*: 146 1/2 miles

The Thames enjoys a special place in the hearts and minds of the English. Stretching for 215 miles from west to east and flowing past the seat of government, it links the Cotswolds, in the centre of the country, with the nation's bustling capital city. Its importance was recognised by the Romans, who built Watling Street, the Fosse Way, Ermine Street and the Icknield Way to cross the river. When the Romans left,

London's population declined, and its significance diminished. It was not until the 15th C that the capital began to grow into a great trading centre, eventually becoming the largest port in the world. Goods were shipped inland from the capital – carried up-river by horse-drawn or sailing barges.

Weirs were built on the river, often in places where they hindered navigation, to power mills, and these caused constant disputes between millers and the barge men. Some weirs, known as flash locks, had movable sections to allow barges to pass through. But even then the barge men would have to wait for the fierce rush of water to subside before passing the weir, or be pulled upstream by winch. Then they would have to wait on the far side for the depth of water to build up again. Legislation tried unsuccessfully to control the building of weirs, and so allow the river to fulfil its important role as a highway, but navigation did not begin to improve until pound locks were introduced on the Thames, one of the first being built at Swift Ditch, near Abingdon, axround 1620. By the end of the 18th C the Thames had been linked to the main canal network, thereby affording access to many other parts of England. However, the importance of the river as a transport artery began to diminish with the expansion of the railways.

The Thames once also supplied food, and trout and salmon could be caught readily. The latter were indeed so common they were eaten by the poor. The river was also thick with eels. These would swim up the river in such numbers that they could be caught with sieves and buckets, and were made into a form of cake.

But as the population of London grew, the amount of waste grew with it, and began to accumulate in the streets. Gradually various schemes were devised to channel this into rivers which discharged into the Thames, and these water-courses were then covered, becoming known as 'the lost rivers of London'. At this time there were still fish in the river, but from the early 19th C increasing industrial pollution drove all the salmon and eels from the lower Thames, and there were outbreaks of cholera amongst the population of London. The year 1858 was known as 'The Great Stink'. The Commission of Sewers was established in 1847, and gradually the clean-up began. Recently a vigorous campaign has restored the quality of the water: salmon have returned and amateur fishermen are now a common sight right through central London.

In the 17th and 18th C Frost Fairs were held in London whenever the river froze. There were stalls, performing bears, fairground amusements and ox roasting on the ice. The last fair was held in 1814 – the removal of the old London Bridge, which had the effect of a dam, and the building of the embankments in the 19th C, narrowed the river, and deepened and speeded the flow of water, so that it is now no longer possible for the tidal river to freeze over. Since the early 19th C the river has become the scene of regattas in summer, that at Henley being an international event. Many Londoners are now aware that their city is sinking at the rate of about twelve inches every 100 years. As long ago as 1236 the river flooded the Palace of Westminster; in 1928 central London was flooded with the loss of 14 lives; and the disastrous surge tide of 1953 left 300 dead along the east coast and Thames estuary. To protect London from this threat the magnificent Thames Flood Barrier was built at Woolwich. Movable barriers can be raised from the river bed to hold back the tide – the four main gates having a span of 200ft and the strength to withstand a load of more than 9000 metric tons. The stainless steel shells housing the machinery are built on hardwood ribs, their design reminiscent of the Sydney Opera House.

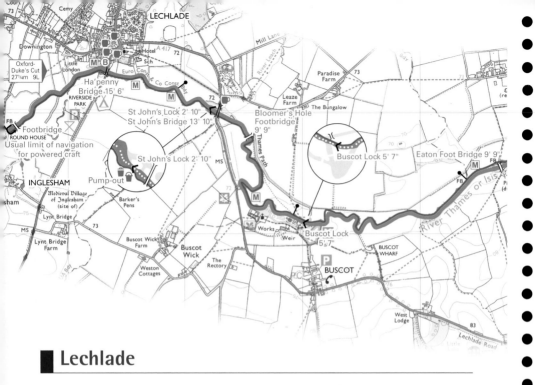

Lechlade

The navigable Thames begins at the Round House, at the junction with the presently unnavigable Thames & Severn Canal near Inglesham – an attractive group of buildings by the river's edge. Moored craft and all the activities of a riverside park are present as the Thames passes Lechlade, flowing under Ha'penny Bridge, so named because a toll was once taken. The church at Lechlade can be seen for miles around – its tall spire always visible as the river meanders to St John's Lock, the highest on the Thames. Note the modern lock house, the quaint miniature buildings in the lock gardens, and the statue of Father Thames, which once marked the river's source at Thames Head, north of Kemble, Gloucestershire. Below the lock the Thames passes under Bloomers Hole Footbridge, the final link in the Thames Path from Lechlade to London. The river's course then becomes quite extravagant – at one point even doubling back before passing the church and beautiful rectory at Buscot. Beyond Buscot Lock the river is once again in open country, delightfully rural and lonely. The church at Eaton Hastings is by the river and provides interest before reaching Grafton Lock, a lonely outpost. A very isolated and rural stretch of river then follows, meandering through meadowland and having little contact with civilisation.

NAVIGATIONAL NOTES

The limit of navigation for powered craft on the Thames is usually at the junction with the Thames & Severn Canal, marked by the Round House, below Inglesham. Here a full-length narrowboat can wind, taking care to avoid the sandbank on the north side. Those not familiar with the river are urged to proceed no further, even though the right of navigation extends to Cricklade, and craft drawing 2ft 6in may be able to proceed as far as 3 miles above Lechlade. The Thames & Severn Canal is currently undergoing restoration.

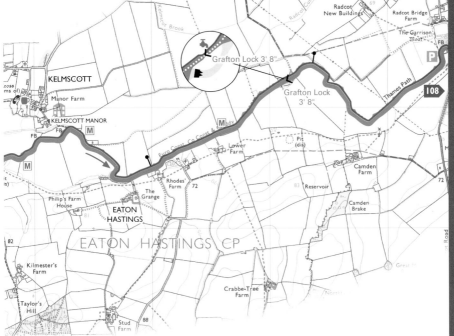

NATURAL HISTORY IN THE THAMES VALLEY

The Thames is a lowland river throughout its length with few of the striking changes in scenery or gradient that one associates with rivers of the north or west of the country. As a result its landscape is gentle and its flood plain contains woodlands, water meadows and grassland with appropriately modest plant and animal inhabitants. However, the scenery is enriched by the Goring Gap, between Goring and Reading, where during the Ice Ages the river cut a new channel through the south western end of the Chilterns, isolating the Berkshire Downs on the south bank. The river here passes through chalk hills with rich grassland and beech woods of spectacular appearance. Through most of its length the water meadows overlie river gravels; in many places these have been excavated to win gravel for roads and buildings, leaving water-filled pits in which the richest animal life of all the Thames valley can be found. As a result of these natural and man-made habitats there is a great deal of fascinating natural history interest in the Thames and its surroundings.

WALKING & CYCLING

Practical walking along the Thames begins at Inglesham. The path is in good shape throughout the length of the river to London. The ambitious could also look to the west, where the Thames & Severn Way traces this currently unnavigable canal's route to the River Severn.

Boatyards

Ⓑ **Riverside Lechlade** Park End Wharf, Lechlade (01367 252229; www.riverside-lechlade.co.uk). 🗑 🚻 ♨ P D E Pump out at St John's Lock. Gas, boat hire, day-hire boats, overnight mooring, long-term mooring, winter storage, slipway, dry dock, crane, boat building, boat and engine sales and repairs, chandlery, toilets, showers, solid fuel. *Emergency call out.*

Upper Thames at Inglesham

Inglesham

Wilts. A marvellous architectural group around the tiny church. Although of Saxon origin, the present building is largely 13th-C. William Morris is responsible for the remarkable original state of the building – he loved it and saved it from 19th-C restoration. A brass to the right of the entrance commemorates his work. The adjoining farm was once the priory. On the north bank the Inglesham Round House is a notable landmark. It once belonged to the lock keeper on the presently unnavigable Thames & Severn Canal, which joins the river at this point.

Thames & Severn Canal (www.cotswoldcanals.com). Stretching almost 29 miles between Inglesham and Wallbridge, Stroud, where it joins the Stroudwater Canal and, in turn, the Goucester & Sharpness Canal. This trade link was initially closed to navigation in 1895, but remedial works were carried out and it re-opened for three months in 1899, but serious leakages in the summit level then again made it unnavigable, and its abandonment was finally confirmed by Act of Parliament in 1901. This heavily locked canal rises to 300ft above sea level, where the Sapperton Tunnel burrows under the Cotswolds for 3808yds. Now undergoing active restoration, it is hoped that it will eventually form part of a Cotswold Ring, linking with the Gloucester & Sharpness, River Avon, Stratford-on-Avon, Grand Union, Oxford and Thames. There are boat trips into Sapperton Tunnel *during the winter months.*

Lechlade

Glos. PO, shops. A golden grey market town dominating the river in all directions and best seen from St John's Bridge, with the tall spire of the Perpendicular wool church rising above the surrounding cluster of buildings. Shelley's Walk leads from the river to the church, where his *Stanzas in a Summer Churchyard* is quoted on a plaque in the churchyard wall. Shelley, Peacock, Mary Godwin and Charles Clairmont stayed in Lechlade in 1815, after rowing from Windsor.

Bloomers Hole Footbridge Completing the Thames Path National Trail, this bridge, although built of steel, is clad with timber. It was lowered into place by a Chinook helicopter from RAF Brize Norton.

Little Faringdon Mill One mile outside Lechlade on the A361 to Burford. A perfect 18th-C mill in its original state, with a farm and outbuildings. Private.

Buscot

Oxon. A small village off the A417, notable for the very beautiful Queen Anne rectory (private) which stands on the riverside by the church, itself unremarkable apart from its Burne-Jones windows. The National Trust owns a picnic site by the weir pool.

Buscot Old Parsonage Buscot, Faringdon, Oxon. A Cotswold stone building of 1703 on the river bank. *Open only by written appointment with the tenant.* NT.

Buscot Park (01367 240786). Built about 1780 in the Adam style by Edward Loveden Townsend, with a park and gardens laid out by Harold Peto. In 1859 the estate was aquired by Robert Tertius Campbell, and he embarked upon a scheme to make it one of the most advanced farms of its time. His major crop was sugar beet, and he installed 6 miles of railway track to aid harvesting. He also built a distillery on Brandy Island (*see* Buscot Wharf, opposite), a gasworks and concrete farm buildings. However these works exhausted his resources, and he became bankrupt. Fine furniture and The Faringdon Collection of Paintings, including works by Rembrandt and Murillo were later bought by Sir Alexander Henderson, First Lord Faringdon. The Second Lord Faringdon continued collecting, and restored much of the original character to the house. The Italianate Water Garden was created by Harold Peto during the 20th C. House *open Apr–Sep, Wed–Fri and second and fourth weekends in month 14.00–18.00.* Grounds *open Apr–Sep, Mon and Tue 14.00–18.00.* Groups should telephone to book. There is a tearoom on site. Charge. NT.

Buscot Wharf Little trace remains of the wharf from which brandy was shipped to France. The short arm was known as Buscot Pill.

Tourist Information Centre 7a Market Place, Faringdon (01367 242191; www.oxfordshire.co.uk/data/018393).

● **Kelmscott**

Oxon. A pristine village of elegant grey stone houses, firmly entrenched against development. The quiet 15th-C church has a strong medieval atmosphere.

Kelmscott Manor (01367 252486; www. kelmscottmanor.co.uk). A beautiful house behind high walls, built in 1570, and added to in 1665. It became the summer home of William Morris from 1871 until his death in 1896, and he adored it, saying it had 'quaint garrets amongst great timbers of the roof, where of old times the tillers and herdsmen slept'. He shared it with Dante Gabriel Rossetti until 1874. William Morris was buried in the churchyard at Kelmscott after his death in Hammersmith; his tomb is the work of Philip Webb. The Manor is *open Apr–Sep, Wed 11.00–13.00 and 14.00–17.00; also third Sat of each month; first and third Sat, Jul–Aug 14.00–17.00.* Charge.

● **Eaton Hastings**

Oxon. Quite inaccessible from the river. The 13th-C church is well situated by the water – the rest of the village is a mile away.

Pubs and Restaurants

🍺 **The Riverside** Lechlade (01367 252229; www.riverside-lechlade.co.uk). This pub sits amidst a pleasant mix of boats and antiques, beside Ha'penny Bridge. Extensive choice of bottled beers. Food (V) is available *all day*. Children's room. Riverside seating. ✗ 🍷 *open Sun L only.* Live music *every Thur.* Mooring.

🍺 **The Swan** Burford St, Lechlade (01367 253571). Cosy and peaceful stone-built pub, the oldest in Lechlade. Real ale. Food (V) served *L and E (not Sun E)*. Children welcome.

🍺 **The Crown Inn** High St, Lechlade (01367 252198). Popular 16th-C coaching inn, with open fires and serving a choice of real ale. Good food (V), such as home-made soups and hamburgers, served *L and E*. Children are welcome and there is a garden.

🍺 ✗ **New Inn Hotel** Market Place, Lechlade (01367 252296; www.newinnhotel.com). Attractive pub by the church and the river. Real ale. Bar and restaurant meals (V) from traditional dishes to the exotic , available *L and E*. Children over 5 years old are welcome and there is a large garden with a play area. There are shower facilities here.

🍺 **The Red Lion** High Street, Lechlade (01367 252373). Friendly old coaching inn with open fires. Real ale. Meals (V) available *L and E*. Children welcome. Outside patio seating.

✗ 🍷 **British Raj** Burford Street, Lechlade (01367 252956). Wide choice of Indian food and takeaways. *Open 12.00–14.30 and 18.00–23.30.*

✗ **The Café** Market Square, Lechlade (01367 253990). Above The Oxford Wine Company. Friendly tearoom and coffee shop, with prints and paintings for sale on the walls. Children welcome, toys available. *Open for food 09.30–16.30.*

🍺 ✗ **The Trout Inn** St John's Bridge, Lechlade (01367 252313; www.thetroutinn. com). A justly famous 13th-C Cotswold stone pub, with plenty of wood panelling, low beams and stuffed fish. Real ale. Tasty home-cooked bar meals (V) served in the bar or dining area *L and E*. Live jazz *Tue and Sun E*. Large riverside garden borders the weir stream, marquee available for special events. An intriguing old Oxfordshire game called Aunt Sally is played in the garden. Children welcome, and there are fishing rights on 2 miles of the Thames. Tractor and steam rally *first weekend in June*. Music weekend *last weekend in June*, a jazz festival is usually held the following weekend (*usually first weekend in July*), and there is a folk festival *last weekend in July*. Rowing boats, punts, electric boats and cruisers for hire. Mooring.

🍺 ✗ **The Plough at Kelmscott** Kelmscott (01367 253543; www.plough-kelmscott. co.uk). A fine 16th-C restaurant and bar with flagstone floors, serving real ale. Restaurant, with à la carte menu, and home-made bar meals (V) served *L and E*. Children are welcome, and there is a garden. Spit roasts *Sun L in summer*. B & B.

Tadpole

A very isolated, rural stretch of river, meandering through meadowland and having little contact with civilisation. The river divides at Radcot where two fine bridges, the ever popular Swan Hotel and a large picnic area opposite are always busy with visitors on summer afternoons. Caravans line the north bank as once more the Thames enters open meadowland around Radcot Lock and then meanders on to the splendid Rushey Lock, with its charming house and fine garden, and the handsome 18th-C Tadpole Bridge. Then again the Thames enters lonely country, passing to the south of Chimney. It is about as far away from it all as you can get on the river.

WALKING & CYCLING
There is a variety of footpaths from either Old Man's Bridge or Rushey Lock to Bampton.

● **Radcot**
Oxon. A small hamlet centred around the popular Swan Hotel. The triple-arched 13th-C bridge is the oldest surviving on the Thames. The single-arched bridge spanning the navigation channel, an artificial cut, was built later, in 1787. The old bridge, made of Taynton stone, was the scene of a Civil War skirmish, when Prince Rupert's Royalist cavalry pounced on Cromwell's men, marching to an attack on Faringdon. Upstream caravans line the north bank – to the south picnics and tents sprawl across the meadow during the summer.
Faringdon House *Oxon.* 2¹/₂ miles south of Radcot

Bridge. An 18th-C house built by George III's 'dogged and dull' poet laureate Henry James Pye. The surrounding parkland is reputedly haunted by a headless Hampden Pye, an earlier member of the family who was decapitated at sea. His story is recalled in *The Ingoldsby Legends*, 1840. The folly on Faringdon Hill, an octagonal Gothic lantern, was built by the artist and author Lord Berners in 1935.

● **Bampton**
Oxon. PO, tel, stores. An attractive greystone town 1¹/₂ miles from the river, easily approached by a variety of footpaths or by road north from Tadpole. It has a timeless appearance in that

Pubs and Restaurants

The Swan Hotel Radcot Bridge (01367 810220). Comfortable and friendly old inn of great character, beside what was once a wharf. The interior is decorated with stuffed fish, a stuffed swan, plenty of brass and a William Morris oak chair. Real ale. Meals (V) available *L and E*. Children are welcome, and there is a pleasant garden.

✕ The Trout at Tadpole Bridge Buckland Marsh, Faringdon (01367 870382; www.trout-inn.co.uk). Fine traditional riverside pub serving real ale, along with modern British food (V) *L and E (not Sun E)*.

Excellent wine list. Children welcome, and there is a well-tended riverside garden. Camping and fishing rights. B & B.

Morris Clown High Street, Bampton (01993 850217). Fine 12th-C pub, with a wonderful sign, serving real ale. Children welcome.

✕ The Romany Inn Bridge Street, Bampton (01993 850237). There are Saxon arches in the cellar of this fine old pub, which is a 19th-C listed building. Real ale. Meals (V) available *L and E*. Children welcome. Garden and play area.

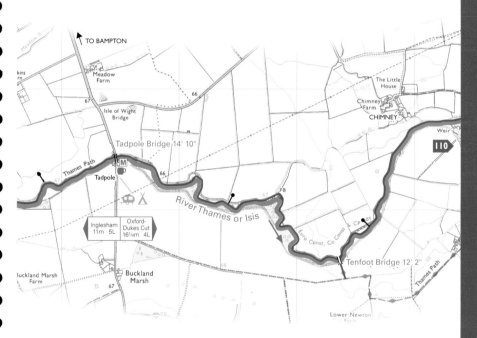

much of the new development is built from the same materials as, and often in a style similar to, the old. The result is both unusual and pleasing. The church, largely 13th- and 14th-C, has a slightly uneasy octagonal spire. Beside the church is the old grammar school, founded in 1653. At one time the town was called Bampton in the Bush – a description dating from before the 18th C when no roads served the community. Morris dancing is reputed to have originated here.

● **Buckland**
Oxon. Stores. About a mile south of Tadpole Bridge. A village intimately connected with Buckland House, and best approached from the river, as there is a fine view over the Thames Valley.
Buckland House Built in 1757 by Wood of Bath, it is one of the most imposing 18th-C homes in Oxfordshire, although the wings were added in 1910. There is a Gothic stable in the park. Private.

Newbridge

The navigation channel passes through a tree-lined cut to Shifford Lock, the last lock to be built on the Thames, in 1898. Again the countryside is flat, glimpsed here and there over the steep river banks which are in places heavily overgrown. Electricity pylons do little to improve the scene. Welcome relief appears at Newbridge, with a fine pub on each side of the handsome old bridge. The nearest village is Standlake, a mile to the north. As the hills close in from the east the countryside gradually loses much of the bleakness of the upper reaches and the villages come a little closer. There are attractive woods below Northmoor Lock, and Bablock Hythe, with another riverside pub, is soon reached. To the north, the grassy banks of the vast Farmoor Reservoir, much loved by anglers, come down to the river's edge.

● **Shifford**
Oxon. A church and a few houses surrounded by lush pastureland are all that remain of what was once an important town. Alfred held a meeting of the English Parliament here in AD890. The church is situated in the middle of a field less than quarter of a mile from the river.

● **Hinton Waldrist and Longworth**
Oxon. Two pleasant straggling villages up on a ridge overlooking the valley. Longworth church contains a good example of Arts and Crafts stained glass by Heywood Sumner, 1906. The Old Rectory, Longworth, was the birthplace of Dr John Fell, 1625–86, who participated in the early development of the Oxford University Press, especially with regard to printing types; and also Richard Doddridge Blackmore, 1825–1900, author of *Lorna Doone* (1869), who spent only the first four months of his life here – sadly his mother died shortly after his birth.

● **Newbridge**
Oxon. A fine 13th-C stone bridge with pointed arches, one of the oldest on the river. The River Windrush joins the Thames here.

● **Northmoor**
Oxon. The 13th-C church contains a restored bell loft, dated 1701. Behind the church is a Tudor rectory.

● **Appleton**
Oxon. PO, store. A meandering thatch and stone village, with new development to the west. Appleton Manor, situated beside a splendid weather-boarded barn and gateway, was built at the end of the 12th C. An astonishing amount remains, including a fine doorway.

● **Bablock Hythe**
Oxon. Mentioned by Matthew Arnold in *The Scholar Gypsy*, 1853, who was seen:

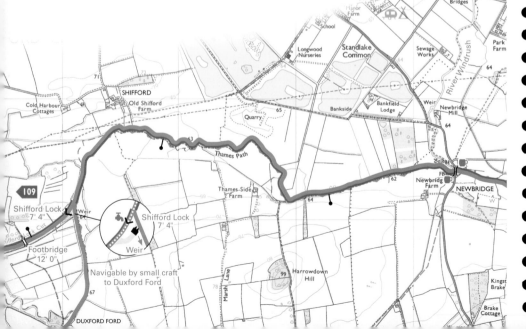

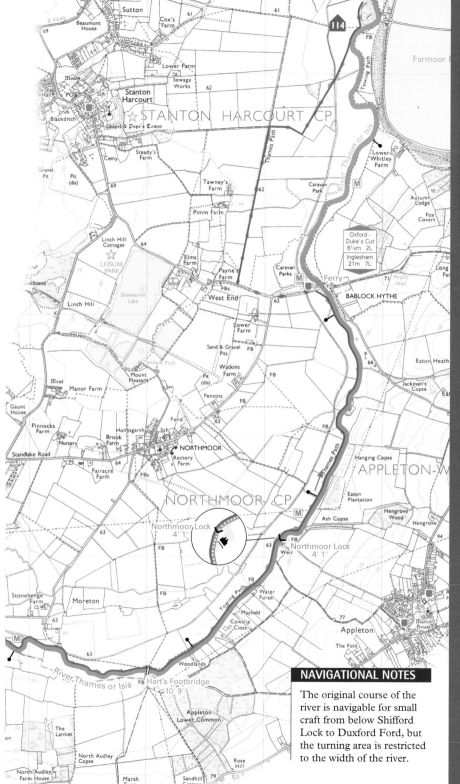

Oxford -
Duke's Cut
6¼m   2L
Inglesham
21m   7L

Northmoor Lock
4' 1"

Northmoor Lock
Weir
4' 1"

Hart's Footbridge
10' 9"

River Thames or Isis

NAVIGATIONAL NOTES

The original course of the
river is navigable for small
craft from below Shifford
Lock to Duxford Ford, but
the turning area is restricted
to the width of the river.

'In hat of antique shape, and cloak of grey, crossing the stripling Thames at Bab-lock-hithe'. A Roman stone altar, now in the Ashmolean, was dredged from the river here. There has been a ferry here since AD904, and although it has been a little erratic in recent years, it is, at the time of writing, operating again, courtesy of the pub. The area is surrounded by an unappealing estate of temporary homes.

● **Stanton Harcourt**
Oxon. PO, tel, stores. A superb grey stone village between the Thames and the Windrush, the waters reflecting the quiet glory of the buildings. The grand cruciform church has fine monuments in the Harcourt Chapel.
Stanton Harcourt Manor (01865 881928; www.stantonharcourt.net). The Harcourts built this manor, one of the earliest unfortified manor houses in England, between 1380–1470, with a Gatehouse being added in 1540. Now only Pope's Tower, the scene of Alexander Pope's translation of the *Iliad*, and the unique Great Kitchen, survive. The Kitchen is unique in England, in that smoke escaped through vents which were opened manually – there is no chimney. The 12 acres of gardens as seen today date from 1948, and consist of three distinct areas: formal gardens; fruit, vineyard and rose gardens and and a romantic 'wild' garden. Stew ponds once supplied fish for the table. *Open Easter–Sep fortnightly on Thur, Sun (and B Hol Mons) 14.00–18.00* (telephone to confirm). Charge. Well worth the walk from the river.

WALKING & CYCLING
The prominent dome-shaped Harrowdown Hill can be approached by footpath from the river about a mile west of Newbridge. Views from the top amply repay the modest effort.

Pubs and Restaurants

🍺 **Blue Boar** Tuck's Lane, Longworth (01865 820494; blueboarox@aol.com). Busy 16th-C country pub. Real ale. Home-cooked restaurant meals (V) *L and E*. Children welcome. Garden.

🍺 **Maybush Inn** Newbridge (01865 300624). Historic riverside pub serving real ale. Bar meals and an à la carte menu (V) available *all day*. Terrace overlooks the river, attractive grassy garden. Children welcome. Caravan and camping site.

🍺✕ **Rose Revived Inn** Newbridge (01865 300221; www.greenking.tablesir.com). Old Cotswold stone inn. Real ale. Bar meals and snacks (V) served *all day*. Children welcome, and there is a tidy garden. Mooring.

🍺 **Thatched Tavern** Appleton (01865 864814). Attractive 17th-C village pub, where the sign displays its earlier thatched roof. Real ale. Meals (V), with Portugese specialities, available *L and E*. Children welcome and Aunt Sally can be played. Garden.

🍺 **Red Lion** Northmoor (01865 300301). Good informal village pub by the church, serving real ale. Wide range of meals (V) available in the bar or dining area *L and E (not Sun or Mon E)*. Children welcome *if you are eating*. Garden. Steak nights *Wed and Thur*, fish suppers *Fri*.

🍺✕ **The Ferryman Inn** Bablock Hythe (01865 880028; kelland@oxfree.com). A famous and welcoming pub, serving real ale. Meals (V) available *L and E (not Tue E)*. Children welcome. Riverside garden. The pub operates the ancient foot ferry and also organise a raft race. The Mikron Theatre visits in *June*. B & B.

🍺✕ **Harcourt Arms** Main Road, Stanton Harcourt (01865 881931; antony@auty.com). Handsome 16th-C food-oriented inn, with inglenook fireplaces. Real ale. Good, interesting food (V), including fish and game, served *L and E*. Children welcome, and there is an all-weather terrace.

🍺 **The Fox** Main Road, Stanton Harcourt (01865 881551). Real ale is served in this traditional village pub. Food (V) available *L (E bookings only)*, *not Sun E or Mon*. Children welcome. Garden with children's play area. Aunt Sally is played. Music *last Sat of month*.

🍺 **The Vine** 11 Abingdon Road, Cumnor (01865 862567; thevineinn@aol.com). Pretty pub with the aforementioned vine growing along the front wall. Real ale. Bar meals (V) available *L and E*. Children welcome. Large garden with a play area.

🍺✕ **Bear & Ragged Staff** Appleton Road, Cumnor (01865 862329). A large, traditional 13th-C pub close to the village pond. Real ale. Good restaurant meals from varied and imaginative menu, and bar meals (V) available *L and E*. Children welcome. Garden with play area.

🍺✕ **Eight Bells** High Street, Eaton (01865 862983). About 1 mile south east of Bablock Hythe. Welcoming pub and restaurant with a log fire. Real ale. Bar meals (V and vegan) can be selected from a large menu, and are available *L and E*. Children are welcome. *Closed Mon in winter*.

Godstow

The Thames meanders extravagantly past Farmoor Reservoir and the very pretty Pinkhill Lock, with its picnic site, towards Swinford. Below Eynsham Lock the entrance to the Wharf Stream can be seen on the east side, followed by the Cassington Cut, which bypassed the lower reaches of the Evenlode, when that river was navigable. Opposite are the dense woodlands of Wytham Great Wood, falling steeply down Wytham Hill to the river's edge. The Seacourt Stream leaves the Thames at Hagley Pool, and a short distance below is King's Lock. Access to the Oxford Canal can be gained via a backwater and the Duke's Cut, which join the weir stream. Pixey Mead lies to the west, its peace shattered by the incessant traffic of the Oxford bypass, which crosses the river above Godstow. On the weir stream is the old Trout Inn: overlooking the lock cut are the ruins of Godstow Abbey. By Port Meadow the river is now significantly wider, flowing between sandy banks to Binsey, where a small jetty indicates the presence of the village and its handsome thatched pub. The navigation channel below Binsey becomes comparatively narrow and tree-lined after Medley Footbridge. Soon a water crossroads is reached, with the unnavigable Bulstake Stream running off to the west, while to the east a short, narrow cut to the Oxford Canal branches off under a very low railway bridge. A smart terrace of railway houses stands beside the river, all with doors opening onto the towpath. The journey through Oxford proper begins at the notoriously low (7ft 6in) Osney Bridge, an obstacle which makes it impossible for larger Thames cruisers to penetrate upstream.

Pubs and Restaurants

The Talbot Oxford Road, Eynsham (01865 881348). North west of Swinford Bridge. Busy and attractive pub on the now unnavigable Wharf Stream, serving real ale. Meals, including fresh fish (V), are available *L and E*. Children are welcome away from the bar, and there is a garden.

The Trout Inn Godstow Road, Wolvercote, Oxford (01865 302071). A lovely ivy-covered stone building, with a riverside terrace, built in 1138 as a hospice for Godstow Nunnery. Peacocks roam the large gardens, and the weir stream – not fished for many years – is full of shoals of large fish, swimming tamely near the surface amongst the ducks. Real ale is served, and hot and cold bar meals (V) are available *L and E*. Children are welcome if eating.

The White Hart Wytham (01865 244372). Friendly old thatched village pub with flag-stone floors, a 16th-C dovecote and walled garden. Real ale. Bar meals (V) available *L and E*. Children welcome.

The Perch Inn Binsey Lane, Binsey (01865 728891). Moor at the jetty and walk 50yds along a path to this large and handsome 800-year-old thatched pub, standing in a superb large garden with willow trees and good children's play area. Real ale is served in the low-ceilinged bar, where the ghost of a sailor is said to appear. Food (V), from ploughmans to exotic fish dishes – fish is the speciality – is available *L and E (not Sun E)*. *Summer* barbecue on *Sun and fine evenings*. Giant chess can be played. Morris dancing *in summer*.

Swinford Toll Bridge A fine stone balustraded bridge and toll house, where a small toll is collected. It was built in 1777.

Eynsham
Oxon. PO, tel, stores, launderette. ³/4 mile north west of Swinford Bridge. Once a town of considerable importance, boasting a Benedictine Abbey founded in the 11th C. Today Eynsham has a good selection of shops

in the Market Square, around the old town hall.
Wytham Great Wood A marvellous wood of over 600 acres, owned by Oxford University, whose field station is a good example of English vernacular architecture. A haven for birds; the hobby has nested here, nightingales and warblers sing, and teal visit in winter. There is a heronry at Wytham. Private, permit required.

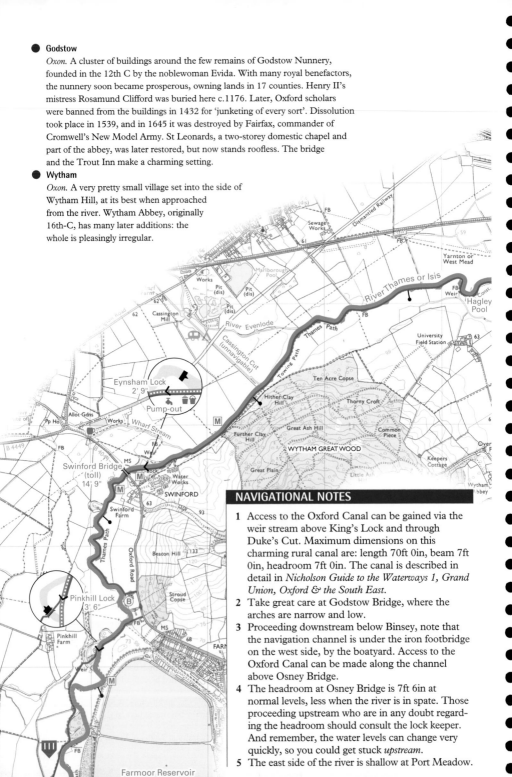

- **Godstow**

Oxon. A cluster of buildings around the few remains of Godstow Nunnery, founded in the 12th C by the noblewoman Evida. With many royal benefactors, the nunnery soon became prosperous, owning lands in 17 counties. Henry II's mistress Rosamund Clifford was buried here c.1176. Later, Oxford scholars were banned from the buildings in 1432 for 'junketing of every sort'. Dissolution took place in 1539, and in 1645 it was destroyed by Fairfax, commander of Cromwell's New Model Army. St Leonards, a two-storey domestic chapel and part of the abbey, was later restored, but now stands roofless. The bridge and the Trout Inn make a charming setting.

- **Wytham**

Oxon. A very pretty small village set into the side of Wytham Hill, at its best when approached from the river. Wytham Abbey, originally 16th-C, has many later additions: the whole is pleasingly irregular.

NAVIGATIONAL NOTES

1 Access to the Oxford Canal can be gained via the weir stream above King's Lock and through Duke's Cut. Maximum dimensions on this charming rural canal are: length 70ft 0in, beam 7ft 0in, headroom 7ft 0in. The canal is described in detail in *Nicholson Guide to the Waterways 1, Grand Union, Oxford & the South East*.

2 Take great care at Godstow Bridge, where the arches are narrow and low.

3 Proceeding downstream below Binsey, note that the navigation channel is under the iron footbridge on the west side, by the boatyard. Access to the Oxford Canal can be made along the channel above Osney Bridge.

4 The headroom at Osney Bridge is 7ft 6in at normal levels, less when the river is in spate. Those proceeding upstream who are in any doubt regarding the headroom should consult the lock keeper. And remember, the water levels can change very quickly, so you could get stuck *upstream*.

5 The east side of the river is shallow at Port Meadow.

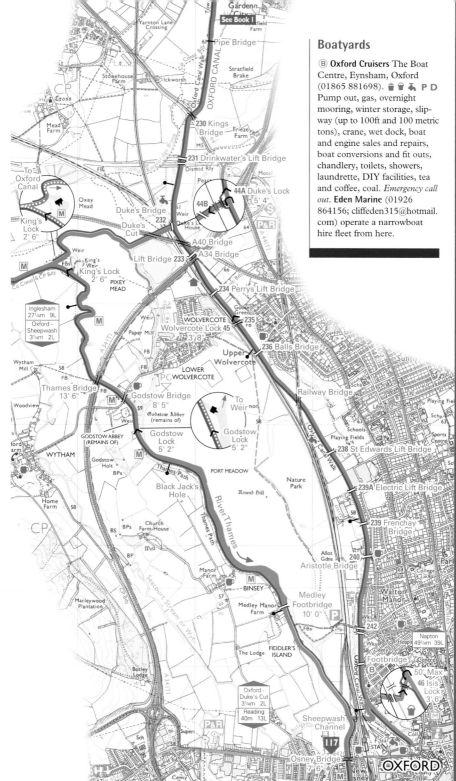

Boatyards

Ⓑ **Oxford Cruisers** The Boat Centre, Eynsham, Oxford (01865 881698). 🚽 🛢 🏊 P D Pump out, gas, overnight mooring, winter storage, slipway (up to 100ft and 100 metric tons), crane, wet dock, boat and engine sales and repairs, boat conversions and fit outs, chandlery, toilets, showers, laundrette, DIY facilities, tea and coffee, coal. *Emergency call out.* **Eden Marine** (01926 864156; cliffeden315@hotmail. com) operate a narrowboat hire fleet from here.

Oxford

This section, while not particularly picturesque, provides plenty of interest, in stark contrast to the miles of water meadows above the town. Below Osney Bridge is a lovely stretch of urban waterway, with terraced houses facing the river, a handsome pub and a lock – an environment much appreciated by the local workers who spend their lunch-breaks here in the summer. There are many access points to the towpath, which is well used by cyclists, joggers and walkers. Just above Osney Railway Bridge stands a touching memorial to Edgar Wilson who, on 15 June 1889, saved the lives of two boys here, at the cost of his own. Folly Bridge is always a hive of activity during the summer; Salter's trip boat base is here, along with a large riverside pub. Punts are available for hire and small motor and rowing boats proceed up and down. Christ Church Meadow lies to the east, and is thronged with tourists and sunbathers when the weather is fine. Below is a long row of boathouses, facing the mock Tudor of the University Rowing Club building. Downstream of Donnington Road Bridge suburbia keeps its distance and the river proceeds along a green passage to Iffley Lock, with its pretty balustraded footbridges and fine lock house, all surrounded by trees, with a white-painted pub nearby. There is an area of parkland to the west, on an isthmus created by the Weirs Mill Stream, followed by the functional steel of Kennington Railway Bridge. As the river dog-legs past Rose Isle pylons run parallel, but still the houses and factories, for the most part, keep away. Gradually the Oxford conurbation is left behind as the river passes through a mixture of woodland, suburbia and light industry, then curves through a maze of backwaters, used as boat club moorings, to Sandford Lock, the deepest on the river above Teddington and distinguished by the presence of large mill buildings. Below here the Thames passes through open country criss-crossed by electricity pylons. An absolutely fascinating stretch of river.

City of Oxford
Oxon. All shops and services. The town was founded in the 10th C and has been a university city since the 13th C. Today it is a lively cosmopolitan centre of learning, tourism and industry.
Tourist Information Centre The Old School, Gloucester Green, Oxford (01865 726871; www.visitoxford.org). Here you will find a good selection of city guides and maps, and helpful and informative staff.
Colleges
It is, of course, the colleges which give Oxford its unique character – they can all be visited, but opening times vary, so consult with the Tourist Information Centre. Those noted here have been selected as being particularly representative of their periods.
Merton College
One of the earliest collegiate foundations, dating from 1264, the buildings are especially typical of the Perpendicular and Decorative periods. The chapel was begun in 1294 and Mob Quad was the first of the Oxford quadrangles. The library, mainly 14th-C, has a famous collection of rare books and manuscripts. During the Victorian era, the college was enlarged, and the Grove Buildings are by William Butterfield, with alterations in 1929 by T. Harold Hughes.

New College
The college was founded by William of Wykeham, Bishop of Winchester, in 1379. The chapel, a noble example of early Perpendicular, was greatly restored by Sir George Scott in the 19th C. The great west window, after a cartoon by Reynolds, and Epstein's *Lazarus* are noteworthy. The 14th-C cloister and the workmanship of the wrought-iron screen, 1684, between the Garden Quad and the Garden, are outstanding memorials of their times.
Keble College
Built by William Butterfield in 1870, Keble is the only Oxford college entirely in the Victorian Gothic style. The frontage of red and grey patterned brickwork and the tracery windows display great self-confidence. The chapel, with its glass and mosaics, bricks, tiles and brass, contains Holman Hunt's *The Light of the World*.
St Catherine's College
An important and interesting example of a new college, designed by the Danish architect, Arne Jacobsen in 1964. The entrance to the college is reached through an unprepossessing car park area, but in the main quadrangle the effect is one of stark impact. The mass of glass windows with their bands of ribbed concrete stretch like concertinas on either side of the quadrangle. All is bleak but full of atmosphere. The furniture and college plate were also designed by Jacobsen.

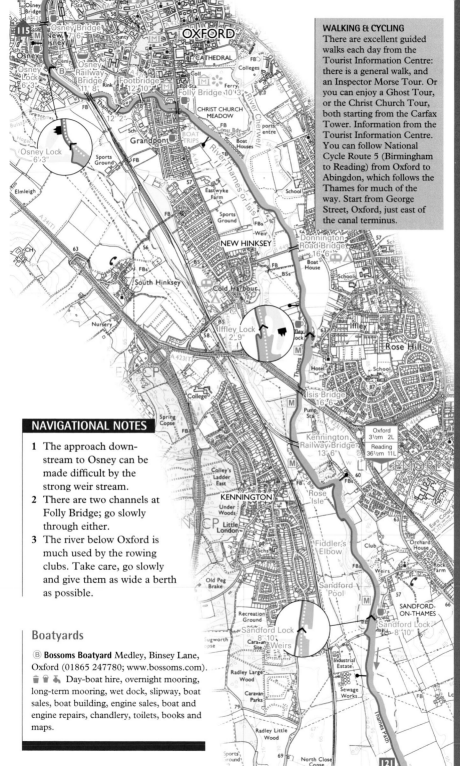

River Thames

Oxford

WALKING & CYCLING

There are excellent guided walks each day from the Tourist Information Centre: there is a general walk, and an Inspector Morse Tour. Or you can enjoy a Ghost Tour, or the Christ Church Tour, both starting from the Carfax Tower. Information from the Tourist Information Centre. You can follow National Cycle Route 5 (Birmingham to Reading) from Oxford to Abingdon, which follows the Thames for much of the way. Start from George Street, Oxford, just east of the canal terminus.

NAVIGATIONAL NOTES

1 The approach downstream to Osney can be made difficult by the strong weir stream.

2 There are two channels at Folly Bridge; go slowly through either.

3 The river below Oxford is much used by the rowing clubs. Take care, go slowly and give them as wide a berth as possible.

Boatyards

Ⓑ **Bossoms Boatyard** Medley, Binsey Lane, Oxford (01865 247780; www.bossoms.com). Day-boat hire, overnight mooring, long-term mooring, wet dock, slipway, boat sales, boat building, engine sales, boat and engine repairs, chandlery, toilets, books and maps.

St Anne's College

This college reflects some of the most exciting modern building in Oxford. The Wolfson block in the main quadrangle was designed by Howell, Killick and Partridge, 1964. With its two curving wings and square jutting windows, all of pre-cast concrete, this building is impressive and original. Facing the block is the Dining Hall by Gerald Banks, 1964, and to one side is Hartland House, mainly 1930s but with 1951 additions by Sir Giles Gilbert Scott.

Other interesting buildings include:

Radcliffe Camera

Radcliffe Square. Dr Radcliffe left £40,000 for the building of this library by James Gibbs, 1739, to house his Physic library. It is a vast domed Italianate rotunda, now a Bodleian reading room, and not open to the public. The staircase and skylight can be admired through the doorway.

Sheldonian Theatre

Broad Street (01865 277299; www.sheldon.ox. ac.uk). Built by Christopher Wren in 1669 under the auspices of Gilbert Sheldon, Archbishop of Canterbury, the theatre was designed to be used for university ceremonies and degrees, which are still awarded here. For many years it also housed the workshops of the University Press. The interior, with its ceiling by Robert Streeter, is delightful. *Open Mon–Sat 10.00–12.30 and 14.00–16.30. Closed when in use for University ceremonies, meetings and concerts.* Charge.

The Old Bodleian

Cattle Street (01865 277000; www.bodley.ox.ac.uk). Named after Thomas Bodley, who died in 1613 leaving a fine collection of rare manuscripts, the old Bodleian buildings, mainly 16th-C and early 17th-C, also incorporate Duke Humfrey's library, dating from the 15th C. Bodley extended Duke Humfrey's library and also financed the rebuilding of the Schools Quadrangle. Under the Copyright Act the Bodleian is entitled to claim a copy of every book published in the British Isles. It currently holds over 6½ million volumes and 160,000 manuscripts. *Open for guided tours (University ceremonies permitting) Nov–mid March, Mon–Fri 14.00 and 15.00, Sat 10.30 and 11.30; mid Mar–Oct, Mon–Fri 10.30, 11.30, 14.00 and 15.00.* The tour lasts 45 mins and tickets are sold in the Divinity School. Charge. Please note that children under 14 years of age *are not permitted on the tours.* The Divinity School is *open Mon–Fri 09.00–16.45 and Sat 09.30–12.30,* and the Exhibition Room is *open Mon–Fri 09.30–16.45 and Sat 09.30–12.30.* Free.

Christ Church Cathedral

Christ Church. The cathedral, with its inconspicuous entrance in Tom Quad, was originally part of the Priory of St Frideswide. It is mainly 12th-C with later additions and is typically Romanesque. The most splendid feature is the 16th-C stone-vaulted fan roof of the choir. There is medieval glass and also 19th-C glass by Burne-Jones. The Chapter House is a 13th-C masterpiece.

St Mary the Virgin

High Street. The fine 14th-C spire is a landmark. The church is typical of the Perpendicular style, apart from the magnificent Baroque porch with its twisted columns by Nicholas Stone, 1637.

Ashmolean Museum

Beaumont Street (01865 278000; www.ashmol. ox.ac.uk). The oldest public museum in Britain (opened in 1683) and one of the most rewarding outside London. It has an outstanding collection of Near Eastern and European archaeology, as well as the Farrer collection of 17th- and 18th-C silver. The Herberden Coin Room has a vast display of early coins, while in the Department of Fine Art, the Michelangelo and Raphael drawings are to be admired. The museum also has the bulk of the archaeological material from the Upper Thames. *Open Tue–Sat 10.00–17.00, Sun and B Hols 14.00–17.00. Free. Café on site open until 17.00.*

Christ Church Gallery

Canterbury Quadrangle at the end of Merton Street, by Oriel Square (01865 276172; www.chch.ox.ac.uk/gallery). Built by Powell and Moya in 1968, the gallery displays Christ Church's private collection. Exceptional Renaissance drawings by Michelangelo, Leonardo da Vinci and Rubens, as well as 14th–18th-C paintings, mainly Italian. *Open Mon–Sat 10.30–13.00 and 14.00–16.30, Sun 14.00–16.30 (Easter–end Sep open until 17.30).* Charge. Shop.

The Oxford Story

6 Broad Street (01865 728822; www.oxfordstory. co.uk). Automated cars take you on a journey through eight centuries of Oxford University's history. The exhibition also includes a recreation of a 1950s street scene, and an audio-visual show of University life today. *Open Apr–Oct, 09.30–17.00; Nov–Mar, 10.00–16.30 (Sat and Sun 17.00).* Charge.

University Museum of Natural History

Parks Road (01865 272950; www.oum.ox.ac.uk). The building by Deane and Woodward, 1855–60, in high Victorian Gothic was much admired by Ruskin. The interior is a forest of columns and skeletons covered by a glass roof. One great rarity is the head and claw of a dodo. *Open daily 12.00–17.00. Free.*

Christ Church Meadows

The meadows lie behind Christ Church and Merton and have fine views and a path leading down to the river. The path is lined with college barges (not many remaining) and boathouses. In the afternoons you can often watch the rowing Eights. Enter the Meadows from St Aldates.

University Botanic Garden

High Street, by Magdalen Bridge (01865 276920; postmaster@botanic-garden.oxford.ac.uk). The oldest botanic garden in Britain, founded by Henry Lord Danvers in 1621. The garden was originally intended for the culture of medicinal plants, but today it fosters an extensive collection of rare plants for research and teaching. The gateway is by Inigo Jones. *Open daily 09.00–17.00 (16.30 in winter).* Charge.

BOAT TRIPS

Salter Bros Folly Bridge, Oxford (01865 243421; www.salterbros.co.uk). Scheduled services *daily mid May–mid Sep,* from Oxford, Abingdon, Reading, Henley, Marlow, Windsor and Staines, with some intermediate stops. These trips are heavily booked in the main holiday season, so telephone first, don't just turn up. Boats also available for party hire. Bar on board. **Rosamund the Fair** Castlemill Boatyard, Cardigan Street, Jericho, Oxford (01865 553370; www.rosamundthefair.co.uk). A stylish cruising restaurant, offering excellent new British cuisine (V), using organic produce, and a well chosen wine list. *Cruises Tue–Sun 19.45–22.45; Fri–Sun 12.15–15.15.* Advance booking required.

Pubs and Restaurants

There are many fine pubs and restaurants in Oxford. Those listed here are on or near the river, with one notable exception.

🍺 **The White House** 2 Botley Road (01865 242823; thewhitehouseoxford@btinternet. com). Situated between Osney Bridge and Oxford Station, this building was once a city gatehouse. Real ale. Home-made bar meals (V) served *L and E.* Children welcome and there is a large garden.

🍺 **The Watermans Arms** 7 South Street, Osney (01865 248832). A very fine riverside local near Osney Lock, once used by the bargees. Real ale is served along with meals (V) *L and E (not Sun E).* Children welcome. Outside seating on patio area. There is also some grass to sit on by the river, in summer. Moorings.

🍺 **The Head of the River** Folly Bridge (01865 721600). A three-storey pub and dining complex built in a converted grain warehouse, with an upstairs bar opening onto a balcony, and which contains the winning 1908 Olympic twin scull. Real ale and bar meals (V) are available *all day.* Children welcome *until 21.00.* Large patio with outside seating at the front of the pub. B & B. Punts for hire close by, *Apr–Oct.*

🍺 **The Folly Bridge Inn** 38 Abingdon Road (01865 790106; stevens@follybridge38.fsnet.co.uk). South of Folly Bridge. A pleasant pub with outside seating, serving real ale and bar meals (V) *L and E (not Sun E).* Children are welcome *until 21.00.* Live music *once a month.*

🍺 ✕ **The Chequers** 131 High Street (01865 726904; thechequers@virgin.net). A 15th-C inn, with the original panelling and fireplace in the Monks bar at the front. Real ale, and meals (V) *L.* Children are welcome if dining. Garden with seating.

🍺 ✕ **The Mitre** 17 High Street (01865 244563). Parts of this building date from the 13th-C, but the majority is 17th-C. Past patrons include Peel, Gladstone and Elizabeth Taylor.

Real ale. Restaurant (V) *open all day,* bar meals are available. Children welcome and there is a courtyard to the rear.

🍺 **The Turf Tavern** Bath Place, off Holywell Street (01865 243235; turftavern@whitbread. com). Surprisingly secluded from the bustle of the city this pub is one of the most distinctive in Oxford. Made famous through Hardy's *Jude the Obscure,* this 13th-C tavern has become popular with both students and tourists. Real ale. Bar meals (V) available *all day until 19.00.* Three gardens, warmed by braziers *in winter.* Children welcome away from the bar.

✕ 🍷 **Restaurant Elizabeth** 82 St Aldates (01865 242230). A restaurant in a very old building of great character, specialising in French traditional cuisine (V). Delicious sweets and a good wine list. Children welcome. Just a short walk up from Folly Bridge. *L and E, closed Mon.*

✕ **Heroes** 8 Ship Street (01865 723459). Home-made soup, hot sandwiches and breakfasts (V). Children welcome. No dogs. *Open Mon–Fri 08.00–19.00, Sat 08.00–18.00, Sun 10.00–17.00.*

🍺 **The Isis Tavern** Riverside, Iffley Lock (01865 247006). Large, white, isolated pub, once a farmhouse, in a pleasant garden (floodlit, and heated in winter) with mature trees and a children's play area. With no direct road access, the beer was once delivered from the river, and during the 19th C they received 5 shillings, or 7 shillings and 6 pence for each corpse removed from the river (it depended upon which side the body was found!). Friendly, family oriented pub, where the bars contain memorabilia of university boat races. Real ale and meals (V) *L and E.* Skittle alley

🍺 ✕ **The King's Arms** Church Road, Sandford Lock, Sandford-on-Thames (01865 777095). A fine lockside pub serving real ale, with ceiling beams of old barge timbers. Family-style restaurant serving food (V) *all day.* Garden with riverside seating.

Abingdon

Hills close in from the east as Radley College Boathouse is passed and the land-scaped grounds of Nuneham House come into view, followed by the steeply wooded slope of Lock Wood. After Nuneham Railway Bridge the river passes the entrance to the Swift Ditch – once the main navigation channel, where one of the earliest pound locks on the Thames was built about 1620. Its remains were incorporated into an overspill weir in 1967. Above Abingdon Lock a handsome river frontage faces the open fields and sports grounds of Andersey Island, in an area noted for mute swans. The River Ock enters the Thames under a bridge (dated 1824) by the Old Anchor Inn, a mellow and welcoming building. Now the river heads for open country and enters Culham Reach, passing the wooden bridge across the Swift Ditch, standing beside the old road bridge and its more modern replacement. A sharp turn east marks the entrance to Culham Cut, overlooked by the 17th-C greystone manor.

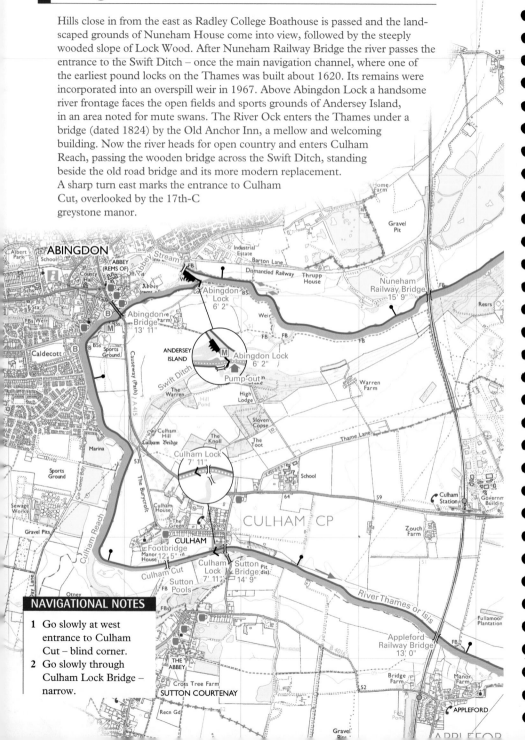

NAVIGATIONAL NOTES

1 Go slowly at west entrance to Culham Cut – blind corner.
2 Go slowly through Culham Lock Bridge – narrow.

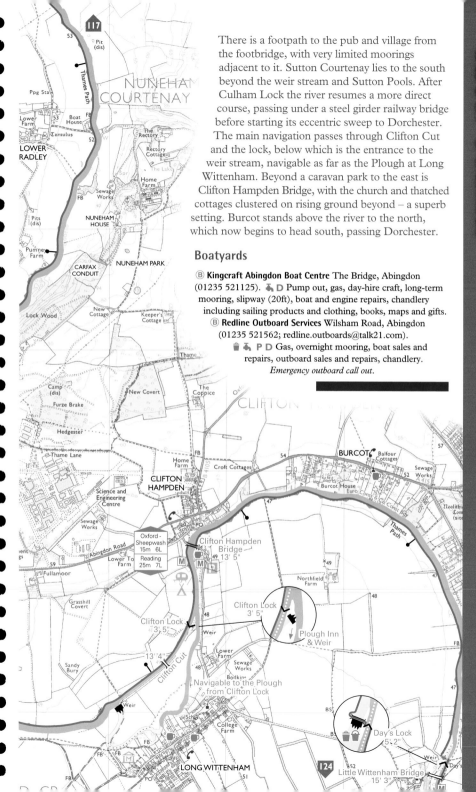

There is a footpath to the pub and village from
the footbridge, with very limited moorings
adjacent to it. Sutton Courtenay lies to the south
beyond the weir stream and Sutton Pools. After
Culham Lock the river resumes a more direct
course, passing under a steel girder railway bridge
before starting its eccentric sweep to Dorchester.
The main navigation passes through Clifton Cut
and the lock, below which is the entrance to the
weir stream, navigable as far as the Plough at Long
Wittenham. Beyond a caravan park to the east is
Clifton Hampden Bridge, with the church and thatched
cottages clustered on rising ground beyond – a superb
setting. Burcot stands above the river to the north,
which now begins to head south, passing Dorchester.

Boatyards

Ⓑ **Kingcraft Abingdon Boat Centre** The Bridge, Abingdon
(01235 521125). Pump out, gas, day-hire craft, long-term
mooring, slipway (20ft), boat and engine repairs, chandlery
including sailing products and clothing, books, maps and gifts.

Ⓑ **Redline Outboard Services** Wilsham Road, Abingdon
(01235 521562; redline.outboards@talk21.com).
P D Gas, overnight mooring, boat sales and
repairs, outboard sales and repairs, chandlery.
Emergency outboard call out.

● **Radley**
Oxon. PO, tel, stores. A straggling commuter suburb.
Radley College Founded in 1847. The college is
based on Radley Hall, 1721–7, with many later
additions. It is famed as a rowing school.
Nuneham Park Nuneham Courtenay, Oxon.
An 18th-C Palladian mansion by Leadbetter,
splendidly situated in landscaped grounds (*see*
Nuneham Courtenay, below) by Mason and
Brown. Rousseau stayed here in 1767, and planted
foreign wild flowers in the gardens. The Temple is
by Athenian Stuart. Particularly noticeable from
the river, standing on a wooded slope, is the Carfax
Conduit, an ornamental fountain built in 1615 and
once part of Oxford's water supply system.
Originally situated in Carfax, it was moved here in
1786. In times of celebration wine and beer were
run through it.

● **Nuneham Courtenay**
Oxon. PO, tel. An 18th-C model village of startling
regularity along the main road, the result of a mass
upheaval around 1760 when the 1st Earl of Harcourt
required the original village site as part of his landscaped garden. Oliver Goldsmith (1730–74) wrote
bitterly of this practice in *The Deserted Village* (1770):
'The man of wealth and pride
Takes up a space that many poor supplied'.
However, whether the early villagers, moving from
ancient clay-built cottages into far more modern
houses, would have seen it that way is open to
question. The site of the original village is by the
estate road.

● **Abingdon**
*Oxon. All shops and services, and an extensive shopping
precinct with laundrette.* An attractive 18th-C
market town which grew up around the abbey,
founded in AD675. Little of the original building
now remains, except the Gateway, Long Gallery
and Checker, which has a 13th-C chimney, and is
used as an Elizabethan-style theatre. What appear
to be stone structural remains, in the park, is a
folly, built about 100 years ago. Abbey Meadow,
by the river, is a public park with a swimming pool,
toilets, café and putting green. The best views of
the town are from the river or the bridge, which is
of medieval origin but was rebuilt in 1927. The
river is dominated by the gaol, an impressive stone
bastille built 1805–11 (now a leisure and sports
centre) and St Helen's Church. Set among
almshouses, the church has five aisles, making it
broader than it is long. Long Alley Almshouses,
beside the Old Anchor Inn, were built 1446–7 by
the Fraternity of the Holy Cross. John Mason of
Abingdon created Christ's Hospital, which has
administered them since. The porches and lantern
were added in 1605 and 1618. Each year in
Abingdon, *on the Saturday closest to 19 June,* the
people of Ock Street elect a Mayor for the day.
Morris dancers perform outside each inn along the
street, a custom of uncertain origin.
Abingdon Museum (01235 523703). What is
recognised as one of the finest town halls in
England stands in the Market Place. Built 1678–82
by Christopher Kempster, one of Wren's city

masons, it is high and monumental with an open
ground floor, once used as a market. The upper
floor, which was a court room, now houses a
varied and interesting museum. *Open daily
11.00–17.00 (16.00 in winter); closed Easter Mon,
Xmas and Boxing Day.* Free. There is a modest
charge for roof visits *Sat, Apr–Sep.*
Swan Upping In the *third week of July,* the
Queen's Swan Keeper, 19 other men (including
representatives of the Vintners' and Dyers'
Companies) and a supply of 'tea' (an intoxicating
mixture of dark rum and milk) take to the river
in double sculling skiffs, to ceremonially mark
the swans. The men wear colourful uniforms,
and 'round up' the swans, which are then
checked, weighed and tagged with a stainless
steel leg ring (beak-marking ceased a while ago).
The count is carried out between Abingdon and
Sunbury, and these days performs an important
conservation role. This tradition dates from the
12th C, when swans were an important source
of food. David Barber is currently Her Majesty's
Swan Keeper – a unique appointment. Swans
on the river now number around 1200.
Tourist Information Centre 25-27 Bridge Street,
Abingdon (01235 522711). Very helpful and
friendly service.

● **Culham**
Oxon. PO, tel. A pretty village with a fine green
and replica stocks.

● **Sutton Courtenay**
Oxon. Tel. A large village, both wealthy and
rewarding, built around a green. Eric Blair
(George Orwell) and Henry Asquith (Prime
Minister of the Liberal government, 1908–16)
are buried in the churchyard here. Overlooking
the weir stream is Norman Hall, a remarkably
original late 12th-C manor house. The 14th-C
abbey was never used as such, but as a grange.

● **Long Wittenham**
Oxon. PO tel. Access by boat along the weir
stream from Clifton Lock. A fine straggling
village along the original course of the river.
The 13th-C church contains choir stalls from
Exeter College, Oxford.
Pendon Museum At the far end of Long
Wittenham village (01865 407365; www.
pendonmuseum.com). A museum of miniature
landscapes and transport. The main display is an
ambitious recreation of the Vale of White Horse
area in the 1930s, with 25 miniature trains
running automatically, controlled by a computer.
There are also miniature recreations of a Great
Western Railway branch on Dartmoor, John
Ahern's famous Madder Valley layout, and a row
of shops based upon The Shambles in York.
*Open weekends and Jun–Aug Wed, 14.00–17.00;
B Hols, including Good Fri–Easter Mon, May and
Aug B Hols 11.00–17.00; closed Dec.* Charge.

● **Clifton Hampden**
Oxon. PO, tel, store. A cluster of thatched cottages
away from the brick bridge (a Norman folly built
in 1864). The small church on a mound is very
picturesque.

Pubs and Restaurants

There are many pubs and eating places to be found in Abingdon.

🍺 **The Nags Head on the Thames** Bridge Street, Abingdon (01235 536645). Well situated on the bridge, this friendly pub serves real ale, along with food (V) *L and E*. Children welcome. Barbecue in the huge gardens. Baby-changing room.

🍺 ✕ **The Crown & Thistle** Bridge Street, Abingdon (01235 522556). Bar and restaurant in old 19th-C coaching inn, with attractive cobbled courtyard. Real ales. Meals (V) served *L and E*. Outside seating in the courtyard. Children welcome.

🍺 **The Broad Face** 30 Bridge Street, Abingdon (01235 524516). Friendly corner pub with lovely sign. Real ale. Bar meals (V) available *L and E (not Sun or Mon E)*. Children welcome. Patio.

🍺 ✕ **The Old Anchor** St Helens Wharf, Abingdon (01235 521726). Handsome and welcoming pub by the confluence of the Rivers Ock and Thames. Real ale is served, and meals (V) are available *L and E*. Children are welcome. Outside seating in the garden. Bar billiards, skittles and other pub games. Music quiz *Mon*, general knowledge *Thur*. Short-stay mooring.

✕ ♀ **Brasserie at the Upper Reaches** Thames Street, Abingdon (0870 400 8101; www. heritage-hotels.com). Relaxed restaurant in converted mill on the Abbey Stream. Meals (V) *L and E*. Patio overlooking the river, and a working water wheel indoors. Children welcome.

🍺 ✕ **The George & Dragon** 4 Church Street, Sutton Courtenay (01235 848142). Traditional country pub with log fires, serving real ale and traditional home-cooked food (V) *L and E*. Children welcome. Terrace.

🍺 **The Swan** The Green, Sutton Courtenay (01235 847446). A quiet, red brick local with a large garden, which has a play area. Real ale. Bar meals (V) available *L and E*. Children welcome.

🍺 **The Fish** 4 Appleford Road, Sutton Courtenay (01235 848242). A pub/restaurant serving real ale, and a fine selection of wines. Excellent fresh food, with a wide range of fish, every *L and E (not Sun E, booking recommended)*. Bistro menu at the barn, in the conservatory and in the large garden and patio *L only*. Children welcome. A short walk across fields from Culham Lock (but please leave muddy boots outside!).

🍺 **Carpenters Arms** Main Road, Appleford (01235 848328). Real ale and bar meals (V) *L and E*. Children are welcome (*but not Sat eve*), and there is a garden.

🍺 **The Lion** High Street, Culham (01235 520327). Traditional pub on the village green, just a short walk from Culham Cut. Real ale. Freshly cooked English food (V) available *L and E*. Traditional pub games. Garden with a children's play area and Aunt Sally.

🍺 **The Waggon & Horses** Main Road, Culham (01235 525012; www.morrellsofoxford.co.uk). On the main road. Real ale. Meals (V) available in the bar or in separate eating area *all day*. Children are welcome, and there is a garden with a play area.

🍺 ✕ **The Plough Inn** 24 High Street, Long Wittenham (01865 407738; the.plough@ virgin.net). The weir stream is navigable from Clifton Lock to this attractive pub, which serves real ale. Meals (V) are served *L and E*. Children are welcome – they will enjoy the massive garden and aviary. The folk club meets here *every Wed*, and it is handy for the Pendon Museum.

🍺 **The Vine** High Street, Long Wittenham (01865 407832; www.thevineinn_countrypub.co.uk). Cosy, welcoming pub/restaurant, bedecked with flowers in the summer. Real ale, and meals (V) served *L and E*. Children welcome. Garden.

🍺 ✕ **Barley Mow** East of Clifton Hampden Bridge (01865 407847). Deservedly famous and superbly old-fashioned thatched pub built in 1350. It was described by Jerome K. Jerome as having 'quite a story book appearance'. Real ale. Bar and restaurant meals (V) available *all day, every day*. Children are welcome away from bar area. Pleasant garden.

🍺 **The Chequers** Burcot (01865 407771). Well worth the walk from Clifton Hampden or Dorchester to visit this handsome and totally civilised thatched pub. A large log fire is surrounded by settees, bookcases, and settles, spaciously arranged. The grand piano is occasionally played live. Excellent food (V) with fresh bread baked on the premises, served *L and E*. Real ale. Children are welcome, and there is a garden.

WALKING & CYCLING
Abingdon Town Council publish a free leaflet giving details of cycling opportunities around the town. Telephone (01235) 522642 to obtain a copy. There are excellent walks across the weir at Sutton Courtenay, by Sutton Pools.

Dorchester

The river now turns south to pass
Dorchester and takes an extravagant
winding route, passing the massive 114 acres of
earthworks known as the Dyke Hills. It then takes a
sharp turn to the east below Day's Lock, where the
World 'Poohsticks' Championships are held *each March*.
This unique event was the brainchild of Lynn David, the
former lock keeper, who introduced it as a fund-raising event for
the RNLI. The River Thame joins opposite Little Wittenham Wood –
very small craft can pass under the footbridge to moor below Dorchester
Bridge. Above the confluence, the Thames is sometimes romantically
known as the Isis. Open, flat farmland flanks the river on its approach to
Shillingford, marked by the smart hotel and accompanying stone bridge, which
replaced an earlier wooden structure built in 1784. A caravan park and many
moored boats then announce the presence of Benson and the lock. Below here the
river makes a beeline for Wallingford, passing Howbery Park Institute of Hydrology,
once the home of Jethro Tull (1674–1741), a pioneer of mechanised farming who
conducted experiments with seed at nearby Crowmarsh. The combine harvester
underwent its first trials in Britain at nearby Long Wittenham. The river then passes
through only a few of Wallingford Bridge's 17 arches. Flowing by some attractive
Georgian buildings, the river continues south.

Boatyards

Ⓑ ✕ **Benson Waterfront** Benson Cruiser Station, Benson (01491 838304). 🚽 🚽 🔧 D E Pump out, gas, boat hire, electric day-boat hire, overnight and long-term mooring, winter storage, slipway, boat and engine repairs, public telephone, toilets, showers, laundrette, shop, café, coal/logs.

Ⓑ **Swancraft** Benson Waterfront, Benson (01491 836700). 🚽 🔧 D E Pump out, gas, hire craft, day-boat hire, overnight and long-term mooring, winter storage, slipway, boat and engine repairs, telephone, toilets, showers, books, maps and gifts, café.

NAVIGATIONAL NOTES

1 Take care at the blind corner below Little Wittenham Bridge.
2 Wallingford Bridge – use the central arch.

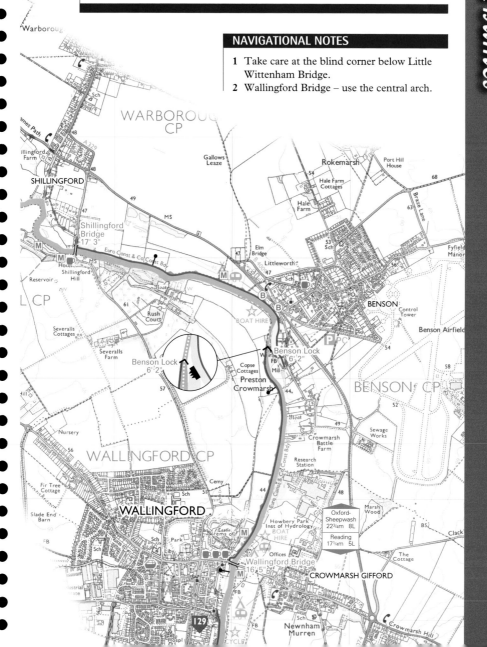

● **Little Wittenham**
Oxon. The church here is nicely situated amongst the woods.

● **Dorchester**
Oxon. PO, tel, stores. This large village of antique shops and hotels was once a small Roman town sited on the River Thames. It is accessible from the river by footpath over the Dyke Hills from Day's Lock. Small craft may navigate up the River Thame to Dorchester Bridge. The town is quite quiet, now it has a bypass, and today only the abbey Church of SS Peter and Paul, founded in the 7th C, reveals that this was once the cathedral city of Wessex, then Mercia. Approached through a Butterfield lych gate, the mostly Decorated abbey gives little clue to the splendid size and proportion of its interior. The most important feature is the Jesse window, with stonework imitating trees. The figures seem to grow organically from the body of Jesse. Note also the tomb of Sir John Holcombe: the realism and fluidity of the effigy has inspired many modern sculptors. The Old Monastery Guest House, built c.1400 and used in the 17th C as a grammar school, now houses the Abbey Museum, although most Roman finds are in the Ashmolean (*see* below).

Dorchester Abbey Museum The Abbey Guest House (01865 340056). *Open May–Sep, Tue–Sat 11.00–17.00, Sun 14.00–17.00; Easter 11.00–17.00; Apr and early Oct weekends only).* Free. Shop.

● **Shillingford**
Oxon. Tel. The extremely handsome triple-arched bridge and the hotel stand away from the village, a discreet residential area to the north.

● **Benson**
Oxon. PO, tel, stores. A friendly town with a pleasant river frontage, although it is hard to believe this was once a seat of the Kings of Mercia. The church is 13th-C.

● **Wallingford**
Oxon. All services. One of the oldest Royal Boroughs, the town received its charter in 1155. Well-preserved banks and ditches of Saxon defences still remain. From the river the town is dominated by the unusual openwork spire of St Peter's Church, built by Sir Robert Taylor in 1777. At the rear of the George Hotel is the entrance to the splendid Castle Gardens, where footpaths lead to the remains of the Norman castle built on a mound by Robert D'Oilly in 1071, held for the Empress Matilda during her fight with King Stephen for the English crown, and finally destroyed by Fairfax in 1646. The town hall, built in 1670, has a typical open ground floor. The 17-arched bridge is of medieval origins (possibly as early as 1141), and was rebuilt in 1809 when the balustrade was added. It still has a Bridge Chamberlain, appointed each year by the town council. There is a music festival held at St Peter's Church *May–Sep*, and an illuminated river pageant in *Sep*.

Wallingford Museum (01491 835065). Housed in Flint House, in the traffic-choked High Street. *Open Mar–Nov, Tue–Fri 14.00–17.00; Sat 10.30–17.00, Sun and B Hols 14.00–17.00.* Charge for adults.

The Corn Exchange Market Place, Wallingford (01491 825000). Theatre and cinema.

The Cholsey and Wallingford Railway 15 minutes walk west of Wallingford (01491 652842 for information; www.ukhrail.uel.ac.uk/cwr). This line opened in 1866 to link the Great Western Railway's main line with the Wycombe Extension Railway. The last British Rail service ran on 31 May 1981. Now 2¹/₂ miles of track have been purchased, and steam and diesel trains are run between Cholsey and St John's Road, Wallingford.

Tourist Information Centre Town Hall, Market Place, Wallingford (01491 826972).

AND BABY MAKES THREE . . .

Babies who are not yet walking can be coped with fairly easily on a boating holiday. Children between the ages of one and five are probably the most difficult to deal with, and the following points may be helpful:

1 Mum, Dad and two toddlers on a heavily locked length of canal will have problems. If you cannot gather a larger crew to help, a river such as the Thames, where the locks are operated by keepers, is ideal.
2 Ensure buoyancy aids are worn by children when they are up on deck.
3 Avoid traditional style narrowboats with a small unprotected rear deck. Thames cruisers, with an enclosed cockpit, are ideal.
4 Airing cupboards are useful for drying all the washing produced by small children.
5 Pack the favourite toys and games.
6 Allow time for plenty of stops, where children can run off their excess energy.

From the age of six, children, properly supervised, can become useful crew members.

There are great walks from either side of Little Wittenham Bridge. To the south there are paths to the hill fort at the summit of the Sinodun Hills, returning over Round Hill. To the north you can follow the riverside path to the River Thame, turning north towards Dorchester. You then return via the Dyke Hills.

Pubs and Restaurants

The George Hotel High Street, Dorchester (01865 340404). Built in 1495 as the brew-house of the nearby abbey, this comfortable galleried inn is one of the oldest privately owned coaching inns in the country. Real ale, along with bar meals (V), *L and E* and a restaurant serving English à la carte *E*. The hotel is set in pleasant grounds. Children welcome in the lounge and restaurant.

White Hart Hotel High Street, Dorchester (01865 340074; www.oxford-restaurants-hotels.co.uk). A 16th-C coaching inn serving real ale and modern European food (V) *L and E*. Children welcome (and look for the goldfish in the well).

Dorchester Abbey Tearoom High Street, Dorchester (01865 340054; www.dorchester-abbey.org.uk). Next to the abbey. Delicious biscuits, cakes and scones, all home baked and including lemon drizzle cake and Dorset gooseberry cake. *Open 15.00–17.00 Wed, Thu, Sat and Sun, May–Sep.* Quiet enclosed garden. Children welcome. Run by the village ladies, and all the profits go to charity.

Chesters Queen Street, Dorchester (01865 341467). Charming coffee shop, serving fine cakes, and *L* (V). Cobbled courtyard. Everything home-baked. *Open daily 10.00–17.00.*

Shillingford Bridge (01865 858567). Smart riverside hotel with excellent moorings (modest fee). Patrons may use the squash courts, and the outdoor heated swimming and paddling pools, *closed after 19.00.* Real ale. Bar and restaurant meals (V) available *L and E, daily.* Children welcome. Pleasant riverside garden. *Every Sat* there is a disco or a dinner/ dance, but you will need to dress smartly!

The Crown Inn 52 High Street, Benson (01491 838247). Welcoming, comfortable 16th-C inn with inglenooks, log fires and a resident ghost. Real ale, and meals (V) *L and E (not Sun E).* Children welcome, garden. Music on *some Fridays.*

The Three Horseshoes Oxford Road, Benson (01491 838242). Traditional 17th-C pub serving real ale. Restaurant (V) open *L and E*, and bar meals are served. Children welcome. Large garden with adventure playground.

The Boathouse 103 High Street, by Wallingford Bridge (01491 833188). Lively riverside pub, with terrace and conservatory. Food (V) *L and E*, and there is a lovely riverside terrace. 60s/70s/80s live music *each Thur E*.

The George Hotel High Street, Wallingford (01491 836665; www.george-hotel-wallingford.com). An attractive 15th-C inn with restaurant. The Teardrop Room recalls a Civil War story of the landlord's daughter's grief at the loss of her love, a Royalist sergeant. Real ale. Bar and restaurant meals, cooked in French and English style (V), are available *L and E.* Children welcome. Sheltered courtyard.

House of Spice 31 High Street, Wallingford (01492 835394). Indian and Bangladeshi cuisine (V) *L and E.* Children welcome. Takeaways and delivery service.

The Bell 75-79 The Street, Crowmarsh Gifford (01491 835324). Large family pub serving real ale. Meals (V), with steak a speciality, *L and E.* Children welcome *until 21.00.* Regular entertainment includes quiz night *Wed*, darts and pool. Garden.

Moulsford

A broad stretch of river, pleasant but unremarkable. The buildings of Carmel College stand in wooded grounds in Mongewell Park, which fronts the Thames for a mile. North Stoke lies back from the river to the east. The islands above Brunel's lovely skewed brick arched railway bridge are supposedly haunted. Gradually the hills close in as the valley narrows towards Goring. The Beetle & Wedge Hotel marks the site of the old ferry which once linked Moulsford and South Stoke. These villages face each other across the river, but they are now totally separate.

● **North Stoke**
Oxon. An attractive red brick village among trees. The church is pleasingly original and unrestored, with notable wall paintings.

● **Cholsey**
Oxon. PO, tel, stores. An undistinguished village, but there is a pub and a shop.

● **Moulsford**
Oxon. Tel. A roadside village with large houses by the river. The small, secluded church was rebuilt by Gilbert Scott in 1846: his fee was reputedly £64.

● **South Stoke**
Oxon. A pretty residential village among trees. St Andrew's Church is 13th-C. Access can be gained from the river opposite the Beetle & Wedge Hotel.

ROW, ROW, ROW YOUR BOAT . . .

In the early part of the 20th C it was not uncommon for those who were lucky enough to live by the river to own a camping boat. The Thames Gig was typical of such craft, and could have been 25ft long with a 4ft beam, constructed perhaps by Hammertons of Thames Ditton. Clinker built in mahogany and propelled by two pairs of sculls, it would have two rowing thwarts, passenger seats in the stern and bows, a camping cover and, for comfort, a carpet! A crew of two could propel such a craft at 6mph over still water for considerable distances, with the added options of a small sail on a mast stepped at the bow if the wind was favourable, or a tow line to haul from the bank when the current was adverse.

Pubs and Restaurants

▯ ✗ **Morning Star** Papist Way, Cholsey (01491 651413). Unspoilt and friendly village pub. Bar and restaurant meals (V) available *L and E (no food Mon)*. Children are welcome and there is a garden. Monthly food theme evenings *during summer*.

▯ ✗ **Beetle & Wedge Hotel** Ferry Lane, Moulsford (01491 651381; www.beetleandwedge.co.uk). A *beetle* is a mallet used to hit the *wedge* which split trees into planks for floating down river to London; a practice last recorded in 1777 but recalled in the name of this justly famous pub, where H.G. Wells stayed while writing *Mr Polly* – it features in the book as the Potwell Inn. The building is a former manor house, standing in a superb riverside situation, with a lovely garden and a jetty. Choice of two (three in summer) smart restaurants, all with à la carte menu: The Boat House has a large open

fire on which many items from the menu (V) are cooked, and real ale is served; The Dining Room, in the main hotel building, is more formal (set price menu *Sun*). *Open L and E*. The Water Garden open *in summer, weather permitting*. Booking advisable for all restaurants. Children are welcome and the large garden is a plus. Moorings. Slipway, but get prior permission to use it. B & B.

▯ **The Perch & Pike Inn** The Street, South Stoke (01491 872415; www.perchandpike.co.uk). Cosy 18th-C red brick and flint pub, with low beams, open log fires, antique furniture and, perhaps, a ghost. Real ale. Extensive home-cooked menu (V), served *L and E*. Boaters and quiet children are welcome, and there is a pleasant garden. Entertainment on Burns Night, St Patrick's Day and so on. B & B.

Boatyards

Ⓑ **Sheridan Marine**
Moulsford (01491 652085;
www.sheridanmarine.com).
⚓ **E** Gas, long-term
mooring, winter storage,
crane, boat and engine sales
and repairs, chandlery,
books and maps and
gifts, café, DIY facilities.
Stockist of traditional
boat and engine fittings:
British Seagull,
Freeman Cruisers,
Watermota,
Worthen Blake
and others.

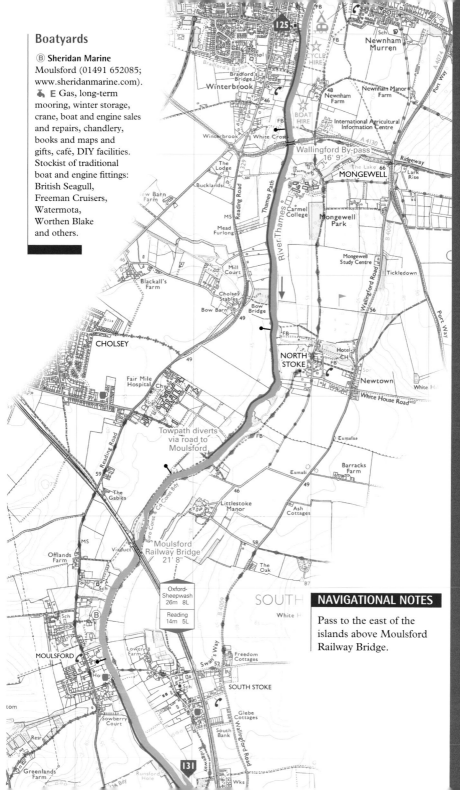

NAVIGATIONAL NOTES

Pass to the east of the
islands above Moulsford
Railway Bridge.

Goring

Approaching Cleeve Lock the valley narrows, with Lardon Chase rising steeply to the west behind Streatley. Little of Goring can be seen from the river – boathouses, the mill and a glimpse of the church as the river enters one of its most attractive parts. In the meadows to the east of Basildon there is a picturesque group of buildings around a church, while on the east bank beech woods rise steeply from the river's edge. The brick Gatehampton Railway Bridge was built by Brunel – beyond this Basildon House stands in wooded grounds, to the west of Beale Park.

Pubs and Restaurants

✕☿ **Leatherne Bottel Restaurant** Bridle Way (01491 872667). Riverside, above Cleeve Lock. There was a well here in Roman times which produced medicinal water. Now it is a smart riverside restaurant, serving fresh local produce (V) *L and E*, in idyllic surroundings. Riverside terrace. Mooring.

● ✕ **Swan Diplomat Hotel** Streatley (01491 878800). Beautifully situated and very pleasant hotel/restaurant serving brasserie light lunches (V) *all day*, with à la carte *Mon–Sat 12.00–14.00 and 19.00–22.00*. Plush interiors and fine riverside gardens. Children welcome.

● ✕ **The Bull** Reading Road, Streatley (01491 872392). Friendly 16th-C restaurant/pub at a busy crossroads. In 1895, when the Thames froze over, the pub sold water at 6d a bucket. Real ale. Bar meals (V) available *L and E (not Sun E)*. Children and dogs welcome, and there is a large garden, where a yew tree was planted to commemorate the 'gross misconduct' of a nun and a monk in 1440.

● ✕ **The Miller of Mansfield** High Street, Goring (01491 872829; www. millerofmansfield.co.uk).

Up the road from the bridge, this is a very comfortable brick and flint pub, where parts of the building are 13th-C. Real ale, separate restaurant and excellent bar meals (V) *L and E*. Children welcome. Seats outside. B & B.

● ✕ **The John Barleycorn** Manor Road, Goring (01491 872509). A beamy 16th-C village pub serving real ale. Bar and restaurant meals (V) available *L and E*. Children welcome in the dining area and restaurant only. Large attractive garden. B & B.

● ✕ **Catherine Wheel** Station Road, Goring (01491 872379). This attractive 15th-C pub claims to be Goring's oldest, and has an open fire in winter. Excellent meals (V) available *L and E (not Sun E)*. Children welcome in the restaurant, and there is a garden.

● **Goring**
Oxon. PO, tel, shops and supermarket in High Street, laundrette. One of the most important prehistoric fords across the river, linking the Icknield Way and the Ridgeway. The village is set in a splendid deep wooded valley by one of the most spectacular reaches on the river. A holiday paradise of indeterminate age, it retains many pretty brick and flint cottages. The church, of handsome proportions, is well situated by the river. Its bell, dating from 1290, is one of the oldest in England. Goring Mill stands below the bridge, an approximate replica (built 1923) of the earlier timber structure. Between Goring and Henley, the Thames passes through the Chilterns Area of Outstanding Natural Beauty, which covers 309 square miles.

● **Streatley**
Berks. Shops. A continuation of Goring on the west bank, its 18th-C charm is diminished by the traffic roaring through. Of note are the old malt houses converted into a village hall by W. Ravenscroft in 1898. Lardon Chase (*NT*) rises to the north.

● **Lower Basildon**
Berks. An attractive group of buildings surround the church in a superb riverside situation. The 13th-C church contains a portrait group of two boys drowned in 1886. Jethro Tull (1674–1741), pioneer of agricultural mechanisation, lies buried in the churchyard.
Basildon Park (0118 984 3040; www.nationaltrust. org.uk). Built by John Carr of York for Sir

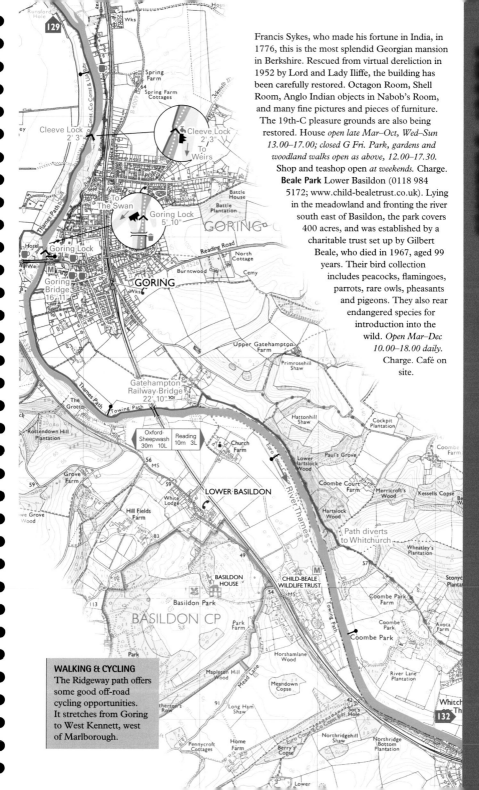

Francis Sykes, who made his fortune in India, in 1776, this is the most splendid Georgian mansion in Berkshire. Rescued from virtual dereliction in 1952 by Lord and Lady Iliffe, the building has been carefully restored. Octagon Room, Shell Room, Anglo Indian objects in Nabob's Room, and many fine pictures and pieces of furniture. The 19th-C pleasure grounds are also being restored. House *open late Mar–Oct, Wed–Sun 13.00–17.00; closed G Fri. Park, gardens and woodland walks open as above, 12.00–17.30.* Shop and teashop open *at weekends.* Charge. **Beale Park** Lower Basildon (0118 984 5172; www.child-bealetrust.co.uk). Lying in the meadowland and fronting the river south east of Basildon, the park covers 400 acres, and was established by a charitable trust set up by Gilbert Beale, who died in 1967, aged 99 years. Their bird collection includes peacocks, flamingoes, parrots, rare owls, pheasants and pigeons. They also rear endangered species for introduction into the wild. *Open Mar–Dec 10.00–18.00 daily.* Charge. Café on site.

River Thames

Goring

WALKING & CYCLING
The Ridgeway path offers some good off-road cycling opportunities. It stretches from Goring to West Kennett, west of Marlborough.

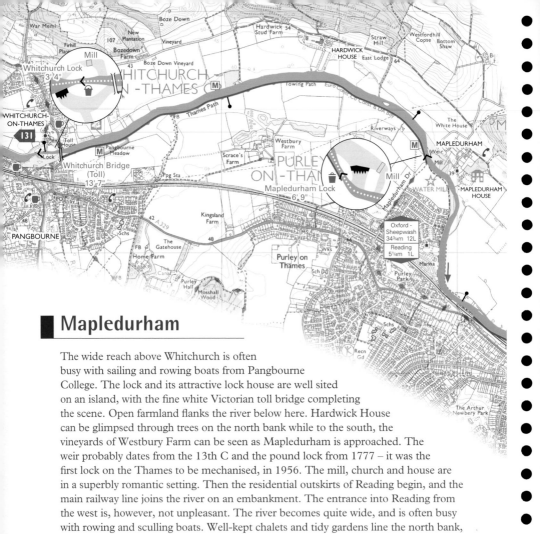

Mapledurham

The wide reach above Whitchurch is often
busy with sailing and rowing boats from Pangbourne
College. The lock and its attractive lock house are well sited
on an island, with the fine white Victorian toll bridge completing
the scene. Open farmland flanks the river below here. Hardwick House
can be glimpsed through trees on the north bank while to the south, the
vineyards of Westbury Farm can be seen as Mapledurham is approached. The
weir probably dates from the 13th C and the pound lock from 1777 – it was the
first lock on the Thames to be mechanised, in 1956. The mill, church and house are
in a superbly romantic setting. Then the residential outskirts of Reading begin, and the
main railway line joins the river on an embankment. The entrance into Reading from
the west is, however, not unpleasant. The river becomes quite wide, and is often busy
with rowing and sculling boats. Well-kept chalets and tidy gardens line the north bank,
followed by landscaped public gardens above Caversham Bridge.

● **Pangbourne**
Berks. All services. A large, well-equipped
commuter town, still preserving traces of
Edwardian elegance, built at the confluence of
the Thames with the Pang, which is a famous
trout stream. The Nautical College, an imposing
William and Mary style mansion, is by Sir John
Belcher, built 1897–8. Pangbourne Meadow is
now a National Trust property of 7 acres. The
Scottish author of *The Wind in the Willows*,
Kenneth Grahame (1859–1932), who was also
Secretary to the Bank of England, lived in
Church Cottage, Pangbourne, and told this story
to his four-year-old son Alastair in 1904.

● **Whitchurch**
Oxon. Tel, stores. Quiet and attractive with a good
group of mill buildings, overlooked by the mainly

Victorian church. A small toll for motor vehicles is
collected at the Victorian iron bridge.

● **Mapledurham**
Oxon. A cluster of period houses and cottages
stand in the water meadows close to the restored
and working water mill, one of the oldest corn and
grist mills on the Thames. The scene is typical of
an early 19th-C landscape painting and should be
visited (but *see* below).
Mapledurham House (0118 972 3350;
www.mapledurham.co.uk). Still occupied by
descendants of the Blount family, who purchased
the original manor in 1490 and built the present
Elizabethan manor house, with grounds sweeping
down to the Thames. The estate is private and
there are no rights of way from the river to the
village, nor any footpaths alongside the river on

Pubs and Restaurants

🍺 ✕ **Appletons at the Swan** Shooters Hill, Pangbourne (0118 984 4494). Above the weir. Jerome K. Jerome, his two colleagues and a 'shamed looking dog' abandoned their *Three Men in a Boat* journey here (on the way back), and took the train to London. Real ale. Food (V) *L and E*. Children welcome. Riverside patio seating.

🍺 ✕ **Copper Inn Hotel** Church Road, Pangbourne (0118 984 2244; www.copper-inn. co.uk). Old coaching inn with restaurant. Real ales. Bar meals and à la carte (V) available *L and E*. Children welcome. Garden.

🍺 ✕ **George Hotel Best Western** The Square, Pangbourne (0118 984 2237). South of the bridge, under the railway. Regularly changing choice of real ale and food (V) *L and E (not Sun E)*. Restaurant open *E (not Sun E)*. B & B.

🍺 **Greyhound** High Street, Whitchurch (0118 984 2160). North of Whitchurch Bridge. Real ale. Bar food (V) *L and E (not Sun E)*. Garden.

🍺 ✕ **The Ferryboat Inn** High Street, north of Whitchurch Bridge (0118 984 2161). Real ale and food (V) *L and E (not Sun E)*. Children are welcome away from the bar. Covered patio.

NAVIGATIONAL NOTES

1 You can pass either side of the island ¼ mile above Mapledurham Lock.
2 Pass to the east of the island ¼ mile below Mapledurham Lock.

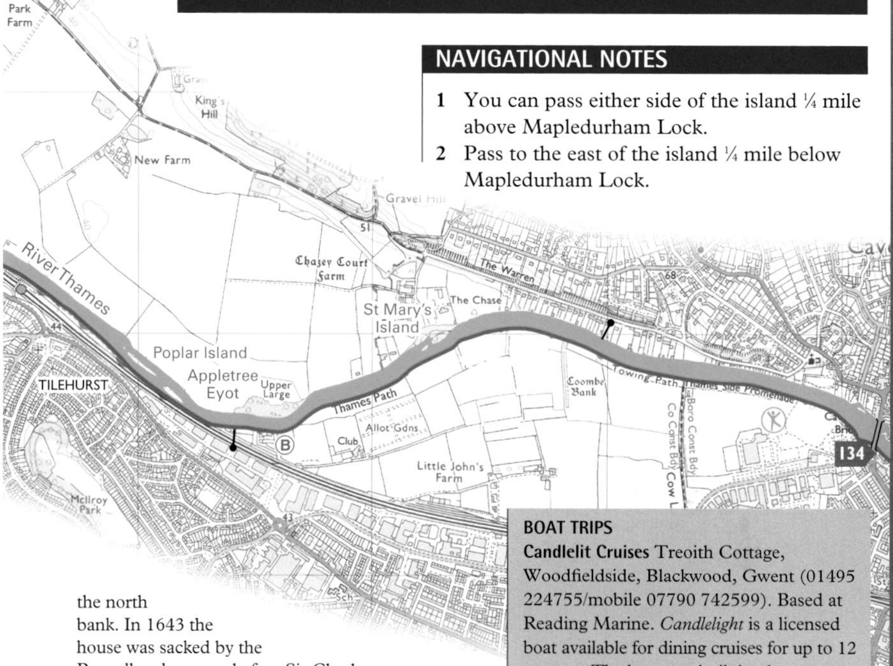

the north bank. In 1643 the house was sacked by the Roundheads, a year before Sir Charles Blount was killed during the siege of Oxford. Following a period of relative impoverishment, the house was restored to what we see today by Michael Henry Blount (1789-1874). Mapledurham has interesting literary connections with Alexander Pope, Galsworthy's *Forsyte Saga* and Grahame's *The Wind in the Willows*. More recently it has been the setting for the film *The Eagle has Landed*, and has appeared in various television series including *Inspector Morse*. Open

BOAT TRIPS

Candlelit Cruises Treoith Cottage, Woodfieldside, Blackwood, Gwent (01495 224755/mobile 07790 742599). Based at Reading Marine. *Candlelight* is a licensed boat available for dining cruises for up to 12 persons. The boat was built by the owner.

Easter–Sep, Sat, Sun and B Hols 14.00–17.30. Charge. On these days a boat can be taken from Caversham Pier (0118 948 1088) to the landing stage on the Mill island. All passengers alighting must purchase an entrance ticket, as do any passengers from private boats, who are allowed to moor only for this purpose, and *only on open days.*

Boatyards

Ⓑ **Reading Marine Services** Scours Lane, Tilehurst (0118 942 3877; www.drivelinemarine. co.uk). 🐟 D Gas, overnight mooring, long-term mooring, slipway, crane, boat and engine sales and repairs, chandlery, books, maps and gifts.

Reading

Caversham Bridge was built in 1926. The original bridge on this site was erected in the 13th C, and at one time had a chapel on it. Fry's Island is situated between the bridges; there are two boatyards on it. Reading lies to the south, a busy modern town which does little to welcome visitors from the river. Just below Reading Bridge is Caversham Lock, on the edge of King's Meadow. A little further down, to the east and under the railway bridge, is the entrance to the Kennet & Avon Canal (*see* page 98). Beyond this junction the scenery is initially uninspiring but this all changes when Sonning Lock and Mill appear amongst the willows. The 18th-C bridge and the large white hotel beside it mark the western extremity of Sonning village, which lies back from the river. About a mile below Sonning, St Patrick's Stream (unnavigable, with the River Loddon flowing in), makes its detour around Borough Marsh. The main course of the river passes numerous islands and skirts Warren Hill, a chalk ridge, before reaching Shiplake Lock. It then passes Shiplake and weaves through a group of islands to the west of Wargrave Marsh, a low-lying area enclosed by the Hennerton Backwater (navigable only by small boats).

BOAT TRIPS
Thames River Cruises Mapledurham House, Mapledurham (0118 948 1088). *Caversham Lady* available for private charter. Also regular *summer* trips to Mapledurham, when the house is open.
Salter Bros Caversham Bridge Road, Reading (0118 957 2388). Scheduled *summer* service up and down river, with various stops.
The Waterman Available for private charter for up to 100 people. Food and a bar can be provided, with a disco if required. Telephone 0118 940 2162 for details.

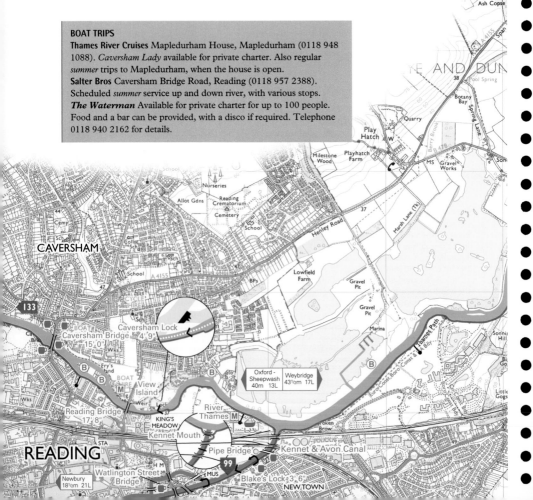

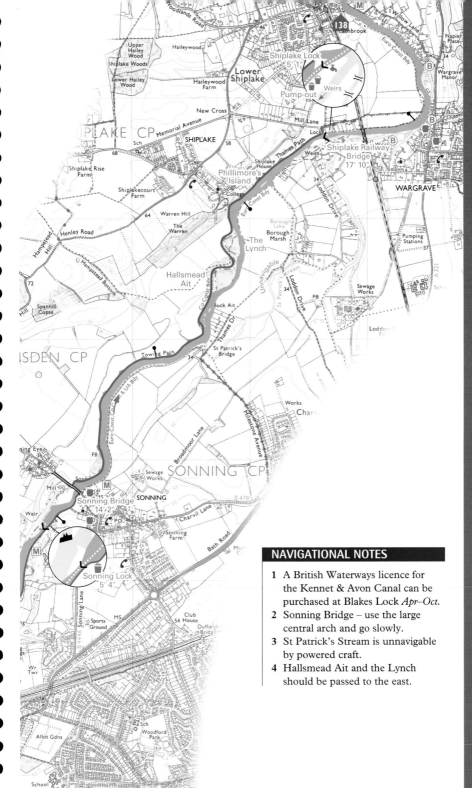

NAVIGATIONAL NOTES

1 A British Waterways licence for the Kennet & Avon Canal can be purchased at Blakes Lock *Apr–Oct*.
2 Sonning Bridge – use the large central arch and go slowly.
3 St Patrick's Stream is unnavigable by powered craft.
4 Hallsmead Ait and the Lynch should be passed to the east.

Boatyards

(B) **Bridge Boats** Fry's Island, Reading (0118 959 0346; www.bridgeboats.com). 🛏 🛏 🔧 D E Pump out, hire craft, overnight and long-term mooring, slipway, boat building, boat and engine repairs, books, maps and gifts.

(B) **Caversham Boat Services** Fry's Island, Reading (0118 957 4323). 🛏 🛏 🔧 D E Pump out, gas, hire craft, day-hire boats, long-term mooring, winter storage, boat and engine repairs, telephone, toilets, books, maps and gifts. Slipway for hire.

(B) **Better Boating** Mill Green, Caversham, Reading (0118 947 9536). 🛏 🛏 🔧 D Pump out, gas, long-term mooring, engine sales and repairs, boat repairs, chandlery, toilets. Walker Outboards (0118 947 8641) are also based here.

(B) **Thames & Kennet Marina** Caversham Lakes, Henley Road, Reading (0118 948 2911). 🛏 🛏 🔧 D E Pump out, gas, overnight and long-term mooring, winter storage, chandlery, telephone, toilets, showers, books and maps, DIY facilities, coal/logs.

(B) **Val Wyatt Marine** Willow Lane, Wargrave (0118 940 3211; www.valwyattmarine.co.uk). 🔧 Pump out, gas, overnight and long-term mooring, winter storage, slipway, crane, boat and engine sales and repairs, chandlery, public telephone, books, maps and gifts, DIY facilities.

(B) **John Bushnell** Thameside Marina, Waterman's Way, Station Road, Wargrave (0118 940 2161; www.bushnells.co.uk). 🛏 🛏 🔧 D E Pump out, long-term mooring, winter storage, dry storage, 25 tonne travel lift, boat building, boat sales and repairs, toilets, showers, DIY facilities.

● **Reading**
Berks. All services. A very busy town lacking a cohesive centre – it is an amalgam of university and industry with a constant stream of traffic scything through. The university buildings are uninspiring, but some of the Victorian buildings are better, and the museum houses one of the most fascinating archaeological collections in the country.
Abbey Ruins Fragmentary remains of the 12th-C abbey, built by Henry I, lie on the edge of Forbury Park. The Abbey was one of the largest in England and at one time comparable with Bury St Edmunds. The 13th-C gatehouse still stands. It was once the Abbey School where Jane Austen studied in 1785–7, although the structure was greatly altered by Gilbert Scott in 1869. The Church of St Lawrence near the Market Place was originally attached to the outer gate.
Gaol Forbury Road. Designed by Scott & Moffat, 1842–4 in Scottish Baronial style. Oscar Wilde (1854–1900) wrote *De Profundis* in 1897 while imprisoned here for homosexual practices (the *Ballad of Reading Gaol* was actually written in Paris in 1898).
Reading Museum The Town Hall, Blagrave Street (0118 939 9800; www.readingmuseum. org.uk). Features *The Story of Reading*, tracing the town's development from a Saxon settlement on the River Kennet to the present day. Special features include a reconstructed section of the abbey and the Oracle gates entrance to the 17th-C workhouse. In the upper gallery is a full 230ft sweep of Britain's Bayeux Tapestry, Reading's faithful replica of the 11th-C original. Huntley & Palmers, the Reading biscuit makers, display a collection of 300 biscuit tins. *Open Tue–Sat 10.00–16.00 (19.00 Thur), Sun 11.00–16.00.* Free.
Museum of English Rural Life Royal History Centre, Whiteknights, University of Reading (0118 931 8661). The first museum in England to specialise in rural life as it was lived about 150 to 175 years ago, before the invention of the tractor. The majority of exhibits date from the period 1850–1950, and include farm equipment, beekeeping equipment, corn dollies, sewing machines and so on. *Open Tue–Sat 10.00–13.00 and 14.00–16.30.* Modest charge.
Tourist Information Centre Church House, Chain Street, Reading (0118 956 6226; www.readingtourism.org.uk).

● **Caversham**
Berks. PO, tel, stores, laundrette, fish & chips. A residential continuation of Reading, which is at its best by the river, where parks and gardens stretch alongside. The library in Church Street is worth a look – it is a jolly Edwardian building, built in 1907, with a central green copper clock supported by an angel.

● **Sonning**
Berks. PO, tel, stores and café. A very pretty and meticulously preserved village. The largely 19th-C church has remarkable monuments, and

some good 15th-C brasses. The most interesting house in the town is Lutyens' Deanery Gardens, built for Edward Hudson in 1901. To the west of Sonning is Holme Park – the Reading Blue Coat School; its wooded grounds drop steeply to the river. The railway passes in a spectacular cutting to the south, built by Brunel.

Valley Vineyards Stanlake Park, Twyford (0118 934 0176). These well-established vineyards may be visited by groups of a *minimum of 25 people*. Book in advance for a tour and wine tasting. The shop is *open Mon–Sat 11.00–17.00, Sun 12.00–17.00*. Charge for the tours.

● **Wargrave**
Berks. PO, tel, stores. A well-situated town on rising ground among trees and overlooking the Thames. The church was burnt down in 1914 by the Suffragettes – some say it was because the vicar refused to take the word 'obey' out of the marriage service. The striking Woodclyffe Hall, in the High Street, was built in 1901. Henry Kingsley (1830–76), the novelist, often stayed here. East of the town is Wargrave Manor, an early 19th-C building. The River Loddon joins St Patrick's Stream to the south west – here, in black swampy soil, the Loddon Lily (*Leucojum aestivum*), or summer snowflake, is native. Loddon Pondweed (*Potamogeton nodosus*, now a threatened species) its leaves beautifully veined, may also be found.

Pubs and Restaurants

If you do not mind dodging the traffic, there are plenty of pubs in Reading (*see* page 101 for a selection) – those visiting from the Thames may wish to travel a couple of miles up- or downstream, where the surroundings are a little more congenial.

● **Pipers Island Bar** (0118 948 4573; www.thamesrivercruise.co.uk). A pub in a lovely situation – right in the middle of the river. Real ale. Food (V) served *L and E (all day during summer holidays)*. Children are welcome, and there is a riverside patio.

● **The Griffin** 10-12 Church Road, Caversham (0118 947 5018). North of Caversham Bridge. Real ale is served in this friendly pub, along with bar meals (V) *L and E*. Children are welcome *until 20.00*. Patio.

● ✕ **Three Men in a Boat Tavern** Richfield Avenue, Reading (0118 925 9988). In the basement of a smart riverside hotel. Bar meals served *L and E*. Terrace overlooking the river.

● ✕ **Great House Hotel** Thames Street, Sonning Bridge (0118 969 2277; www.greathouseatsonning.co.uk). Beautifully situated riverside hotel and restaurant of great character, with fine gardens and lawns, and terrace lined with lime trees. One dining room is 700 years old; the main bar is a beamed room with a stone fireplace. The Ferryman's Bar has choice of real ale. Meals (V) are served *L and E*. Children are welcome. Mooring.

● **The Bull Inn** By Sonning church (0118 969 3901). Lovely, friendly, old half-timbered pub in a 15th-C church house covered with wisteria, used by locals and visitors alike. There are comfy cushioned settles, massive beams and inglenook fireplaces inside, with wooden tables in a flower-decorated courtyard facing the church outside. Real ale. Bar meals (hot and cold, V) are served *L and E* (and please don't ask for chips – they are *not* served here!). Children welcome, and there is a garden.

● ✕ **The Bull** High Street, Wargrave (0118 940 3120; www.thebullatwargrave.co.uk). Friendly 15th-C coaching inn. Real ale. Excellent bar and restaurant meals (V) *L and E*. Children welcome in the dining areas, and there is a garden. Look out for the 19th-C ghost of an ex-landlady. B & B.

● ✕ **The White Hart Inn** 45 High Street, Wargrave (0118 940 2590; www. maidenheadweb.com/whitehart). A fine old inn serving real ale, and bar and restaurant meals (V) *L and E (not Sun E)*. Coffee and afternoon teas. Children welcome if you are eating. B & B.

● **The Greyhound** 79 High Street, Wargrave (0118 940 2556). A half-timbered corner pub serving real ale. Bar lunches *L*. Children welcome away from the bar. Garden. Outside seating on patio. There is an old forge at the back of the pub.

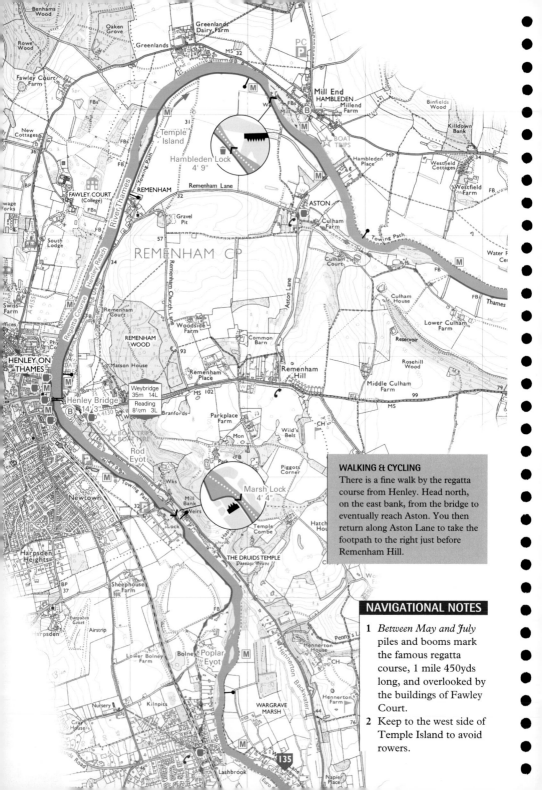

WALKING & CYCLING

There is a fine walk by the regatta course from Henley. Head north, on the east bank, from the bridge to eventually reach Aston. You then return along Aston Lane to take the footpath to the right just before Remenham Hill.

NAVIGATIONAL NOTES

1 *Between May and July* piles and booms mark the famous regatta course, 1 mile 450yds long, and overlooked by the buildings of Fawley Court.

2 Keep to the west side of Temple Island to avoid rowers.

Henley on Thames

The Thames continues north towards Temple Combe Woods, which rise steeply to the east. This part of the river is noted for

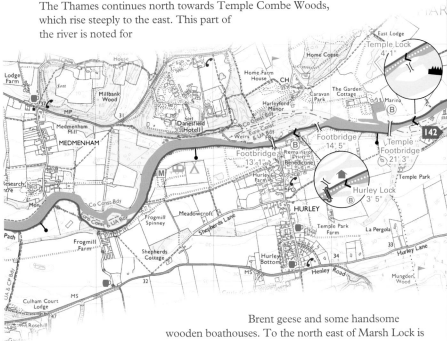

Brent geese and some handsome wooden boathouses. To the north east of Marsh Lock is Park Place; in the grounds is part of Wren's original spire for St Bride's Church, Fleet Street. The house was once occupied by General Conway, whose daughter, Mrs Damer, sculpted the masks of Thames and Isis on Henley Bridge. The town of Henley lies to the west of the river, with an attractive waterfront, many moored boats and resident swans, facing the rise of Remenham Wood to the east. Below Temple Island the river passes the immaculate grounds of the Henley Management College before reaching Hambleden Lock, beautifully situated with an extensive weir (footpath over) and a fine weatherboarded mill, now converted into flats. The tiny village of Aston can be seen on a hillside to the south below the lock; the Thames then divides around thickly wooded islands and meanders past Medmenham and St Mary's Abbey. Beyond the next group of islands a large caravan site heralds the approach of Hurley, where the weir streams rush among more islands by the lock. To the north is Danesfield, a home built at the turn of the 20th C by a Manchester millionaire.

Boatyards

ⓑ **Hobbs & Sons** Station Road, Henley (01491 572035; www.hobbs-of-henley.com). ⚓ P D Gas, day-boat hire, long-term mooring, winter storage, trailboat slipway, crane, boat building, boat sales, outboard engine sales and repairs, chandlery, telephone, toilets, books, maps and gifts.

ⓑ **Peter Freebody's Boatyard** Mill Lane, Hurley (01628 824382; www.boatbuilder. co.uk). Overnight and long-term mooring, winter storage, boat and engine sales and repairs. Primarily a boat builder, this is a very famous yard, building many boats, including steam launches and electric boats.

Shiplake

Oxon. Stores. A village of desirable commuter houses climbing up into the hills that border the river. The splendidly situated Church of SS Peter and Paul contains some medieval Belgian glass of great beauty. Tennyson married Emily Sellwood here in 1850. To the north, near the station, George Orwell lived as a boy at Roselawn, Station Road.

Henley on Thames

Oxon. All shops and services, laundrette, swimming baths, theatre. A fine market town and one of the most popular resorts on the river, described by Dickens as 'the Mecca of the rowing man'. The main street, running down to the Thames from the Victorian town hall, has a feeling of timeless-ness and Edwardian elegance almost out of place today. From the river the most obvious features are the 18th-C stone bridge (note the masks of Thames and Isis) and the church, a large and gloomy building. The Red Lion Hotel, near the church, has received some notable visitors, including King Charles I (1632 and 1642), the Duke of Marlborough (early 18th C), the poet William Shenstone (1750) and Johnson and Boswell (1776). The Kenton Theatre in New Street is the fourth oldest in the country, being built in 1805. The first Oxford and Cambridge boat race was rowed between Hambleden and Henley on 10 June 1829 – the race is now rowed between Putney and Mortlake. The first Henley Regatta (01491 572153) was held in 1839, becoming Royal in 1851, with Prince Albert as patron. This is now held *annually in the first week of July;* the town becomes very busy indeed, and everyone seems to be on a picnic. The epitome of an English summer (when the sun shines).

The River and Rowing Museum Mill Meadows, Henley-on-Thames (01491 415600; www.rrm.co.uk). In a new building, clad with green oak and set upon columns in the water meadows just outside Henley, the museum has three galleries illustrating the river, the town of Henley, and rowing. Exhibits range from the world's oldest rowing boat to a state-of-the-art monocoque racing machine, and include a river gallery, with an aquarium of Thames fish. It also has a very fine painting of Henley by Jan Siberechts, dated 1698, showing the river busy with barges. *Open May–Aug 10.00–17.30; Sep–Apr 10.00–17.00.* Charge. Café, shop, library.

Fawley Court Marlow Road, Henley on Thames (01491 574917). The court, in a fine riverside situation, was designed by Wren and built in 1684 on the arched basement of an earlier fortified manor house. It was later to be decorated by Grinling Gibbons and classicised by James Wyatt. The grounds were laid out by 'Capability' Brown in 1770. It now owned by the Marian Fathers and has a museum founded by Father Joseph Jarzebowski, consisting of a library, various documents of the Polish monarchy, including Laksi's *Code of Laws* dating from 1506, and Polish militaria, and paintings and sculpture illustrating ancient history and the Middle Ages. *Open Mar–Oct, Wed, Thur and Sun 14.00–17.00; closed Whitsun and Easter weekends.* Charge. Tea shop and gift shop. Very limited moorings in the old canal, and nearby.

Temple Island The temple was built by James Wyatt in 1771 as a vista for Fawley Court, and has a set of hand-painted wall decorations by him. It is thought to be the earliest example in England of the Etruscan style. Owned by the Mackenzie family for over 130 years, the island was sold in 1988. Visited by King Edward VII and Queen Alexandra, it is very pretty, with views down the river to Henley.

Tourist Information Centre King's Arms Barn, Kings Road, Henley-on-Thames (01491 578034; henleytic@hotmail.com).

Hambleden

Bucks. PO, tel, stores. Set back from the river and surrounded by heavily wooded hills, this is one of the most attractive villages – all mellow flint and brick – in Buckinghamshire, and worth the walk up from the river. The 14th-C church and the houses round the green make it a perfect village setting, with the 17th-C Manor House in the background. The mill and mill house look good by the lock.

Medmenham

Bucks. A village straggling up from the now defunct ferry into the woods behind.

Medmenham Abbey (St Mary's Abbey) is a charming agglomeration of building styles: 1595, 18th-C Gothic and mostly 1898. It was the house of the orgiastic Hell Fire Club, under the patron-age of Sir Francis Dashwood. It was decorated in a suitably pornographic and sacrilegious style, but understandably none of this survived the 19th C.

Hurley

Berks. PO, tel, stores. In the old part of the village the long, dark and narrow nave of the church is all that remains of Hurley Priory (St Mary's), founded before 1087 for the Benedictine Order. Opposite the church are a 14th-C tithe barn (now a dwelling) and a dovecote.

Harleyford Manor Henley Road, Marlow (01628 471361) On the north bank opposite Hurley. The red-brick Georgian manor was built in the late 1740s by Sir Robert Taylor for Sir William Clayton, and has been recently restored. Notable amongst visitors to The Manor have been Emperor Napoleon III, Prime Minister Disraeli and author Kenneth Grahame. The superbly landscaped grounds contain an ice house and the ruins of a Georgian temple. The whole estate is an Area of Outstanding Natural Beauty, and is now used as a leisure environment, with holiday lodges and a golf course.

Pubs and Restaurants

🍺 ✕ **The Baskerville Arms** Station Road, Shiplake (0118 940 3332). Real ales served. Restaurant with wide-ranging menu (V) *L and E*. Children welcome. Garden. Live jazz *Tue*, quiz *Wed*. B & B.

Henley has a fine selection of pubs, the majority serving real ale brewed by Brakspear in their 18th-C brewhouse in New Street, by the river. In warm, calm weather the aroma of malt and hops wafts over the water tempting all devotees of good beer to search hastily for a mooring.

🍺 **The Anchor Inn** 58 Friday Street, Henley (01491 574753; www.loud-n-clear.com/anchor). Cosy and friendly 15th-C pub, haunted by a friendly cleaning lady! Real ale. Traditional English food and home-baked bread (V) available *L and E*. Children welcome. Garden and patio. No dogs.

🍺 ✕ **The Red Lion Hotel** Hart Street, by the bridge (01491 572161; www.redlionhenley.co.uk). A very auspicious and much-visited (*see* Henley, opposite) 15th-C red brick hotel with a restaurant serving meals (V) *L and E*. Children welcome.

🍺 ✕ **The Angel on the Bridge** Thameside, Henley Bridge (01491 410678; www.angelonthebridge.com). Beautiful and historic 14th-C inn adjoining the bridge. Real ale. Bistro restaurant serving fresh fish from Billingsgate and fresh meat from Smithfield. Bar and restaurant meals (V) available *L and E*. Children welcome. Riverside terrace.

🍺 **The Little White Hart Hotel** Riverside, Henley (01491 574145; www.honeypotinns.com). Half-timbered riverside inn with jetty moorings across the street. Real ale. Food (V) *L and E (not Sun E)*. Children welcome away from the bar. Garden.

🍺 **The Rose & Crown** New Street (01491 578376). Traditional local next door to the Brakspear brewery and the Kenton Theatre. Real ale. Bar meals (V) *L and E (not Sun E)*. *Fish & chip specials on Tue and Fri (book)*. Garden. B & B.

🍺 ✕ **The Little Angel** Remenham Lane, east of Henley Bridge (01491 574165; www.thelittleangel.com). A 17th-C pub serving modern English and Mediterranean food, including fish and tapas (V) *L and E (not Sun E in winter)*. Children welcome. Outside seating on the patio, overlooking the cricket ground. It is haunted by Marie Blandy, who poisoned her father.

🍺 **The Flower Pot Hotel** Aston (01491 574721). Attractive, old-fashioned pub built about 1890 and decorated with a vast collection of cased fish. Real ale. Meals (V), including fresh fish and local game (in season) are available *L and E (not Sun E)*. Children welcome. Large garden. Mooring.

🍺 ✕ **The Stag & Huntsman Hotel** Hambleden (01491 571227). Traditional brick and flint pub. Real ale. Good menu (V), including game in season, served *L and E (not Sun E)*. Children welcome. Large garden. B & B.

🍺 ✕ **The Dog & Badger** Henley Road, Medmenham (01491 571362). This fine old pub dates from 1390 and has historical associations with the Hell Fire Club (*see* Medmenham opposite). Real ale. Bar meals (V)are available *L and E (not Sun E)*. Restaurant with à la carte menu *Tue–Sat E*. Children are welcome in the front bar and restaurant. Outside seating on the terrace.

🍺 **The Black Boy** Henley Road, Henley (01628 824212). Traditional country pub about ¼ mile from Frogmill Farm. Real ale and an extensive range of bar meals (V, and vegan with prior notice) are available *L and E*. Children welcome. Large garden.

🍺 ✕ **The Rising Sun** High Street, Hurley (01628 824274). A dark and beamy village pub with a log fire. Real ale. Bar and restaurant meals (V), with fresh fish a speciality, *L and E*. Regular theme nights.

🍺 ✕ **The East Arms** Henley Road, Hurley (01628 823227). This pub serves food (V) *L and E*, and real ale. Children's play areas and a garden. Karaoke/disco *Fri and Sat*.

BOAT TRIPS
Hobbs & Sons (01491 572035). They have three boats available for trips and private charter: The ***New Orleans*** is available for corporate hire, and two river-buses make *1 hour* trips.

Marlow

On the reach below Temple Lock you may well see canoeists and dinghy sailors from the National Sports Centre at Bisham Abbey, so take care. At the end of this long wide stretch is the elegant white Marlow suspension bridge, with the lock just beyond. The Marlow-Bisham bypass crosses below here, and this is followed by the Scouts Boating Centre, so once again the river is often full of small craft.

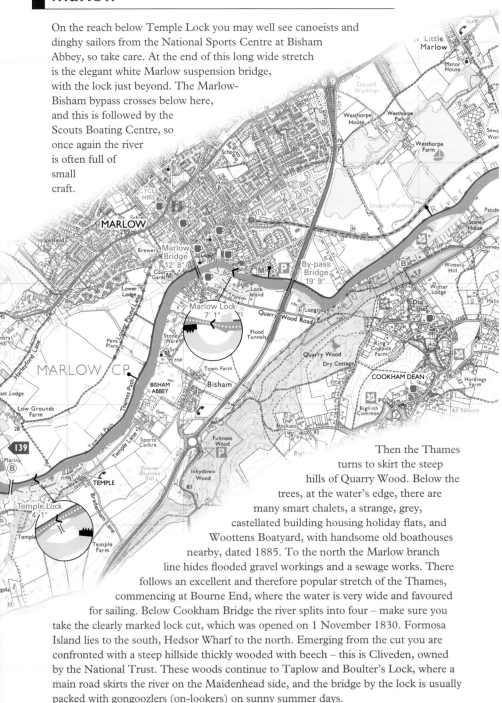

Then the Thames turns to skirt the steep hills of Quarry Wood. Below the trees, at the water's edge, there are many smart chalets, a strange, grey, castellated building housing holiday flats, and Woottens Boatyard, with handsome old boathouses nearby, dated 1885. To the north the Marlow branch line hides flooded gravel workings and a sewage works. There follows an excellent and therefore popular stretch of the Thames, commencing at Bourne End, where the water is very wide and favoured for sailing. Below Cookham Bridge the river splits into four – make sure you take the clearly marked lock cut, which was opened on 1 November 1830. Formosa Island lies to the south, Hedsor Wharf to the north. Emerging from the cut you are confronted with a steep hillside thickly wooded with beech – this is Cliveden, owned by the National Trust. These woods continue to Taplow and Boulter's Lock, where a main road skirts the river on the Maidenhead side, and the bridge by the lock is usually packed with gongoozlers (on-lookers) on sunny summer days.

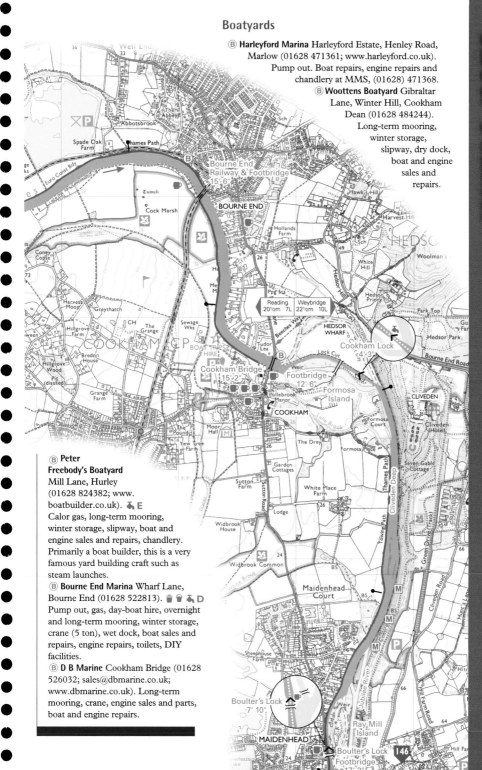

Boatyards

Ⓑ **Harleyford Marina** Harleyford Estate, Henley Road, Marlow (01628 471361; www.harleyford.co.uk). Pump out. Boat repairs, engine repairs and chandlery at MMS, (01628) 471368.

Ⓑ **Woottens Boatyard** Gibraltar Lane, Winter Hill, Cookham Dean (01628 484244). Long-term mooring, winter storage, slipway, dry dock, boat and engine sales and repairs.

Ⓑ **Peter Freebody's Boatyard** Mill Lane, Hurley (01628 824382; www. boatbuilder.co.uk). ⚓ E Calor gas, long-term mooring, winter storage, slipway, boat and engine sales and repairs, chandlery. Primarily a boat builder, this is a very famous yard building craft such as steam launches.

Ⓑ **Bourne End Marina** Wharf Lane, Bourne End (01628 522813). ⛽ 🛢 ⚓ D Pump out, gas, day-boat hire, overnight and long-term mooring, winter storage, crane (5 ton), wet dock, boat sales and repairs, engine repairs, toilets, DIY facilities.

Ⓑ **D B Marine** Cookham Bridge (01628 526032; sales@dbmarine.co.uk; www.dbmarine.co.uk). Long-term mooring, crane, engine sales and parts, boat and engine repairs.

Map labels

Well End

The Abbey

Abbotsbrook

Spade Oak Farm

Thames Path

Euro Const Bdy

Tumuli

Cock Marsh

BOURNE END

Bourne End Railway & Footbridge 15' 6"

Hollands Farm

Sch

HEDSOR

Hawk's Hill

Harvest Hill

White Hill

Woolman's

Coney Copse

Harvest Moor

Greythatch

Hillgrove Farm

Hillgrove Wood

Bredon House

Pit (disused)

Grange Farm

COOKHAM CP

BOAT HIRE

Cookham Bridge 15' 2"

Sewage Wks

Tudor Lea

Beeches Way

Hedsor Hill

Hedsor Priory

Park Top

Hedsor Park

	Reading	Weybridge
	20½m 7L	22½m 10L

HEDSOR WHARF

Cookham Lock

Bourne End Road

The Grange

CH

Weir

Footbridge 12' 6"

Bullebrook Manor

Formosa Island

CLIVEDEN

COOKHAM

Cliveden (Hotel)

Lulle Brook

The Pound

Moor Hall

Yew Tree Farm

Formosa Court

The Drey

Formosa Place

Cliveden Deep

Seven Gable Cottage

Sutton Farm

Garden Cottages

White Place Farm

Thames Path

Green Drive (track)

Widbrook House

Lodge

Sutton Road

Widbrook Common

White Brook

B5

Cliveden Road

Maidenhead Court

Towing Path

Sheephouse Farm

Jubilee River

Hunt's La

Hurley

Hill Farm Road

Boulter's Lock 7' 10"

Weir

Ray Mill Island

MAIDENHEAD

Boulter's Lock Footbridge 17' 3"

146

There is good riverside walking south of Marlow Bridge – turn right just before Temple Lock, and return via Lower Pound Lane. There is also a stiff walk to the top of Winter Hill, but it is worth the effort. Walk north west from Cookham across the golf course, then along Alleyns Lane to Cookham Dean. Follow the path to Quarry Wood, turn right and walk to the summit of Winter Hill, for splendid views. Continue with the river to your left to return to Cookham, passing The Moorings pub on the way.

Pubs and Restaurants

✕♀**The Compleat Angler Hotel** By Marlow Bridge, Marlow (01628 484444). A restaurant and hotel with a riverside terrace, by the famous suspension bridge. It used to be the Anglers Rest; now the name commemorates Izaak Walton's famous book, published in 1653. The Riverside Restaurant serves an à la carte menu (V), in a romantic atmosphere *L and E* (booking preferred). Bistro *L and E, including afternoon tea*. Children welcome.

🍺 ✕ **The George & Dragon** The Causeway, Marlow (01628 483887; www.eatingoutandout. com). A restaurant/pub serving real ale. Meals (V) *all day, every day*. Children welcome. Patio.

🍺 ✕ **The Chequers Inn** High Street, Marlow (01628 482053). Real ale in a 16th-C inn. Restaurant and bar meals (V) available *L and E (not Fri–Sun E)*. Children welcome. Outside seating.

🍺 **The Crown** Market Square, at the top of the High Street, Marlow (01628 487661). Historic pub, once the market, jailhouse and fire station, with the town hall above. Real ale. Bar meals (V) *L and E*. Children welcome. Secluded patio.

🍺 **The Prince of Wales** Mill Road, Marlow (01628 482970). Locals pub serving real ale. Meals (V) in bar or dining area *L and E*. Children welcome when eating. Outside seating. Opposite is the excellent Jolly Frier fish & chip shop. B & B.

🍺 **The Marlow Donkey** Station Road, Marlow (01628 482022). Victorian pub near the station – The Donkey was a famous local train, as the sign indicates. Real ales. Bar meals from full menu (V) available *L and E (not Sun E)*. Children welcome. Garden.

🍺 ✕ **The Jolly Farmer** Church Road, Cookham Dean (01628 482905). Opposite the local church, this friendly pub offers a varying range of real ales. Home-cooked meals (V) served *L and E (not Sun and Mon E)*. Children welcome. Large garden with play area. This pub was bought by the village, for the village, in 1987.

🍺 ✕ **Chequers Brasserie** Dean Lane, Cookham Dean (01628 481232). Historic pub/restaurant, with wooden beams and an open fire. Good selection of wines and real ale. Meals from a daily changing menu (V) *L and E*. Children welcome. Conservatory, and seats outside.

🍺 ✕ **The Hare & Hounds** Cookham Dean Common (01628 483343). Typical old pub serving real ale. Bar and à la carte restaurant meals (V) *L and E (not Sun E)*. Children welcome. Small garden.

🍺 **The Walnut Tree** Hedsor Road, Bourne End (01628 520797). A 16th-C traditional pub with a large garden. Real ale. Superbowl menu (V), with dishes from around the world, *L and E (not Sun E)*. Children welcome. Large patio garden, regular entertainment.

🍺 ✕ **The Bounty** Riverside, Cockmarsh, Bourne End (01628 520056). Old-fashioned pub/ restaurant decorated with an array of naval flags. Real ale. Meals (V) are served *L and E*. Children welcome. Patio overlooking the river, extensive moorings. *Open weekends only in winter.*

🍺 ✕ **The Firefly** Station Approach, Bourne End (01628 521197). Real ale. Bar meals (V) served *L Mon–Fri and Sun*. Large garden, pétanque is played. No children.

🍺 ✕ **The Ferry** Sutton Road, Cookham (01628 525123). Relaxed restaurant by the bridge, with separate low-ceilinged pub. The restaurant has a patio, river views and children are welcome. Bar and restaurant meals (V) available from separate menus *L and E*. Folk music *Thur*.

🍺 ✕ **Bel & The Dragon** High Street, Cookham (01628 521263; www.belandthedragon.co.uk). An attractive pub dating from 1417. Real ale. Freshly prepared meals (V) served *L and E*. Children welcome, and there is a garden with a terrace.

✕♀ **Out & Out** High Street, Cookham (01628 530667; www.eatingoutandout.com). Fashionable and lively restaurant and wine bar, serving real ale. Food (V), including steaks and seafood, *L and E*. Children welcome. Superb patio garden with a play area.

✕♀ **Boulters Lock Hotel** Boulters Island, Maidenhead (01628 621291). Hotel, bar and restaurant right by the lock in the Old Ray Flour Mill, built 1726 and converted in 1950. The Terrace Bar upstairs serves light meals, and the restaurant serves fine English and French cuisine *L and E (not Sun E)*. Children welcome, *but not after 22.00 on Fri*.

Bisham

Berks. A largely Georgian village set back from the river, behind the abbey. The church is set apart from both, being superbly sited almost at the river's edge. Although rebuilt, it still has a Norman tower.

Bisham Abbey The abbey, built mainly in the 14th and 16th C, was a private house from 1540. It is now a sports centre of the Central Council of Physical Recreation, a hive of activity where young players and coaches come together under the aegis of their respective governing bodies of sport. They train in the sport of their choice, ranging from archery to weight lifting. River activities feature strongly in the training programme. *The centre is not open to casual visitors.*

Marlow

Bucks. All shops and services, laundrette. A very handsome and lively Georgian town, with a wide tree-lined High Street connecting the bridge with the Market Place. A marvellous view of the weir can be had from the white suspension bridge, built by Tierny Clarke in 1831–6 and reconstructed, retaining its original width, in 1966. The town's most ancient building is the Old Parsonage, once part of a great 14th-C house and containing panelled rooms and beautifully decorated windows. West Street, at the top of the High Street, has great literary associations – Thomas Love Peacock wrote *Nightmare Abbey* at no. 47, Shelley wrote *Revolt to Islam* in Albion House, while his wife Mary Godwin created *Frankenstein* there. T. S. Eliot also lived in West Street for a while, after World War I.

Cookham Dean

Berks. PO, stores. Large parts of Cookham Dean are owned by the National Trust. The village stands above steep beech woods by the river. Winter Hill has one of the best views over the Thames Valley, and is well worth the steep walk. Kenneth Grahame, who wrote *The Wind in the Willows,* published 1908, lived at Mayfield between 1906–10. It is thought that Quarry Wood may have been the wild wood mentioned in the story.

Bourne End

Bucks. PO, shops. A riverside commuter village, famous for Bourne End Sailing Week. Cock Marsh opposite, 132 acres, is owned by the National Trust.

Cookham

Berks. PO, tel, no grocery shops. A pretty village of pubs, antique shops, restaurants and boutiques, with bijou cottages filling the gaps in between. Cookham is famous as the home of the artist Stanley Spencer, who was born in 'Fernlea', in the High Street – the quite amazing variety of his work is splendidly exhibited in the old Wesleyan Chapel. His *Last Supper,* painted in 1920, hangs in the splendid square-towered Holy Trinity Church, built by the Normans in 1140 on the site of a Saxon building. There are fine 16th-C monuments, and the church is floodlit after dark. The bridge, an iron structure, was built in 1867.

Stanley Spencer Gallery The Kings Hall, High Street, Cookham (01628 471885; www.cookham.com/about/spencer). Opened in 1962, this is the only gallery devoted to an artist which is situated in the village of his birth, and where he attended Sunday school. Along with his paintings, there is a collection of memorabilia associated with this remarkable man. *Open Easter–Oct, daily 10.30–17.30; Sat, Sun and B Hols in winter 11.00–17.00.* Modest admission charge.

Odds Farm Park Wooburn Common, High Wycombe (01628 520188; www.oddsfarm.co.uk). The best approach is by taxi from Maidenhead. One of only 20 rare breeds centres in the country, where children (and adults) can observe the animals in close proximity. Tractor rides, log play and a calendar of special events throughout the summer. *Open Feb half-term–Oct, daily 10.00–17.00; Nov–Feb half-term, Thur–Sun 10.00–16.00.* Charge. Tea room, gifts.

Hedsor

Bucks. A priory and an over-restored church on the hill. It is worth the walk up for the splendid views over the beech woods. Hedsor House was rebuilt in 1862 in an Italianate style. Lord Boston's Folly, an 18th-C structure, faces the church from the opposite hill.

Hedsor Wharf An important shipping point for timber, paper and coal for over 500 years until the lock cut bypassed it in 1830. At the lower end of Hedsor Water there was once a lock – the original cottage still stands, a single room cut from the chalk and fronted with brick. Hedsor Water is private.

Cliveden Taplow, Maidenhead (01628 605069). A most marvellous stretch of beech woods from Hedsor to Taplow surrounds the house, which was built in 1851 by Charles Barry for the Duke of Sutherland. It was the home of Nancy, Lady Astor, and was the background to many 20th-C political intrigues and scandals, ending with the Profumo affair in 1963. Fine tapestries and furniture, and a theatre which heard the first performance of *Rule Britannia.* It is now a stately home/hotel, leased from the National Trust. B & B prices start at over £300 per night. *House open Apr–Oct, Thur and Sun 15.00–17.30. Garden: mid Mar–Oct, daily 11.00–18.00; Nov–Dec 11.00–16.00.* Charge. Restaurant. Temporary moorings (charge).

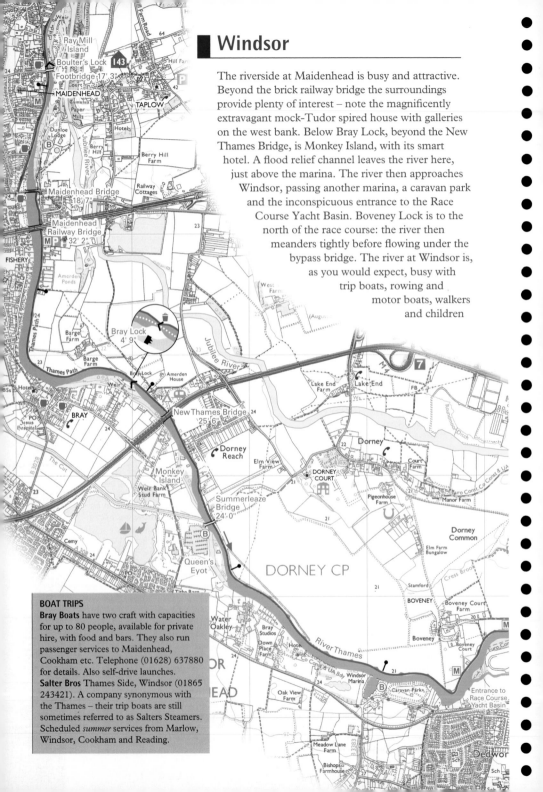

Windsor

The riverside at Maidenhead is busy and attractive. Beyond the brick railway bridge the surroundings provide plenty of interest – note the magnificently extravagant mock-Tudor spired house with galleries on the west bank. Below Bray Lock, beyond the New Thames Bridge, is Monkey Island, with its smart hotel. A flood relief channel leaves the river here, just above the marina. The river then approaches Windsor, passing another marina, a caravan park and the inconspicuous entrance to the Race Course Yacht Basin. Boveney Lock is to the north of the race course: the river then meanders tightly before flowing under the bypass bridge. The river at Windsor is, as you would expect, busy with trip boats, rowing and motor boats, walkers and children

BOAT TRIPS

Bray Boats have two craft with capacities for up to 80 people, available for private hire, with food and bars. They also run passenger services to Maidenhead, Cookham etc. Telephone (01628) 637880 for details. Also self-drive launches.

Salter Bros Thames Side, Windsor (01865 243421). A company synonymous with the Thames – their trip boats are still sometimes referred to as Salters Steamers. Scheduled *summer* services from Marlow, Windsor, Cookham and Reading.

feeding the ducks. On the north bank is Eton College Boat House, while Windsor Castle dominates the river for miles around. Leaving Windsor, the Thames winds around Home Park, passing the famous college, on the north bank.

Boatyards

Ⓑ **Bray Boats** Lockbridge Boathouse, Ray Mead Road, Maidenhead (01628 637880). 🛏 🚻 ⚓ Pump out, day-boat hire, long-term mooring, outboard repairs, toilets. Tug hire. *Closed Sun in winter.*

Ⓑ **Peter Freebody** Boulters Island, Maidenhead (01628 824382; www.boatbuilder.co.uk). Boat building and repairs. This is the Maidenhead yard of the very famous boat builders, who also construct steam launches.

Ⓑ **Bray Marina** Monkey Lane, Bray (01628 623654; 07885 189805 between 19.00–07.00; bray@mdlmarinas.co.uk). 🛏 🚻 ⚓ P D E Gas, overnight and long-term mooring, winter storage, crane (10 ton), boat and engine sales and repairs, telephone, chandlery, toilets, showers, books, maps and gifts, café, DIY facilities.

Ⓑ **Windsor Marina** Maidenhead Road, Oakley Green, Windsor (01753 853911;

bray@mdlmarinas.co.uk). 🛏 🚻 ⚓ P D E Pump out, gas, overnight and long-term mooring, winter storage, slipway, crane (10 ton), boat sales and repairs, engine repairs, chandlery, telephone, toilets, showers, DIY facilities. *Emergency call out.*

Ⓑ **Racecourse Yacht Basin** Maidenhead Road, Windsor (01753 851501; www.ryb.co.uk). 🛏 🚻 ⚓ P D Pump out, gas, overnight and long-term mooring, winter storage, crane, boat and engine sales and repairs, large chandlery, telephone, toilets, showers, café, books, maps and gifts.

Ⓑ **Stanley & Thomas** Romney Lock Boat House, Windsor (01753 833166/mobile 07831 862729; www.stanleyandthomas.co.uk). Long term mooring, winter storage, crane, boat building, boat and engine sales and repairs, painting.

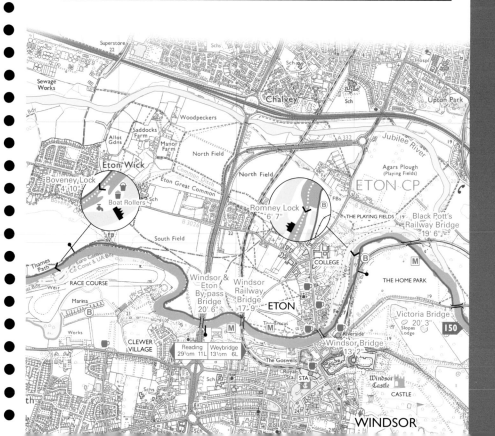

WINDSOR

Maidenhead

Berks. All services. A dormitory suburb of London, close to the M4 motorway, and with much new development.

Tourist Information Centre The Library, St Ives Road, Maidenhead (01628 781110; www.maidenhead.gov.uk).

The Jubilee River An imaginative solution to the ever-present threat of flooding in the Thames Valley, this newly constructed 7-mile river takes full account of environmental considerations. Built at a cost of £100 million, it passes under the main railway line from Paddington, and the M4 motorway, before rejoining the Thames near Eton College. Over 250,000 native trees have been planted – creating habitat for mandarin ducks, reed and sedge warblers, bittern, bearded tit and marsh harriers. A footpath and cycleway accompanies its course, and there are hides for birdwatchers. Boating activity is restricted to canoeing. But should a drought occur, as in 1976, this new river would be sacrificed to the more long-standing demands of the Thames, whatever the environmental cost.

Maidenhead Railway Bridge These two beautiful arches, each 123ft long, are reputedly the largest brickwork spans in the world. They were built in 1839 by Brunel.

Bray

Berks. Tel, stores. Despite commuter development, Bray still retains its village centre. The largely 13th-C church is approached via a fine brick gatehouse of 1450. Simon Alwyn, the 16th-C vicar of Bray, who changed his creed three times to hold the living under Henry VIII, Edward VI, Mary and Elizabeth I, lies buried in the churchyard. Just outside the village is the Jesus Hospital, founded in 1627.

Monkey Island On the island are the fishing lodge and pavilion of the 3rd Duke of Marlborough, built in 1744 on rubble salvaged from the Great Fire of London. The Lodge was constructed from wooden blocks, cut to look like stone and still in good condition; the nearby Temple has a fine Wedgwood-style ceiling. In one of the restaurant rooms of the Pavilion there are monkey paintings on the ceiling, completed by Andie de Clermont before 1738. The name of the island, however, is a corruption of 'Monk's Eyot'. The Pavilion became an inn around 1840, and was fashionable at the start of the 20th C when Edward VII and Queen Alexandra had afternoon tea on the lawn. It is now a hotel.

Down Place A pretty 18th-C riverside mansion, once the meeting place of the Kit Kat Club. Steele, Addison, Walpole and Congreve were members. Nearby is Oakley Court, a magnificent Victorian Gothic castle of 1859.

Dorney Court and Church (01628 604638; palmer@dorneycourt.co.uk). A gabled and timbered Tudor manor house, built c.1440, and occupied by the Palmer family for 400 years. Restorations have not altered the original feeling of the house which contains fine furniture and paintings. The church contains a Norman font, 17th-C woodwork and a Garrard monument. It is reputedly haunted by a cavalier, a Turk and a young girl in white. Cream teas and shop. *Open May, Sun and B Hols; Aug, Sun–Fri 13.00–16.30.* Charge.

Boveney

Bucks. A village scattered around a green, with Tudor buildings and a pretty flint and clapboard church.

Windsor

Berks. All shops and services. The main street curves around the castle and is full of pubs, restaurants and souvenir shops. The Church of St John the Baptist in the High Street, built 1820–2, has three galleries supported by delicate cast iron piers. The town hall was built by Wren in 1689–90 after a design by Sir Thomas Fitch. The ceiling appears to be supported by four Tuscan columns which stop two inches short: a private joke of the architect's at the expense of a doubting mayor. To the west of the town there is a fine riverside park. Theatre at the Theatre Royal (01753 853888).

Tourist Information Centre 24 High Street, Windsor (01753 743900; www.windsor.gov.uk). *Open daily.*

Windsor Castle

(www.royal.gov.uk). The largest inhabited castle in the world, first built by Henry II, 1165–79. Most succeeding monarchs have left their mark, notably Charles II, and Queen Victoria who spent over £1 million on modernisation. It has been meticulously restored following the disastrous fire of 20 November 1992 (the Queen and Duke of Edinburgh's 45th wedding anniversary!). The building falls into three sections:

Lower Ward St George's Chapel, the finest example of Perpendicular architecture in the country, containing the tombs of ten sovereigns. The Albert Memorial Chapel, originally built by Henry VII and turned into a Victorian shrine.

Middle Ward The Round Tower, with a panoramic view over twelve counties.

Upper Ward The Private Apartments and the State Apartments, containing a collection of paintings. The castle is surrounded by parks; Home Park borders on the river and contains Frogmore House, built by Wyatt in 1792 out of an earlier house, and the Royal Mausoleum. *The castle precincts are open daily – other parts of the castle are often open to the public but times do vary: telephone for a recorded message on (01753) 831118.* Charge.

Legoland Winkfield Road, Windsor (08705 040404; www.lego.com). A building-brick fantasy covering over 150 acres, with 40 rides, shows and attractions, including Lego Traffic, and Miniland, built from 32 million Lego bricks. *Open early Mar–Oct, daily.* Charge. Doors close if it gets crowded!

Windsor Great Park

A total area of 4800 acres between the Thames and Virginia Water. There has been a starling roost in the park for over 100 years, and a heronry at Fort Belvedere.

● **Eton**
Berks. PO, tel, shops. The long and rambling
High Street is a pleasant place to walk.
Eton College Eton High Street (01753 671177;
www.etoncollege.com). Founded by Henry VI in
1440 to provide education for 70 poor scholars.

The buildings date from 1441 to the present day.
Now 1280 boys attend. Eighteen former British
prime ministers have been educated here. *Parts
open to the public Apr–Oct daily, 14.00–16.30
during term-time, 10.30–16.30 during school
holidays. Tours at 14.15 and 15.15.* Charge.

Pubs and Restaurants

◗ ✕ **Taplow House Hotel** Berry Hill, Taplow
(01628 670056). A Georgian mansion standing in 6 acres of grounds and housing a hotel,
an excellent restaurant and two bars. The
new à la carte restaurant serves English and
continental cuisine (V) *L and E (unless there is a
function)*. Children welcome.

◗ ✕ **The Thames Hotel** Ray Mead Road,
Maidenhead (01628 628721). Cosy and
relaxed riverside hotel and restaurant, built in
the 1880s by a prosperous local boat builder –
indeed at one time it had a telegraph office.
Princess Frederika of Hanover, and many
other distinguished guests, have stayed here.
Real ale. Bar meals (V) and restaurant meals
E (not Sun E). Bar meals served overlooking
the river. Children welcome. Terrace with
outside seating.

✕ ♀ **Topogigio** 2 Ray Mead Road, Maidenhead
(01628 777555). By the bridge. Modern
Italian restaurant overlooking the river. *Open L
and E, closed Sun.*

◗ **The Thames Riviera Hotel** (Jerome's Bar)
Bridge Road, Maidenhead (01628 674057;
www.thamesriviera.co.uk). Residential hotel
overlooking the Thames below Maidenhead
Bridge. Bar meals (V) served *L and E*. Coffee
shop *09.00–17.00*. Children welcome. Garden.
Maidenhead town centre, where you will find
more pubs and eating places, lies about 3/4 mile
south west of the bridge.

✕ ♀ **The Waterside Inn** Ferry Road, Bray
(01628 620691; waterinn@aol.com). Smart
riverside restaurant in a beautiful setting,
run by Michel Roux – considered by some
to be the best restaurant in the country.
Exciting menu, attentive waiters, expensive
wine. *Open L and E (closed Mon, and Tue
Sep–May). Booking essential.* Children over
12 welcome.

◗ ✕ **The Crown** High Street, Bray (01628
621936). A beamy old pub serving real ale.
Food (V) *L and E (not Sun or Mon E)*.
Children welcome in the restaurant. Sheltered
courtyard with vines.

◗ ✕ **Sir Christopher Wren's House Hotel**
Thames Street, Windsor (01753 861354; www.
scw.activehotels.com/HEN). A Thames-side
residential hotel, built by Sir Christopher
Wren as a family home, with cocktail bar and
restaurant overlooking the river. Restaurant
serves excellent food (V) *L and E* plus *afternoon
teas*. Children welcome. Outside seating.

Windsor has many fine pubs, the following are
those nearest the river:

◗ ✕ **The Royal Oak** Datchet Road (01753
865179). There was a brewery here in 1539,
when the building was owned by St George's
Chapel and the pub was known as The Crown.
On 8 March 1834 it was reported that Mrs
Bitmead, of The Royal Oak, was fined ten
shillings for allowing her pig to escape, and
rampage around the town. Real ale is served in
the bar, and there is a separate restaurant (V) *L
and E*. Children welcome. Garden.

✕ ♀ **La Taverna** 2 River Street, Windsor
(01753 863020; www.lataverna.co.uk).
Excellent Italian food (V) and wine *L Mon–Fri
and E Mon–Sat*. Booking recommended.
Children welcome. River views from the first
floor.

The following five pubs are easily found in
Eton High Street, straight up from the
bridge:

◗ **The Crown & Cushion** 84 High Street, Eton
(01753 861531). Friendly pub serving real
ale, and bar meals (V) *L and E (not Fri–Sun
E)*. Children welcome in the back bar.
Garden. B & B.

◗ ✕ **The Christopher Hotel** 110 High Street,
Eton (01753 852359; www.christopher-hotel.
co.uk). Friendly old coaching inn. Real ales.
Meals (V) available *L and E*. Children welcome.
Small patio.

◗ **The New College** 55 High Street, Eton
(01753 865516). Friendly refurbished pub
serving real ale, with bar meals (V) available *L
and E*. Children welcome. Outside seating on
the terrace.

◗ **Hog's Head Ale House** Eton (01753
861797). Traditional pub serving real ale.
Food (V) available *L and E*. Large garden. No
children.

✕ ♀ **The House on the Bridge** 71 High Street,
by Windsor Bridge, Eton (01753 860914;
www.house-on-the-bridge.co.uk). International
restaurant with its own moorings. Meals (V) *L
and E*. Children welcome. Outside seating on
riverside terrace.

◗ ✕ **The Watermans Arms** Brocas Street,
Eton (01753 861001). Situated near the Eton
College Boat House, the restaurant serves
traditional English cuisine and bar meals
(V) *L and E (not Sun E)*. Real ale. Children
welcome. Conservatory seating area. Live
music *Wed*.

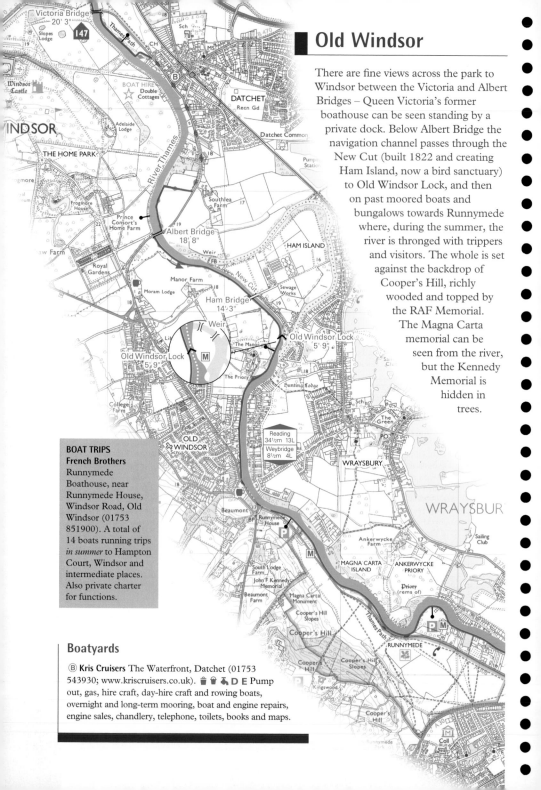

Old Windsor

There are fine views across the park to Windsor between the Victoria and Albert Bridges – Queen Victoria's former boathouse can be seen standing by a private dock. Below Albert Bridge the navigation channel passes through the New Cut (built 1822 and creating Ham Island, now a bird sanctuary) to Old Windsor Lock, and then on past moored boats and bungalows towards Runnymede where, during the summer, the river is thronged with trippers and visitors. The whole is set against the backdrop of Cooper's Hill, richly wooded and topped by the RAF Memorial. The Magna Carta memorial can be seen from the river, but the Kennedy Memorial is hidden in trees.

BOAT TRIPS
French Brothers
Runnymede Boathouse, near Runnymede House, Windsor Road, Old Windsor (01753 851900). A total of 14 boats running trips *in summer* to Hampton Court, Windsor and intermediate places. Also private charter for functions.

Boatyards

Ⓑ **Kris Cruisers** The Waterfront, Datchet (01753 543930; www.kriscruisers.co.uk). 🚽 🚿 ♿ D E Pump out, gas, hire craft, day-hire craft and rowing boats, overnight and long-term mooring, boat and engine repairs, engine sales, chandlery, telephone, toilets, books and maps.

To the north are the remains of Ankerwyke Priory. Passing Holm Island, the London Stone stands by the river: this marked the former limit of the jurisdiction of the City of London over the Thames. There is some smart and mellow housing on the north bank above Staines Bridge, but for the most part the riverside is lined with a wonderful, and sometimes very eccentric, array of holiday chalets and bungalows, along with houseboats and moored craft of indiscriminate vintage.

● **Datchet**
Berks. Shops. At its best around the green, where there is still a village feeling.

● **Old Windsor**
Berks. Tel, shop. A great expanse of suburban houses with no sign of the 9th-C village, built around the site of a Saxon royal palace. The 13th-C church is hidden among trees.

● **Runnymede**
Surrey. Beside the river on the south bank, this is a stretch of open parkland backed by the wooded slope of Cooper's Hill. The paired gatehouses, by Lutyens, introduce an area of memorials. The inspiration is the sealing of the Magna Carta in 1215. On top of the hill is the Commonwealth Air Forces Memorial. This quadrangular structure, built by Sir Edward Maufe in 1953, perfectly exploits its situation.

Below are the Magna Carta Memorial and the Kennedy Memorial, the latter built on an acre of ground given to the American people.This is a popular venue in summer.

Ankerwyke Built on the site of a Benedictine nunnery is Ankerwyke Priory, a low, early 19th-C mansion surrounded by trees, among which is the Ankerwyke Yew, whose trunk is 33ft in circumference.

● **Staines**
Surrey. All services, laundrette, fish & chips. A commuter town which has expanded hugely over the last 30 years. However, the area around the pleasantly situated church has remained virtually unchanged. Clarence Street, which culminates in Rennie's stone bridge, built 1829–32, still has the feeling of an 18th-C market town. To the north are huge reservoirs.

Pubs and Restaurants

● ✕ **The Bells of Ouzeley** Straight Road, Old Windsor (01753 861526). There has been a pub on this site for about 800 years, although it nearly all came to an end during World War II, when a V1 flying bomb destroyed part of the building. Food (V) available in the restaurant *L and E*. Children welcome and there is a garden.

● ✕ **The Leftbank** Windsor Road, Egham (01784 436171; www.runnymedehotel. com). Smart hotel with riverside gardens, conference facilities and the new Leftbank waterfront restaurant,

created by Suchà Design at a cost of £1m, and based upon an aquatic theme. Real ale. Modern Mediterranean dishes (V) *L and E*. Children welcome. Dinner dance *Sat.*

● ✕ **Brasserie, Thames Lodge** Thames Street, Staines (0870 400 8121; www.heritage-hotels. com). A Thames-side hotel, where meals (V) are served *L and E*. Children welcome. Patio/terrace. Mooring.

● **The Bells** Church Street, Staines (01784 454240). Close to the supposedly haunted churchyard. Real ale. Bar meals (V) available *L and E (not Sun E)*. Children welcome. Garden and conservatory.

WALKING & CYCLING
There are excellent walks by the river at Runnymede, where the land is owned by the National Trust.

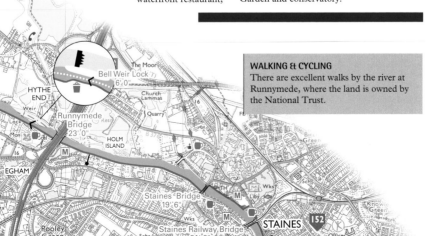

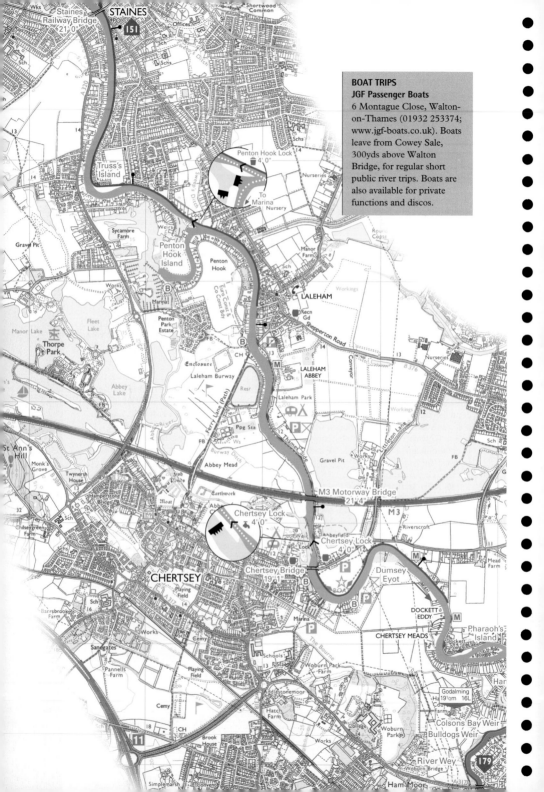

BOAT TRIPS

JGF Passenger Boats

6 Montague Close, Walton-on-Thames (01932 253374; www.jgf-boats.co.uk). Boats leave from Cowey Sale, 300yds above Walton Bridge, for regular short public river trips. Boats are also available for private functions and discos.

Penton Hook Lock 4'0"

Weir

Penton Hook Island

Penton Hook

LALEHAM

Shepperton Road

Thorpe Park

Laleham Burway

LALEHAM ABBEY

Laleham Park

Ferry Lane (Path)

Thames Side

Abbey Mead

Gravel Pit

M3 Motorway Bridge 21'4"

M3

Chertsey Lock 4'0"

Chertsey Lock 4'0"

CHERTSEY

Chertsey Bridge 19'11"

Dumsey Eyot

DOCKETT EDDY

CHERTSEY MEADS

Pharaoh's Island

Colsons Bay Weir

Bulldogs Weir

River Wey

Woburn Bridge

Weybridge

At Penton Hook a large marina has been established in flooded gravel pits – it is approached from below the lock. Laleham follows, and soon the bungalows disappear and Laleham Abbey and park provide a brief breathing space before Chertsey looms large. The river twists and turns on its way to Weybridge, where the River Wey (*see* page 179) flows in from the south joining it, and the Basingstoke Canal (*see* page 11) to the Thames. Desborough Cut removes two large loops from the navigable course before the rivers makes a direct run for Sunbury, leaving Walton-on-Thames to the east.

NAVIGATIONAL NOTES

1 Note that Penton Hook Marina is approached from *below* the lock.
2 The River Wey joins the Thames *below* Shepperton Lock.
3 The old course of the river north of Desborough Island is navigable, but it may be shallow in places.
4 *Nauticalia* runs a ferry service below Shepperton Lock for the National Trust, so walkers can enjoy this ancient crossing, noticing that 'droves of sheep will be carried at the fare of one shilling per score (shepherd to clean up afterwards)'.

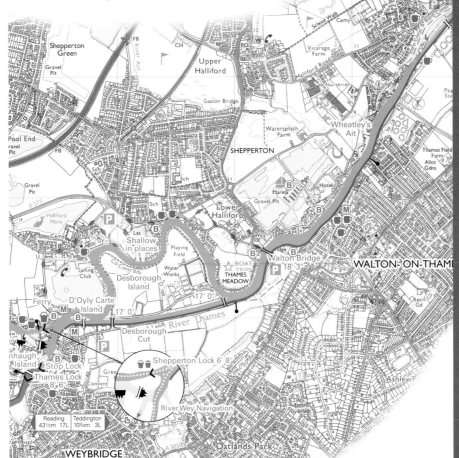

Boatyards

Ⓑ **Penton Hook Marina** Staines Lane, Chertsey (01932 568681; www.marinas.co.uk). A vast marina in flooded gravel pits. 🛏 🚽 🚿 P D Pump out, gas, overnight and long-term mooring, winter storage, slipway, crane, boat and engine sales and repairs, chandlery, telephone, toilets, showers, DIY facilities.

Ⓑ **Chertsey Meads Marine** Mead Lane, Chertsey (01932 564699; www.boatsthames.com). 🚿 D E Pump out, gas, boat hire, day-boat hire, overnight and long-term mooring, winter storage, slipway, crane, boat and engine repairs, DIY facilities, books and maps. *Emergency call out.*

Ⓑ **Nauticalia** Ferry Lane, Shepperton (01932 254844; www.pushtheboatout.com). 🛏 🚿 E Gas, overnight and long-term mooring, winter storage, slipway, hoist, boat building, boat and engine repairs, chandlery, telephone, toilets, café, DIY facilities.

Ⓑ **Eyot House** D'Oyly Carte Island, Weybridge (01932 848586). 🛏 🚽 🚿 Gas, long-term mooring, winter storage, slipway, wet dock, boat and engine repairs, chandlery, toilets, DIY facilities.

Ⓑ **Gibbs Marine Sales** Sandhills, Russell Road, Shepperton (01932 220926; www.gibbsmarine. co.uk). 🚿 Long-term mooring, winter storage, slipway, crane, boat sales, engine repairs, toilets.

Ⓑ **Walton Marine** Walton Bridge, Walton (01932 226266; www.waltonmarine.co.uk). 🛏 🚽 🚿 Pump out, gas, overnight and long-term mooring, winter storage, slipway, crane, boat and engine sales and repairs, chandlery, telephone, toilets, showers, books, maps and gifts, café, DIY facilities. *Emergency call out.*

Ⓑ **Bridge Marine** Thames Meadow, Shepperton (01932 245126; boatyard@chase-signs.com). 🚿 E Gas, winter storage, slipway, crane, boat building, boat and engine sales and repairs, chandlery, telephone, toilets, books, maps and gifts, DIY facilities. *Emergency call out.*

Ⓑ **Shepperton Marina** Felix Lane, Shepperton (01932 243722; www.boatshowrooms.com). 🛏 🚽 🚿 P D Pump out, gas, overnight and long-term mooring, crane, boat and engine sales and repairs, chandlery, telephone, toilets, showers, books, maps and gifts, DIY facilities. *Emergency call out.*

Ⓑ **DBH Marine** Angler's Wharf, Manor Road, Walton (01932 267999; dbh01@aol.com). Long-term mooring (*the yard is for sale as we go to press*).

Laleham
Surrey. Tel, stores. The first impression of Laleham is one of bungalows and houseboats. The village does not exploit the river at all, and the centre lacks the riverside feeling of some other towns hereabouts. The 18th- and 19th-C church is well placed in a wooded graveyard, which contains the tomb of Matthew Arnold (1822–88, see Bablock Hythe, on page 112). To the south of the town is Laleham Park. Formerly the grounds of Laleham House, built about 1805, it is now a wooded public park reaching down to the river.

Thorpe Park Staines Road, Chertsey (www. thorpepark.com). One of the country's first theme parks, which is suitable for all ages. Rides and attractions include Colossus, which hurtles through ten loops over 2800ft long at speeds of 40 mph, along with the highest log flume ride in the UK, Thunder River, Phantom Fantasia and the Canada Creek Railway which takes visitors to Thorpe Farm – a 1930s traditional working farmyard. There is also a Medieval town square and castle. *Open daily Easter–Oct, telephone 0870 444 4466 for recorded details.* Charge.

Chertsey
Surrey. All shops and services. From the river the first sight of Chertsey is James Paine's stone bridge, built 1780–2. Chertsey just manages to retain a feeling of the 18th C, especially around Windsor Street, which runs past the site of the abbey, once one of the greatest in England. Founded in AD666 and rebuilt in the 12th C, it was finally destroyed during the Reformation. It is thought likely that materials from the abbey were used in the construction of Hampton Court.

Weybridge
Surrey. All shops and services, laundrette. A commuter town in the stockbroker belt, built around the confluence of the rivers Wey and Thames – the junction is marked by a pretty iron bridge of 1865. Weybridge represents the frontier of the suburbia that now spreads almost unbroken to London.

Shepperton
Surrey. All shops and services, laundrette. Recognisable from the river by the lawns of the 19th-C manor house, Shepperton is a surprising example of village survival. The square contains a number of relatively intact 18th-C inns. The church, with its fine brick tower, was built in the 17th and 18th C, and has box pews. To the north of the church is the rectory, which has a pretty Queen Anne front. The famous film studios are to the north, near the vast Queen Mary Reservoir.

Walton-on-Thames
Surrey. All shops and services, laundrette, fish & chips.

● **Sunbury**
Surrey. PO, tel, shops and laundrette. Sunbury has a pleasant village feeling. Sunbury Court, the grand mansion of the town, was built in 1770 and is now a Salvation Army Centre.

WALKING & CYCLING
National Cycle Route 4 connects Weybridge with Putney Bridge, using quiet streets and cycle paths. Follow the signs on the Thames towpath from its junction with the River Wey to pass through Kingston and Richmond Park. This is part of the Thames Valley Cycle Route, which stretches all the way to Oxford.

Pubs and Restaurants

🍴 ✕ **The Three Horseshoes** Shepperton Road, Laleham (01784 452617). Having been a police station and a morgue, this is now an characterful, relaxed and comfortable pub, once patronised by the Prince Regent, Sir Arthur Sullivan and Marie Lloyd. Real ale. Excellent home-made food (V) *L and E*. Children welcome. No-smoking conservatory and large garden. Dominoes, cards and Chinese chequers can be played here. Live light music *once a month, telephone for details.*

🍴 ✕ **The Feathers** The Broadway, Laleham (01784 453561). Friendly pub serving real ale, and food (V) *L and E (not Sun E)*. Children welcome, and there is a garden.

🍴 **The Kingfisher** Bridge Road, Chertsey (01932 579811). Cosy traditional pub, with low ceilings, timbered walls and an open fire. Real ale. Meals (V) served *L and E*. Children welcome, and on fine days you can sit by the river.

🍴 ✕ **The Boat House and Bridge Lodge Hotel** Bridge Road, Chertsey (01932 565644; www.galleon-taverns.co.uk). Busy wood and tile riverside pub and restaurant, with a nautical theme. Real ale. Food (V) *L and E*. Children welcome. Riverside seats. Moorings.

🍴 ✕ **The Thames Court** Ferry Lane, The Towpath (01932 221957). Oak-panelled and balconied pub by Shepperton Lock. Real ale. Meals (V) *all day, every day*. Children welcome if eating. Patio.

🍴 ✕ **The Anchor Hotel** Church Square, Shepperton (01932 242748; www.anchorhotel.co.uk). Friendly 400-year-old wood-panelled pub. Real ale. Bar snacks *L* and restaurant meals (V) *E (not Sun E)*. Children welcome, and there are seats outside.

🍴 **The Old Crown** 83 Thames Street, Weybridge (01932 842844). Rambling weather-boarded pub by the old course of the River Wey, with charming nautical decor. It has been run by the same family since 1959. Real ales. Meals (V) *L and E (not Sun, Mon or Tue E)*. Children welcome *until 21.00*. Conservatory containing plants from New Zealand. Riverside garden, patio and landing stage.

🍴 ✕ **The Ship Hotel** Russell Road, Shepperton (01932 227320). Friendly riverside hotel where real ale is served, along with food (V) *L and E*. Children welcome in the lounge. B & B.

🍴 **The Swan** Manor Road, Walton (01932 225964). Imposing and friendly riverside pub, licensed since 1770. Real ale. Meals (V) available *L and E*. Children welcome. Garden. *Summer* barbecues. Live blues evenings *Sep–Apr*.

🍴 ✕ **The Anglers** Anglers Wharf, Manor Road, Walton (01932 223996). Fine riverside pub serving a choice of real ale. Food (V) available *all day, every day*. Children welcome. Riverside seats. Mooring.

🍴 **Old Manor Inn** 113 Manor Road, Walton (01932 221359). Real ale in a local's pub with a fine floral display. Bar meals (V) served *L Mon–Fri and E Tue–Wed*. Children welcome if eating. Garden, and 14th-C manor house to the rear.

🍴 **Flower Pot Hotel** Thames Street, Sunbury (01932 780741). A 14th-C pub/restaurant, offering real ale. Food (V) served *L and E (not Sun E)*. Children welcome if eating.

🍴 ✕ **The Magpie** 64 Thames Street, Sunbury (01932 782024). Real ales. Meals (V) available *L and E (not Sun E)*. Children welcome *until 19.00*. Patio.

🍴 **The Phoenix** 26-28 Thames Street, Sunbury (01932 785358). Friendly local, once two cottages. Real ale. Meals (V) *L and E*. An area is set aside for children. Dominoes, cribbage, chess and draughts can be played. Garden.

Hampton Court

Sunbury Court Island is lined with immaculate chalets and bungalows: opposite and to the east is a vast area of reservoirs and waterworks. Below Platt's Eyot is Hampton, where the ferry still survives. Hampton Church stands on the north bank opposite Garrick's Ait. Bushy Park stretches away to the north east of the river. Tagg's Island and Ash Island are lined with smart moored craft and eccentric houseboats, including a large Swiss chalet behind Tagg's Island. Below Hampton Bridge is Hampton Court Palace, standing close to the river, and separated from it by an extremely long red brick wall. Further downstream, Thames Ditton Island is absolutely packed with yet more bungalows and chalets. The river then becomes very wide as it curves past Thames Ditton, flanked by the parkland of Hampton Court to the west and the housing and industry of Surbiton and

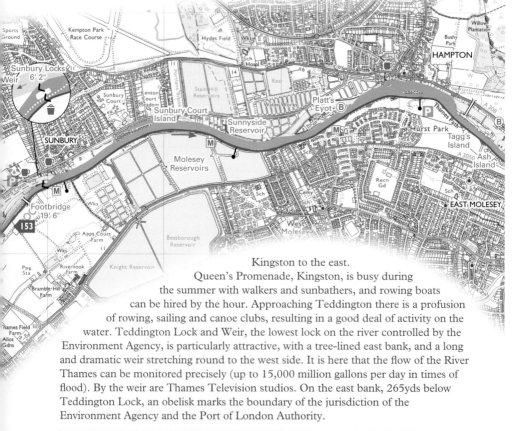

Kingston to the east.

Queen's Promenade, Kingston, is busy during the summer with walkers and sunbathers, and rowing boats can be hired by the hour. Approaching Teddington there is a profusion of rowing, sailing and canoe clubs, resulting in a good deal of activity on the water. Teddington Lock and Weir, the lowest lock on the river controlled by the Environment Agency, is particularly attractive, with a tree-lined east bank, and a long and dramatic weir stretching round to the west side. It is here that the flow of the River Thames can be monitored precisely (up to 15,000 million gallons per day in times of flood). By the weir are Thames Television studios. On the east bank, 265yds below Teddington Lock, an obelisk marks the boundary of the jurisdiction of the Environment Agency and the Port of London Authority.

BOAT TRIPS

Turk Launches Town End Pier, 68 High Street, Kingston (0208 546 2434; www.turks.co.uk) They run a public service to Hampton Court, Kingston and Richmond in *summer*. Also private charter for up to 150 people. Telephone 0208 546 2434 for details.

Lord Aragorn Aragorn Enterprises, 27 Esher Road., East Molesey (0208 339 0609; www.aragornenterprises.com). Built in 1999 in the style of a traditional Edwardian Inspection Launch, but with modern facilities. Teak-lined saloon. Charters for special occasions for up to 12 people.

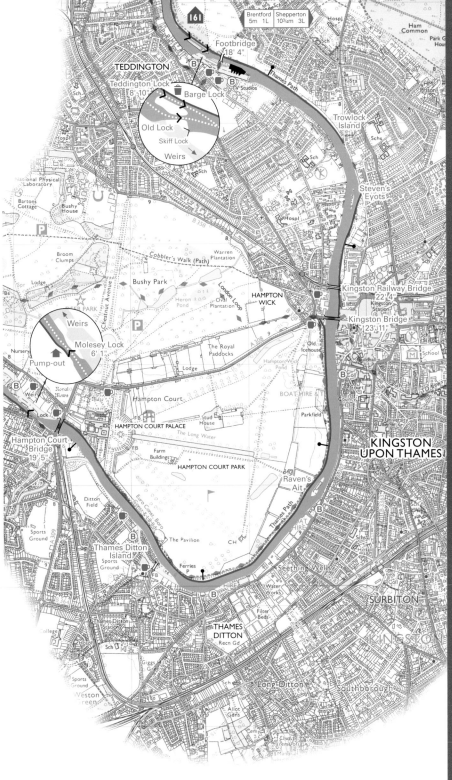

NAVIGATIONAL NOTES

1 Sunbury Locks – The mechanised lock on the south side is normally used. The hand-operated lock on the north side is used only during busy periods in the summer.
2 Teddington Locks (0208 940 8723). Traffic moving upstream *must* observe the light signals at the end of the lock island.
   Two red diagonal crosses – both locks *closed*. Do not proceed.
   One red diagonal cross – lock *closed*.
   White Arrow – *proceed* in direction indicated.
3 Those using the Skiff Lock should follow the lock keeper's instructions.
4 The river below Teddington Lock is tidal for two hours either side of high water.
5 **Teddington to Brentford** – leave Teddington 20 minutes before high water.
6 **Teddington to Limehouse** – leave Teddington 30 minutes before high water.
   Note for both 5 & 6 Arrival time must fall within normal working hours. If it will not, the passage **must** be booked *24 hours* in advance with the appropriate lock keeper. *If you fail to do this, you will be left in the tideway.* Times are approximate and depend upon the speed of your boat. If in any doubt – *check before you leave.*

Boatyards

⒝ **Port Hampton** Platts Eyot, Hampton (0208 979 8116). 🗑 🚻 ⚓ Pump out, long-term mooring, winter storage, crane, toilets, DIY facilities.
⒝ **Geo Wilson & Sons** Ferry House, Thames Street, Sunbury (01932 782067). Day-hire craft, long-term mooring, slipway, traditional boat repairs, DIY facilities.
⒝ **Turks of Sunbury** 10 Thames Street, Sunbury (01932 782028; www.turks.co.uk). Long-term mooring, winter storage, slipway, boat and engine sales and repairs, boat building.
⒝ **T.W. Allen & Son (Yachts)** Ash Island, Hampton Court, East Molesey (0208 979 1997). ⚓ Gas, long-term mooring, slipway, boat sales and repairs, DIY facilities.
⒝ **Ferryline Cruisers** Ferry Yacht Station, Thames Ditton (0208 398 0271). 🗑 ⚓ D Pump out, hire craft, day-hire craft, overnight mooring, crane, boat sales, books and maps.
⒝ **Taggs Boatyard** Summer Road, Thames Ditton (0208 398 2119; maritek@taggsboatyard.co.uk). 🗑 ⚓ E Day-hire craft, overnight and long-term

mooring, winter storage, slipway, boat building, boat sales and repairs, engine repairs, toilets.
⒝ **Thames Marina** Portsmouth Road, Thames Ditton (0208 398 6159; www.thamesmarina.co.uk). 🚻 ⚓ D Pump out, gas, long-term mooring, slipway, crane, boat building, boat repairs, engine sales and repairs, chandlery, toilets, books and maps.
⒝ ✕ **Hart's Boats** Portsmouth Road, Surbiton (0208 399 4009). 🗑 🚻 ⚓ E Gas, electric day boats, overnight and long-term mooring, winter storage, slipway, boat building, boat sales and repairs, engine repairs, telephone, toilets, books and maps. *Summer* ferry to Home Park.
⒝ **Turk Launches** Town End Pier, 68 High Street, Kingston (0208 546 2434; www.turks.co.uk). ⚓ Pump out, long-term mooring, boat building, boat sales and repairs. *Summer* ferry to Hampton Court.
⒝ **Tough's Boatyard** 27 Ferry Road, Teddington (0208 977 4494). Boat and engine repairs, small boat building, surveying, boat safety certificates, valuations. Chandlery next door.

● **Hampton**
Surrey. PO, tel, shops, laundrette. Despite much new development, Hampton remains an attractive late 18th-C village, still linked by ferry to the south bank. The church, built in 1831, is prominent on the riverside. Despite the proximity of Hampton Court, the village owes its existence to Hampton House, bought by David Garrick in 1754, and subsequently altered by Adam. By the river is Garrick's Temple, built to house Roubiliac's bust of Shakespeare. Nearby stands the large Swiss chalet which was brought over from Switzerland in 1899.

● **Hampton Court Palace**
Surrey. (0208 781 9500; www.hrp.org.uk). Probably the greatest secular building in England. Cardinal Wolsey, son of an Ipswich butcher, was graced by ambition and ability to such an extent that at the age of 40 he had an income of £50,000 a year. He was thus able to build the grandest private house in England. Work began in 1514. Henry VIII was offended by the unashamed ostentation of his lieutenant and in 1529, following Wolsey's downfall and his failure to secure the annulment of Henry VIII's first marriage, the king took over the house. Henry

spent more on Hampton Court than on any other building, establishing it as a Royal Palace. Subsequently Wren added to it, but little work, other than repairs, has been done since. Visit the State Apartments, The Tudor Kitchen, The Wolsey Rooms, The King's & Queen's Apartments, The Georgian Rooms, The Courtyards and The Cloisters. In the formal gardens (at their best in *mid May*) are the Great Vine, planted in 1789, and the Maze where Harris, one of Jerome K. Jerome's *Three Men in a Boat*, got hopelessly lost, along with 20 followers and a keeper. *Open 09.30 (10.15 Mon)–18.00 (16.30 winter) daily. Closed Xmas. The gardens close at 21.00, or dusk.* Charge. Teas in the grounds. River launches connect with Westminster, Richmond and Kingston. Behind the palace is Bushy Park, enclosing 2000 acres. It is a formal design reminiscent of Versailles, and is famous for deer.

● **Hampton Green**
Surrey. A fine collection of 18th-C and earlier buildings surround Hampton Green, just to the north of Hampton Court Bridge. The bridge was built by Lutyens in 1933.

● **Thames Ditton**
Surrey. PO, tel, shops, laundrette. The centre of this unspoilt riverside village has managed to avoid the careless development of the surrounding area. The church here has an interesting graveyard, a lovely garden and there are several good brasses inside. Pretty whitewashed houses stand close by the suspension bridge which leads to Thames Ditton Island.

● **Kingston-on-Thames**
Surrey. All shops and services. A Royal Borough where seven Saxon kings were crowned. The coronation stone is displayed outside the Guildhall. There is a good river frontage, centred round the stone bridge built 1825–8 by Lapidge. Away from the river the market place is the centre of the town. The Lovekyn Chapel on London Road dates largely from the Tudor period and is surrounded by many interesting 18th-C buildings. The Italianate town hall, 1838–40, is one of the most striking structures in the area. There are also the five conduit houses built by Cardinal Wolsey to supply water to Hampton Court.

● **Teddington**
Gt London. PO, tel, shops, laundrette. R. D. Blackmore (1825–1900), author of *Lorna Doone,* lived in Teddington from 1860. The site of his home, Gomer House, is at the end of Doone Close, near the station. The riverside, viewed from the Surrey bank, is one of Teddington's most pleasing aspects. The television studios stand in Broom Road, near the weir.

Pubs and Restaurants

🍺 **The Bell** 8 Thames Street, Hampton (0208 941 9799). Right by the church and overlooking the river, this small, cosy pub serves real ale, and food (V) *L (E Tue–Sat)*. Children welcome *until 17.00*. Patio and conservatory.

🍺 **Cardinal Wolsey** The Green, Hampton Court (0208 979 1458). Real ale and bar meals (V) *L*, in a pub by the stables. It is sometimes busy, sometimes empty. Children welcome.

🍺 ✕ **The King's Arms** Lion Gate, Hampton Court Road (0208 977 1729). Superbly situated pub adjoining the palace wall. Real ale. Excellent food (V) *L and E*. Children and dogs welcome. Outside seating.

🍺 **The Crown Inn** Summer Road, Thames Ditton (0208 398 2376). Friendly refurbished pub just over the river from Hampton Court. Real ale. Bar meals (V) *L*. Children welcome. Outside seating.

🍺 ✕ **The Old Swan Hotel** Summer Road, Thames Ditton (0208 398 1814). Riverside pub behind Thames Ditton Island, once visited by Henry VIII. Real ale. Meals (V) available *L and E*. Children welcome. Outside seating.

🍺 ✕ **The King's Head** 123 High Street, Teddington (0208 977 2413; www.massivepub. com). Quiet pub with strong sporting links. Real ale. Bar meals (V) *L and E (not Fri or Sat E)*

and full meals in l'Auberge, an authentically French restaurant *E*. Children welcome. Attractive garden. Across the road is la Petite Auberge, a delicatessen and bistro, where you can get a continental breakfast, or crepes *L*.

🍺 **The White Hart** 70 High Street, Hampton (0208 979 5352). A mock Tudor single bar pub serving only real ale, together with food (V) *L and E*. Children welcome in the Thai restaurant upstairs. Seating on the patio.

🍺 **The Swan** 22 High Street, Hampton Wick (0208 296 0559). Friendly local pub serving real ale, along with a range of international food (V) – Thai, Japanese, British and so on – *L and E (not Sun E)*. Children welcome for *Sat and Sun L*. Outside seating.

🍺 **The Anglers** 3 Broom Road, Teddington (0208 977 7475). Right next door to Thames Television Studios, this pleasant riverside pub overlooking Teddington Lock offers real ale, along with food (V) *L and E (not Sun E)*. Children welcome away from the bar. Large garden with children's play area. Barbecues *in summer*. Mooring.

🍺 **Tide End Cottage** 8 Ferry Road, Teddington (0208 977 7762). Quaint little riverside pub, offering a choice of real ale. Food (V) *L and E*. Children welcome. Pleasant patio, with a grapevine.

Richmond-upon-Thames

As the river passes Eel Pie Island and enters Horse Reach, Richmond Hill can be seen rising gently from the east bank, with the large Star and Garter Home dominating the view. To the west lies Marble Hill Park, where a ferry connects this with Ham House – the last surviving ferry on the tidal Thames. The river is the focal point of Richmond – indeed the view of the river from Richmond Hill is dramatic and much painted and photographed. Richmond Bridge is an elegant, slightly humped, 18th-C structure – one of the prettiest bridges on the river. Beyond the railway bridge is Richmond half-tide lock, movable weir and footbridge, built in 1894. Its brightly painted arches belie its more serious function of tide control. The river curves around Old Deer Park, with Isleworth Ait to the west, and the old village and church close by the river to the north. Behind wooded banks is Syon Park, and opposite are the Royal Botanic Gardens, Kew. Immediately below the park is the entrance to the Grand Union Canal, a direct link with Birmingham (see *Guide 1*).

Boatyards

ⓑ **Hammerton Ferry Boat House** Marble Hill Park, Orleans Road, Twickenham (0208 892 9620). Day-hire craft, overnight and long-term mooring. They run the only ferry surviving on the tidal Thames, between Ham House and Marble Hill Park – *Feb–Oct daily, Nov–Jan Sat and Sun only*.

ⓑ **Swan Island Harbour** Strawberry Vale, Twickenham (0208 892 2861). 🛠 **D E** Long-term mooring, winter storage, slipway, boat sales, boat and engine repairs, toilets, DIY facilities.

ⓑ **Brentford Dock Marina** 2 Justin Close, Brentford Dock (07970 143987/0208 232 8941). 🚻 🛠 Overnight mooring and long-term mooring, boat sales, telephone, toilets, showers, bar and restaurant.

ⓑ **Brentford Marine Services** Ridgeways Wharf, Brent Way, Brentford (0208 568 0287). Gas, overnight and long-term mooring, slipway, crane, tidal grid, boat sales and repairs, engine repairs, DIY facilities.

Pubs and Restaurants

🍺 **The White Swan** Riverside, Twickenham (0208 892 2166). Startlingly attractive black and white balconied pub right by the river's edge. Fine choice of real ales. Excellent bar meals (V) *L*. Children welcome, and there is riverside seating.

🍺 ✗ **The Barmy Arms** Twickenham (0208 892 0863). Lively pub serving real ale, and food (V) *L and E*. Children welcome. Outside seating on the patio. Live music outside, and barbecues *when there are events on the river*.

🍺 ✗ **The London Apprentice** Church Street, Old Isleworth (0208 560 1915). A 15th-C riverside pub with Elizabethan and Georgian interiors, decorated with prints of Hogarth's *Apprentices*. Real ale. Bar meals (V) available *L and E*. Children welcome in the conservatory, and there is a patio.

🍺 **The Rose of York** Petersham Road, Richmond (0208 948 5867). Large, comfortable, typically English pub panelled in oak, warmed by a coal fire and decorated with reproductions of paintings of the famous turn in the river by Turner and Reynolds. Good views of the Thames from the terrace and courtyard. Real ale. Food (V) served *L and E*. Children welcome. Garden overlooking the river. B & B.

🍺 **The Waterman's Arms** Water Lane, Richmond (0208 940 2893). Small cosy and popular pub, in a cobbled riverside street, which was once frequented by the watermen who trudged up from the river. Real ale. Meals (V) available *L*. Children welcome away from the bar. Small garden.

🍺 **The White Cross** Water Lane, Richmond (0208 940 6844). Lively riverside pub with a garden, serving real ale. Food (V), with game a speciality, *12.00–16.00*. Look out for the unusual fireplace. Children welcome upstairs. Large patio.

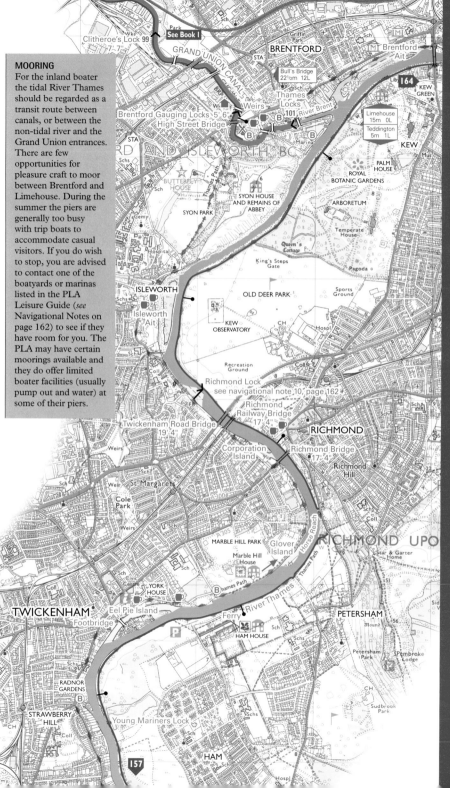

MOORING

For the inland boater the tidal River Thames should be regarded as a transit route between canals, or between the non-tidal river and the Grand Union entrances. There are few opportunities for pleasure craft to moor between Brentford and Limehouse. During the summer the piers are generally too busy with trip boats to accommodate casual visitors. If you do wish to stop, you are advised to contact one of the boatyards or marinas listed in the PLA Leisure Guide (*see* Navigational Notes on page 162) to see if they have room for you. The PLA may have certain moorings available and they do offer limited boater facilities (usually pump out and water) at some of their piers.

1 From **Brentford** to **Limehouse** navigation on the Thames is far more complex than on the upper reaches. The river here is a commercial waterway first and foremost, and pleasure craft must take great care. The River Thames below Teddington is controlled by the Port of London Authority (PLA) which produces a useful set of free notes, the *Pleasure User's Guide*. A separate leaflet (*PLA Leisure Guide*) details facilities on the tidal river and an annual publication – *Handbook of Tide Tables and Port Information* – is available free to boaters. For general navigational enquiries about the river contact the Assistant Harbour Master, Devon House, 58–60 St Katharine's Way, London E1 9LB (0207 743 7900; www.portoflondon.co.uk). It is anticipated that the PLA will make more and more use of their website to disseminate information (especially time-sensitive information) so becoming less dependant on the current printed guides. While hire companies do not usually allow their craft to be taken onto the tideway, owners of pleasure boats may wish to make the passage along the Thames below Teddington Locks and between the canals at Brentford and Limehouse. With proper planning this should present no particular difficulties. However, check with your insurance company who may have special requirements.

2 **Brentford** to **Limehouse Basin** – leave Brentford 1/2 hour before high water to gain the benefit of the ebb tide. Limehouse Basin is fitted with sector gates and is open in line with BW's *List of Opening Times for Brentford, Bow and Limehouse Locks*, published at six-monthly intervals and obtainable from BW London Region 0207 286 6101; www. britishwaterways.co.uk/london. Telephone Limehouse Basin (0207 308 9930) and inform them of your intentions.

3 **Limehouse Basin** to **Brentford** – pass through the entrance lock at Limehouse 2 1/2 hours before high water, to gain the benefit of the flood tide. Thames Lock, Brentford is manned for a period before and after high water (2 hours each side if this falls within normal working hours). Contact the lock keeper to pre-book passage outside normal working hours (as per Limehouse) on 0208 560 1120. Brentford gauging lock is boater-operated using a BW sanitary station key. Brentford listen and operate on VHF channel 74.

4 **Brentford** to **Teddington** – pass through Thames Lock, Brentford 2 hours before high water to gain the benefit of the flood tide. Teddington lock keeper can be contacted on 0208 940 8723 and Richmond lock keeper can be contacted on 0208 940 0634.

5 **VHF Radio** – all vessels of 20 metres (65ft) or more in length must carry a VHF radio capable of communicating with the harbourmaster at port control – channel 14. The exception is narrowboats over 65ft in transit between the Grand Union Canal at Brentford and the non-tidal Thames at Teddington Locks. Such vessels must telephone the PLA duty officer (0208 855 0315) immediately before and on completion of transit, if no radio is available.

6 **Warning lights** – see PLA publication: *Pleasure User's Guide*.

7 **Draught** – the depth at the centre span of Westminster Bridge is approximately 2ft 8in at chart datum (about 4ft 0in at mean low water springs). In practice there is usually a greater depth than this. The depth at all the other bridges is greater than Westminster.

8 **Headroom** – on the tidal river the clearance at bridges is given as the maximum at mean high water springs – this is less than the headroom at chart datum (lowest astronomical tide). In practice this means that there will usually be more headroom than that indicated.

9 **Canals –** those who wish to navigate on the adjoining British Waterways canals will require a licence, available from: Craft Licensing Office, Willow Grange, Church Road, Watford WD1 3QA (01923 226422). Full details of the inland waterways encountered at Brentford and Limehouse can be found on pages 161 and 174.

10 **Richmond Lock –** (0208 940 0634). The weirs are raised from approximately 2 hours before until approximately 2 hours after high water. At all other times, the lock must be used.

Ham House Petersham, Surrey (0208 940 1950; shhgen@smtp.ntrust.org.uk). A superb 17th-C riverside mansion, the exterior largely by Sir John Vavassour. The lavish Restoration interior has a collection of Stuart furniture, and is haunted by a ghostly dog. There are also formal gardens and an ice house. *House open: Easter–Oct Sat–Wed and G Fri 13.00–17.00. Gardens: all year Sat–Wed 11.00–18.00 or dusk if earlier.* Charge. Licensed Orangery with historic menus and tea garden *open Easter–Oct.*

● **Twickenham**
Gt London. All shops and services. Twickenham was one of the most elegant and desirable areas in the 18th C. The church, with its three-storey tower, dates largely from 1714. The poet Alexander Pope, 1688–1744, moved to Twickenham in 1717. Deformed at an early age by a bone disease, his most notable work was the 'Rape of the Lock', although the lock in question was associated with hair, rather than the river. Monuments to him and to his parents can be found in the church. York House, built c.1700, and now Municipal Offices, has an astonishing collection of statues in its riverside gardens.

Strawberry Hill Waldegrave Road. The surviving glory of Twickenham is Walpole's Gothic fantasy, one of the earliest examples of the 18th-C Gothic Revival. Designed first by John Chute and Richard Bentley between 1753–63, and later by Thomas Pitt, it expresses Walpole's appreciation of Gothic forms and spirit. Strawberry Hill now houses St Mary's Training College.

Marble Hill House Richmond Road (0208 892 5115). A restored Palladian mansion, built in 1724–9 by George II for his mistress, Henrietta Howard. Fine collection of paintings and furniture dating from the early 18th C, plus the Lazenby Bequest Chinoiserie (chinese motifs) display. *Open Apr–Sep, daily 10.00–18.00; Oct, daily 10.00–17.00.* Charge. Open–air concerts *in summer – telephone for details.*

Eel Pie Island Twickenham. In Edwardian times the hotel on the island ran tea dances. In the 1960s it housed a noisy night club which featured popular rock groups.

Tourist Information Centre Civic Centre, York Street, Twickenham (0208 891 7272).

● **Petersham**
Surrey. But for the traffic, this would be one of the most elegant village suburbs near London. It is exceptionally rich in fine houses of the late 17th and 18th C. Captain George Vancouver, who sailed with Cook and discovered the island off the coast of Canada which is named after him, lived in River Lane and is now buried in the churchyard here.

● **Richmond-upon-Thames**
Surrey. All shops and services. One of the prettiest riverside towns in the London area. Built up the side of the hill, Richmond has been able to retain its Georgian elegance and still has the feeling of an 18th-C resort. Richmond Green is the centre, both aesthetically and socially; it is surrounded by early 18th-C houses. Only the

brick and terracotta theatre, built in 1899, breaks the pattern; so deliberately that it is almost refreshing. The gateway of Richmond Palace is all that remains of the Royal residence built by Henry VII, out of the earlier Palace of Shene. Behind the gate, in Old Palace Yard, is the Trumpeter's House. This magnificent building, c.1708, was once visited by Disraeli. At the top of Richmond Hill stands Wick House, built for Joshua Reynolds in 1772. It is from here that he painted marvellous views over the Thames.

Richmond Theatre The Green (0208 940 0088; www.theambassadors.com/richmond). Productions from London's West End and touring companies.

Richmond Park The largest of the royal parks, created by Charles I in 1637, it covers 2358 acres. The park remained a favourite hunting ground till the 18th C. Private shooting stopped in 1904 but the hunting lodges can still be seen. White Lodge, built for George II in 1727, now houses the Royal Ballet School. *Park open 07.00–dusk.*

Old Deer Park Kew Observatory was built here in 1729 (by William Chambers for George III) and was used by the Meteorological Office until 1981. The three obelisks nearby were used to measure London's official time.

Richmond Bridge This fine stone bridge with its five arches and parapet is one of the most handsome on the Thames, and was frequently the subject for paintings in the 18th–19th C. Built in the classical style by James Paine, 1777, it replaced the earlier horse ferry, and was a toll bridge until 1859.

Tourist Information Centre Old Town Hall, Whittaker Avenue, Richmond-upon-Thames (0208 940 9125; information.services@richmond. gov.uk).

● **Isleworth**
Gt London. PO. The prettiest view of this village is from the stretch of river just before Syon House. The 15th-C tower of All Saints' Church, the London Apprentice Inn and a collection of fine Georgian houses all make for a delightful setting. Vincent Van Gogh taught here and used the Thames as the subject for his first attempts at painting.

Syon Park Park Road, Brentford (0208 560 0881; www.syonpark.co.uk). Set in 55 acres of parkland, landscaped by 'Capability' Brown, Syon House is built on the site of a 15th-C convent. The present square structure with its corner turrets is largely 16th-C, although the interior was remodelled by Robert Adam in 1762. The house itself is mainly of interest on account of the magnificent neo-classical rooms by Adam. Katherine Howard was confined here before her execution in 1542 and Lady Jane Grey stayed here for the nine days preceding her death in 1554. Conservatory (1827) by Charles Fowler. The Butterfly House houses a huge variety of live butterflies and insects from all over the world. There is also an excellent garden centre. *House open Easter–Oct, Wed, Thur and Sun (also G Fri and Easter Sun) 11.00–17.00. Gardens open daily 10.30–17.30.* Charge.

West London

Immediately below Brentford Dock Marina is the entrance to the Grand Union Canal, a direct link with Birmingham and places north. On the north bank opposite Kew is Strand-on-the-Green, a cluster of desirable houses and fashionable pubs facing

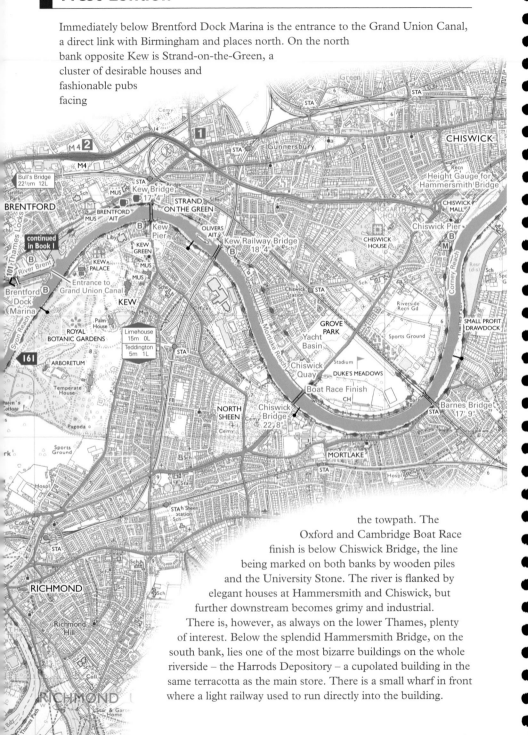

the towpath. The Oxford and Cambridge Boat Race finish is below Chiswick Bridge, the line being marked on both banks by wooden piles and the University Stone. The river is flanked by elegant houses at Hammersmith and Chiswick, but further downstream becomes grimy and industrial.

There is, however, as always on the lower Thames, plenty of interest. Below the splendid Hammersmith Bridge, on the south bank, lies one of the most bizarre buildings on the whole riverside – the Harrods Depository – a cupolated building in the same terracotta as the main store. There is a small wharf in front where a light railway used to run directly into the building.

NAVIGATIONAL NOTES

Boaters joining the tidal Thames at Brentford should read the Navigational Notes on page 162, and the Mooring Note on page 161.

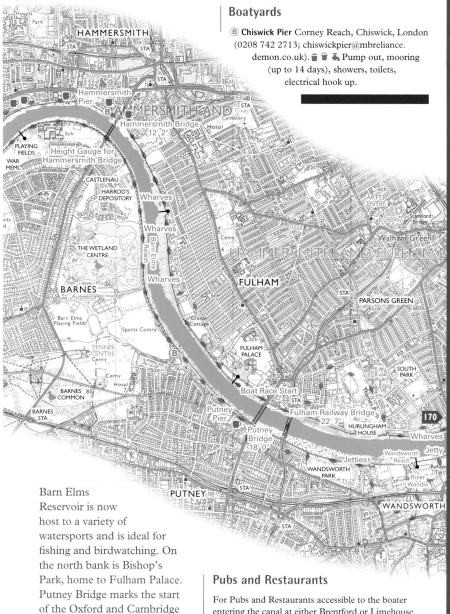

Boatyards

Ⓑ **Chiswick Pier** Corney Reach, Chiswick, London (0208 742 2713; chiswickpier@mbreliance. demon.co.uk). 🎁 🚻 🛁 Pump out, mooring (up to 14 days), showers, toilets, electrical hook up.

Barn Elms Reservoir is now host to a variety of watersports and is ideal for fishing and birdwatching. On the north bank is Bishop's Park, home to Fulham Palace. Putney Bridge marks the start of the Oxford and Cambridge Boat Race and gives way to a stretch of industry.

Pubs and Restaurants

For Pubs and Restaurants accessible to the boater entering the canal at either Brentford or Limehouse see *Guide 1*.

Millennium Bridge (see page 173)

WALKING & CYCLING
This is an absolutely splendid section for walking. The path keeps to the south side throughout and Kew Gardens and Kew Palace are definitely worth a visit. Across the river is Strand-on-the-Green, with its fine houses and pubs. Barnes Railway Bridge has a foot crossing, and walkers can choose which bank they take to reach Hammersmith – the scenic route is on the south bank, the pubs on the north. After the fascinating walk around Barnes to Putney, the Thames towpath terminates, giving way to road as far as Putney Bridge. The course of the river can best be followed through London by keeping to the north side. *Collins London Street Atlas* is a helpful guide when detours are necessary.

● **Royal Botanic Gardens** Kew Road, Kew, Richmond (0208 940 1171). Superb botanical gardens of 300 acres founded in 1759 by Princess Augusta. Delightful natural gardens and woods bounded by the river on one side, and stocked with thousands of flowers and trees. The lake, aquatic garden and pagoda were designed by Sir William Chambers in 1760 and the magnificent curved glass Palm House and the Temperate House, 1844–8, are by Decimus Burton. Beneath the Palm House is a Marine Display which has examples of flowering marine plants and coral reef. The Princess of Wales Conservatory houses orchids, cacti, and water lilies the size of mattresses. Kew's scientific aspect was developed by its two directors Sir William and Sir Joseph Hooker and the many famous botanists who worked here. Cafeteria and gift shop in the Orangery. *One hour* tours available from the Victoria Gate Visitor Centre. Gardens *open daily 09.30–dusk.* Charge.

Kew Bridge Opened by Edward VII in 1903 and officially called the King Edward VII Bridge. A fine stone structure designed by Sir John Wolfe Barry and Cuthbert Brereton, it replaced the earlier granite bridge of 1789.

Kew Railway Bridge When it was opened in 1869 this five-span lattice girder bridge, designed by W. R. Galbraith, was part of the London and South Western Railway extension.

● **Kew**
Surrey. Old Kew centres around the Green, the 18th-C houses built for members of the Court of George III, and the entrance to the Royal Botanic Gardens. The church of St Anne dates from 1714 but was greatly altered in the 19th C.

Musical Museum St George's Church, 368 High Street, Brentford (0208 560 8108). A fascinating collection of around 200 automatic, old and odd musical instruments. Many of the instruments are played during the *one hour* conducted tour. *Open Jul-Aug, Wed-Sat 14.00–17.00; Sep-Jun, Sat and Sun 14.00–17.00.* Charge. No small children.

Kew Bridge Steam Museum Green Dragon Lane, Brentford (0208 568 4757). Huge Victorian building housing six gigantic beam engines, restored to working order by volunteers. In steam at *weekends.* Also a collection of old traction engines and a working forge. Tearoom *(weekends only). Open daily (including B Hols) 11.00–17.00.* Charge (under 5s free).

● **Chiswick**
W4. Chiswick stretches between Kew Bridge and Hammersmith Terrace and provides some of the most picturesque scenery on the London stretch of the Thames. Georgian houses extend along Strand-on-the-Green and again at Chiswick Mall. Between these points, running down to the riverside, originally stood three 18th-C mansions: of the three, only Chiswick House remains. The site of Grove House has been built over, and Duke's Meadows, part of the grounds of Chiswick House, is now a recreation ground. Chiswick Cemetery backs on to St Nicholas Church where Lord Burlington and William Kent are buried.

Chiswick Bridge Built in 1933, designed by Sir Herbert Baker and opened to the public by the Prince of Wales, this bridge has the longest concrete arch of any bridge on the Thames. The centre span measures 150ft.

Chiswick House Burlington Lane W4. 0208 994 3299. Lovely Palladian villa built in the grand manner by 3rd Earl of Burlington 1725–30, modelled on Palladio's Villa Capra at Vicenza.

● **Mortlake**
SW14. In the 17th C Mortlake was famous for its tapestry workshop, established by James I and staffed by Flemish weavers. Some of the Mortlake Tapestries can still be seen in the Victoria & Albert Museum. The riverside here is picturesque along Thames Bank where there is a fine collection of 18th-C houses. Mortlake also marks the end of the Oxford and Cambridge Boat Race at Chiswick Bridge (although the first race took place at Henley in 1829).

Barnes Railway Bridge This light and elegant iron bridge by Locke was opened in 1849 to connect with the Richmond line. Similar in design to Richmond Railway Bridge.

Oxford v Cambridge Boat Race On a *Saturday afternoon in March or April* this famous annual event is held over a 4-mile course from Putney to Mortlake. Get to the riverside early for a good view.

● **NORTH BANK**

Hammersmith Terrace *W6*. A terrace of 17 identical houses on the river bank, built c.1750. The late Sir Alan Herbert, historian of the Thames, lived in the Terrace.

Upper Mall *W6*. Separated from Lower Mall by Furnivall Gardens, Upper Mall boasts some fine 18th-C buildings including the Dove Inn, originally a coffee house. William Morris lived in Kelmscott House between 1878 and 1896.

Lower Mall *W6*. Bustling in the summer months with rowers from the number of boathouses and rowing clubs which have been established here for over a century. Lower Mall is home to the Rutland and Blue Anchor pubs, and a number of pretty 18th-C cottages.

Hammersmith Bridge The first suspension bridge in London. The original, built 1824 by William T. Clarke, was replaced in 1883 by the present splendid construction by Sir Joseph Bazalgette.

Fulham In the 18th and 19th C Fulham was the 'great fruit and kitchen garden north of the Thames', a place of market and nursery gardens, attracting the more prosperous Londoners in search of purer air. Today little is left of the fertile village and the area has become quite built-up. Fulham has, however, remained an attractive area, nowadays better known for its abundance of restaurants and bars. Also home to two of London's most famous football clubs, Fulham and Chelsea. Bishop's Park and Hurlingham House can be seen from the river.

Fulham Palace The palace lies behind the long avenues of Bishop's Park, with grounds stretching to the river. The site was first acquired by Bishop Waldhere in AD704 and continued as a residence of the Bishops of London until 1973.

A fascinating mixture of architectural styles, from the Tudor courtyard with its mellow red brick to the restrained elegance of the Georgian east front.

Putney Bridge The wooden toll bridge of 1729 was replaced by the present bridge designed by Sir Joseph Bazalgette in 1884. Putney Bridge marks the start of the Oxford and Cambridge Boat Race.

Fulham Railway Bridge This trellis girder iron bridge was part of the Metropolitan extension to the District Railway. Designed by William Jacomb, it was opened in 1889 and connects with a footbridge running parallel to it. Part of the London Transport underground system.

Hurlingham House Ranelagh Gardens *SW6*. This is the only large 18th-C residence still surviving in Fulham. The house has a fine river front with Corinthian columns and is now the centre of the Hurlingham Club. Members play tennis, golf and croquet in the grounds.

● **SOUTH BANK**

Barnes Terrace *SW13*. The delightful village of Barnes lies behind the attractive ironwork façade of Barnes Terrace. The terrace was, and still is, a fashionable place to live, with former residents including Sheridan and Gustav Holst.

Castelnau Barnes is rich in Victorian houses and some of the most interesting are to be seen in Castelnau. Remarkably standardised, they are largely semi-detached and typical of early Victorian villa architecture with their arched windows.

Barn Elms Formerly the manor house of Barnes, the estate was later leased to Sir Francis Walsingham, Secretary of State to Elizabeth I. Today, all that remains of the former layout is part of the ornamental pond and the ice house. The Reservoir at Barn Elms now plays host to a variety of watersports, plus fishing and bird-watching.

Putney The Embankment is picturesque. The London Rowing Club and Westminster School have their boathouses here and the eights and sculls can be seen practising most afternoons.

BOAT TRIPS

One of the best ways to understand the layout of a large, water-bound city is to take a boat trip and London is no exception to this rule. There is a large number to choose from, although most originate from Westminster Pier. Broadly speaking the options available encompass a selection of down-river trips as far as the Thames Barrier (and the Visitor Centre) and a range of up-river trips, which can reach as far as Hampton Court. The latter takes a full day. There are also evening dinner and dance cruises. Visit the pier (without your boat) to compare the plethora of options and make a choice.

Central London

The short stretch of intrusive industry, sprawling along the south bank, is soon relieved at Battersea by the splendid St Mary's Church opposite Lots Road Power Station and Chelsea Harbour. Albert Bridge, restored in 1991, is a remarkable sight when illuminated at night by over 4,000 bulbs. From here on the River Thames curves through the heart of the capital, and has been London's lifeline for 2000 years. Indeed it was instrumental in the Roman settlement which created London as an international port. Once used as the local bypass, being cheaper and safer than travel by road, it has carried Roman galleys, Viking longships, Elizabethan barges and Victorian steamers. One of the best ways to see London is still from the Thames. The buildings and sights lining its twisting, turning path are as varied as London itself. It is fascinating by day and magical by night.

● NORTH BANK

Wandsworth Bridge In 1938 the 19th-C bridge was replaced with the existing structure by E. P. Wheeler, now painted a distinctive bright blue.

Chelsea Harbour A modern development dominated by the Belvedere tower block. The golden ball on its roof slides up and down with the level of the river. The development contains offices, restaurants, a luxury hotel, smart shops, apartments and the marina. Chelsea Wharf, just along the bank, has been transformed from old warehouses into modern business units.

Battersea Railway Bridge The West London Extension Railway, of which this bridge was a part, was opened in 1863 to connect the south of England directly with the north. Because it did not end at a London terminus, it became a target for bombing during World War II.

Lots Road Power Station This huge and domi-nating structure was built in 1904 to provide electricity for the new underground railway.

Battersea Bridge The original Battersea Bridge, 1772, a picturesque wooden structure by Henry Holland, has been portrayed in paintings by Whistler and Turner. The replacement iron structure, opened in 1890, was designed by Sir Joseph Bazalgette.

All Saints Church Chelsea Embankment. Rebuilt in 1964 after severe bomb damage during the war. Contains two 13th-C chapels, one restored by Sir Thomas More 1528, a Jacobean altar table and one of the best series of monuments in a London parish church. Henry VIII married Jane Seymour here before their state wedding in 1536.

Cheyne Walk *SW3*. Cheyne Walk, with its houseboats and its row of delightful riverside Queen Anne houses, has been home to Lloyd George, Hilaire Belloc, George Eliot, Isambard Kingdom Brunel, Turner and Whistler.

Carlyle's House 24 Cheyne Row *SW3*. Once the haunt of writers such as Dickens and Tennyson, and the home of Thomas and Jane Carlyle 1834–81.

Albert Bridge A delightful suspension bridge connecting Chelsea and Battersea, built by Ordish 1871–3. The bridge was strengthened in 1973 by a huge solid support under the main span. Illuminated by over 4,000 bulbs, the bridge is particularly beautiful at night.

Chelsea Embankment *SW3*. Chelsea Embankment, stretching between Albert Bridge and Chelsea Bridge, was built in 1871. The embankment is bordered on the north bank by the grounds of the Chelsea Royal Hospital where the Chelsea Flower Show is held annually in *May*. Norman Shaw's famous Old Swan House stands at No. 17 Chelsea Embankment.

Tate Britain Millbank *SW1*. Founded in 1897 by Sir Henry Tate, the sugar magnate and by Sidney HJ Smith. Following the opening of Tate Modern, the Millbank gallery has redefined its role, concentrating on British art over the last 500 years. Five thematic displays portray historic and modern works in an imaginative and often disturbing way which, whilst adding an element of surprise, success-fully demonstrates continuity over the cen-turies. The Clore Gallery houses the works of Turner and Constable and special displays depicting major artists range from Blake to Hockney. *Open daily*. Telephone 0207 887 8000 for further details. Free (except for special exhibitions).

Millbank Tower Millbank *SW1*. The traditional balance of the river bank has been overturned by this 387ft–high office building by Ronald Ward and Partners, 1963.

Victoria Tower Gardens Abingdon Street *SW1*. A sculpture of Rodin's Burghers of Calais, 1895, stands close to the river and near the entrance to the gardens is a monument to Mrs Emmeline Pankhurst and Dame Christabel Pankhurst, champions of the women's suffragette movement in the early 1900s. Emmeline Pankhurst is reputedly the last person to have been incarcerated in the cell at the bottom of Big Ben (1902).

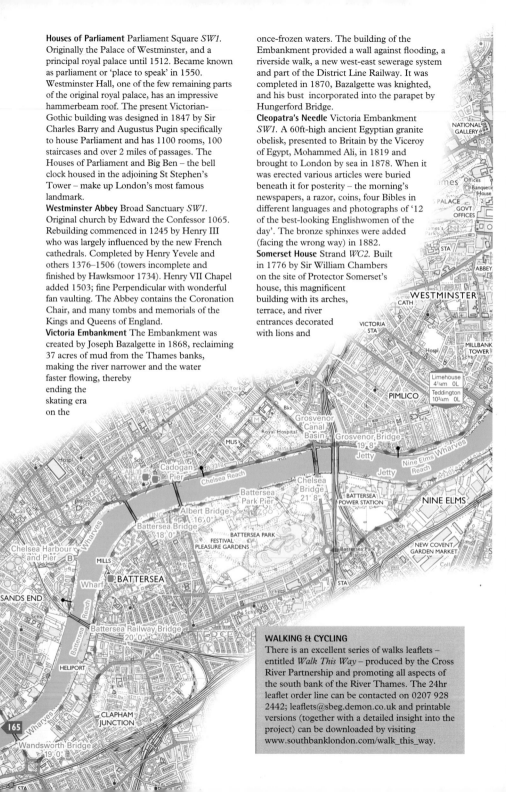

Houses of Parliament Parliament Square *SW1*. Originally the Palace of Westminster, and a principal royal palace until 1512. Became known as parliament or 'place to speak' in 1550. Westminster Hall, one of the few remaining parts of the original royal palace, has an impressive hammerbeam roof. The present Victorian-Gothic building was designed in 1847 by Sir Charles Barry and Augustus Pugin specifically to house Parliament and has 1100 rooms, 100 staircases and over 2 miles of passages. The Houses of Parliament and Big Ben – the bell clock housed in the adjoining St Stephen's Tower – make up London's most famous landmark.

Westminster Abbey Broad Sanctuary *SW1*. Original church by Edward the Confessor 1065. Rebuilding commenced in 1245 by Henry III who was largely influenced by the new French cathedrals. Completed by Henry Yevele and others 1376–1506 (towers incomplete and finished by Hawksmoor 1734). Henry VII Chapel added 1503; fine Perpendicular with wonderful fan vaulting. The Abbey contains the Coronation Chair, and many tombs and memorials of the Kings and Queens of England.

Victoria Embankment The Embankment was created by Joseph Bazalgette in 1868, reclaiming 37 acres of mud from the Thames banks, making the river narrower and the water faster flowing, thereby ending the skating era on the once-frozen waters. The building of the Embankment provided a wall against flooding, a riverside walk, a new west-east sewerage system and part of the District Line Railway. It was completed in 1870, Bazalgette was knighted, and his bust incorporated into the parapet by Hungerford Bridge.

Cleopatra's Needle Victoria Embankment *SW1*. A 60ft-high ancient Egyptian granite obelisk, presented to Britain by the Viceroy of Egypt, Mohammed Ali, in 1819 and brought to London by sea in 1878. When it was erected various articles were buried beneath it for posterity – the morning's newspapers, a razor, coins, four Bibles in different languages and photographs of '12 of the best-looking Englishwomen of the day'. The bronze sphinxes were added (facing the wrong way) in 1882.

Somerset House Strand *WC2*. Built in 1776 by Sir William Chambers on the site of Protector Somerset's house, this magnificent building with its arches, terrace, and river entrances decorated with lions and

WALKING & CYCLING
There is an excellent series of walks leaflets – entitled *Walk This Way* – produced by the Cross River Partnership and promoting all aspects of the south bank of the River Thames. The 24hr leaflet order line can be contacted on 0207 928 2442; leaflets@sbeg.demon.co.uk and printable versions (together with a detailed insight into the project) can be downloaded by visiting www.southbanklondon.com/walk_this_way.

1959 following energetic campaigning by
Lord Bernard Miles. It was rebuilt on a new
site and re-opened in 1981.

● **Fishmongers' Hall**
1 London Bridge Road. Built in the grand
classical manner in 1831–4 by Henry Roberts
to replace the original hall which was burnt
down in the Great Fire of 1666. The
Fishmongers' Company administers the
annual Doggett's Coat and Badge Race for
Thames Watermen. This race, the oldest
annually contested sporting event and the
longest rowing race in the world (1 furlong
short of 5 miles), was introduced in 1715.
Doggett, an Irish comedian and staunch
Hanoverian, who used the services of the
watermen to ferry him to and from the
theatres, decided to mark the anniversary of
the accession of George I to the throne by
instituting an annual race for watermen. The
race is from London Bridge to Cadogan Pier,
Chelsea, and is usually held at the *end of July*.
The victor is presented with a red coat,
breeches and cap, and a silver arm badge
bearing the words 'The Gift of the late
Thomas Doggett'.

Monument *EC4.* A 17th-C hollow fluted
column by Wren, built to commemorate the
Great Fire of London. It marked the northern
end of the original London Bridge and stands
at 202ft, a foot in height for every foot in distance from where the fire started in Pudding
Lane. Gives a magnificent view over the city.

Old Billingsgate Market Lower Thames Street
EC3. The yellow-brick Victorian building
with arcaded ground floor was built by
Sir Horace Jones, 1875, although the first
reference to a market at Billingsgate was
made in AD870. A free fish market was established by statute in 1699, but until the 18th C
coal, corn and provisions were also sold. The
fish-porters wore leather hats with flat tops

Tuscan
columns, was
intended to
compete with the
splendour of
Adam's Adelphi.
Once occupied by
the General Register
Office whose records
of birth and death go
back to 1836, it now
houses offices of the
Inland Revenue and the
Courtauld Institute
Galleries.
The Temple *EC4.* The name
derives from the Order of
Knights Templar who occupied
the site from 1160–1308. In the
17th-C the Temple was leased to
the benchers of the Inner and Middle
Temple, two Inns of Court. These inns,
together with Lincoln's Inn and Gray's Inn,
hold the ancient and exclusive privilege of
providing advocates in the courts of England
and Wales. A visit should be made on foot, as
only a few of the Temple buildings are visible
from the river. On the Embankment, Sir Joseph
Bazalgette's arch and stairs mark the 19th-C
access to the Temple from the river.
City of London A thriving and commercial
centre, stretching between Blackfriars Bridge
and London Bridge, which has within its square
mile such famous institutions as the Bank of
England, the Stock Exchange, the Royal Courts
of Justice and the Guildhall.
Mermaid Theatre Puddle Dock *EC4.* The
original theatre, the first in the City since the
16th C, was opened in a converted warehouse in

and wide brims, formerly known as bobbing hats. Bobbing was the charge made by the porter to carry fish from the wholesaler to the retailer. These hats enabled the porter to carry about a hundredweight of fish on his head. The market moved down river to new premises on the Isle of Dogs in 1982.

The Custom House Lower Thames Street *EC4*. A custom house has stood beside Billingsgate since AD870. The present building is by Laing, 1813–17, but the river façade was rebuilt by Smirke in 1825. Badly bombed in the war, the building has been restored.

Tower of London Tower Hill *EC3*. Although greatly restored and altered over the centuries, the Tower of London is probably the most important work of military architecture in Britain and has been used as a palace, a fortress and a prison since William the Conqueror built the White Tower in 1078.

Tower Bridge This spectacular bridge was built by Sir John Wolfe Barry in 1894 and the old hydraulic lifting mechanism was originally powered by steam.

● SOUTH BANK

Wandsworth Until the 19th C Wandsworth was a village oasis on the River Wandle – a good fishing river – and was noted for a local silk and hat industry. The course of the Wandle can still be traced near the Church of All Saints. The Surrey Iron Railway, whose wagons were drawn by horses, ran alongside the river. Past residents include Defoe, Thackeray and Voltaire, but today little remains to point to the past.

Battersea Many of the old riverside warehouses are now gone and tall tower blocks dominate.

St Mary's Church Church Road *SW11*. The church is one of the few relics of Battersea's 18th-C village. Built in 1775 by Joseph Dixon, it is strangely Dutch in character.

Battersea Park *SW11*. The park was laid out by Sir James Pennethorne as a public garden and opened by Queen Victoria in 1858. Re-designed in the 1950s for the Festival of Britain, there is a boating lake, a deer park, an Alpine showhouse, herb garden and greenhouse, a children's zoo and sculptures by Moore, Hepworth and Epstein. The London Peace Pagoda which stands close to the river was built in 1985 by monks and nuns of the Japanese Buddhist order Nipponzan Myohoji.

Battersea Power Station *SW8*. This vast oblong of brick with its four chimneys was designed by Sir Giles Gilbert Scott, 1932–4. Redundant as a power station, plans are to convert the building into an arts or leisure complex.

Albert Embankment *SE1*. Designed as a broad footwalk by Sir Joseph Bazalgette, 1867, the Embankment stretches between Vauxhall and Westminster Bridges. The upper Embankment was once the site of the 18th-C Vauxhall Gardens, whose Chinese pavilions and walks were the envy of Europe.

Lambeth Palace Lambeth Palace Road *SE1*. The London residence of the Archbishop of Canterbury since 1197. Remarkable Tudor gate-

house, fine medieval crypt. A 14th-C Hall with a splendid roof and portraits of archbishops on its walls. The Guard Room, which houses the library, was rebuilt in medieval style in 1633.

County Hall Westminster Bridge *SE1*. Designed by Ralph Knott in 1911, this was once the imposing headquarters of the Greater London Council. Today it houses the London Aquarium, one of the largest collections of underwater life in Europe swimming in an impressive 450,000 gallons of water. Breath-taking colours abound in tanks depicting sea life from different corners of the globe. The Pacific and Atlantic tanks are spectacular in their sheer size alone, as are the sharks therein. Also touch tanks and the chance to stroke a ray. *Open daily*. Telephone 0207 967 8000 for further details. Charge. Disabled access.

London Eye Jubilee Gardens *SE1*. A gigantic ferris wheel, *open daily 1000–1800*, offering a bird's eye view over London.

Shell Centre *SE1*. Part of the area known as the South Bank, the Shell Centre was designed by Sir Howard Robertson in 1962, and is of greyish white concrete with monotonous little square windows. The central 351ft-high skyscraper rises like a huge grey mountain.

South Bank Arts Centre *SE1*. Royal Festival Hall, the Queen Elizabeth Hall, the Purcell Room, the National Theatre, the National Film Theatre, the Hayward Gallery and the Museum of the Moving Image make up the complex which originated with the Festival of Britain in 1951. The Festival Hall, completed in 1951 and built by Sir Robert Matthew and Sir Leonard Martin, seats 3400. The Queen Elizabeth Hall by Hubert Bennett, 1967, is much smaller and intended for recitals. Bennett also designed the Hayward Gallery which opened in 1968. The Purcell Room is the smallest of the three concert halls; ideal for chamber music and solo concerts. The range of cultural activities on offer at the South Bank Centre is diverse and can be enjoyed by everyone.

Upper Ground *SE1*. The decrepit warehouses that used to line the south bank have been demolished, and replaced by the impressive London Weekend Television building and Gabriel's Wharf – South Bank's answer to Covent Garden. To the east of Gabriel's Wharf stands the fine art deco OXO tower, built in 1928 and decorated thus because advertising was forbidden on buildings.

Bankside *SE1*. In the 16th C the Rose Theatre, the Swan and the Globe were all situated around Bankside, and until the 19th C the area was the site of playhouses and amusement gardens. Today the area has been developed and almost all is changing apart from the few remaining 17th-C and 18th-C houses and the Anchor pub, an historic tavern with strong smuggling connections. A Tudor theatre has been reconstructed near the site of the original Globe Theatre as part of the International Shakespeare Globe Centre, and the Shakespeare Globe Museum illustrates the theatre of the age (*see* below). From Bankside are fine views of St Paul's Cathedral and the City.

Shakespeare Globe Museum 1 Bear Gardens, Bankside *SE1*. Converted 18th-C warehouse on the site of a 16th-C bear-baiting ring and the Hope Playhouse.

Tate Modern *SE1*. The Tate Gallery's international collection of 20th-C art is housed within the former Bankside Power Station, designed in 1935 by Sir Giles Gilbert Scott. Displays are themed and stylistic and historical parallels are drawn between works from different periods to challenge the viewers perception of non-representational art. Genres range from Surrealism and New Reaslism through to Pop Art and Minimal Art. Striking views from the top floor – both of the sculptures inside the building and out over the Thames. Café and restaurant with outdoor river terrace. Open daily. Telephone 0207 887 8888 for further details. Free (except for special exhibitions). Disabled access.

Southwark Cathedral Borough High Street *SE1*. Built by Augustinian Canons but destroyed by fire in 1206 and greatly restored. The tower was built c.1520 and the nave, by Blomfield, 1894–7. In the Middle Ages the cathedral was part of the Augustinian Priory of St Mary Overie. Despite its 19th-C additions, it is still one of the most impressive Gothic buildings in London.

Kathleen & May St Mary Overy Dock. Last surviving three-masted, topsail, trading schooner and now a floating museum.

● **BRIDGES**

Chelsea Bridge The original bridge designed by Thomas Page, 1858, was rebuilt as a suspension bridge in 1934 by Rendel, Palmer & Tritton.

Victoria Railway Bridge When it was opened in 1859, this was the widest railway bridge in the world – 132ft wide and 900ft long – and it provided 10 separate accesses to Victoria Station.

Vauxhall Bridge James Walker's Regent's Bridge which opened in 1816 was the first iron bridge to span the Thames in London. The present structure, designed by Sir Alexander Binnie, was opened in 1906. The bronze figures alongside the bridge represent Agriculture, Architecture, Engineering, Learning, the Fine Arts and Astronomy.

Lambeth Bridge Originally the site of a horse ferry, the first bridge was built here in 1861, designed by P. W. Barlow. This was replaced in 1932 by the present steel-arch bridge designed by George Humphreys and Sir Reginald Blomfield.

Westminster Bridge Built in 1750, Westminster Bridge was the second bridge to be built across the Thames in central London. The present bridge, by Thomas Page, replaced the old stone one in 1862.

Charing Cross Railway Bridge Also known as Hungerford Bridge, it has replaced the original suspension bridge which was demolished in 1864. A separate walkway and cycleway run alongside to Waterloo Station with excellent views of the City.

Waterloo Bridge John Rennie's early 19th-C bridge, a beautiful design of Greek columns and nine elliptical arches, was replaced in 1945 by Sir Giles Gilbert Scott's concrete bridge, faced with Portland stone.

Millennium Bridge Constructed in 1999 and, in conjunction with the new walkway on the upstream side of Hungerford Bridge, forms part of the City's Cross River Partnership initiative to provide an integrated transport and regeneration strategy for Thames side in central London.

Southwark Bridge Southwark Bridge was built in 1814 and was the largest bridge ever built of cast iron. Replaced 1912–21 by the present five-span steel bridge of Mott and Hay, with Sir Ernest George as architect. Southwark Causeway, the steps on the south side, were used by Wren when he travelled across the river to supervise work on St Paul's.

Cannon Street Railway Bridge Built in 1866 as part of the extension of the South Eastern Railway, the bridge's engineers were J. Hawkshaw and J. W. Barry. A prominent structure on account of the 19th-C train shed jutting out to the side of the bridge.

London Bridge Until 1749 London Bridge was the only bridge to span the Thames in London. The first recorded wooden bridge was Saxon, but it is possible that a Roman structure may have existed here. In 1176 the wooden bridge was replaced by a stone structure, with houses, shops and a church built upon it, similar in appearance to the Ponte Vecchio in Florence. The heads of traitors were displayed on the spikes of the fortified gates at either end. In 1831 this bridge was demolished and a new bridge, by John Rennie, replaced it. A granite bridge with five arches, this soon became too narrow to meet the demands of modern traffic and because of structural faults could not be widened. A new bridge, constructed under the direction of the City Engineer, was opened to traffic in 1973. Built out of concrete, it has a flat-arched profile in three spans carried on slender piers. The McCulloch Corporation of Arizona paid £2,460,000 for the facing materials of Rennie's bridge, which has been reconstructed spanning Lake Havasu.

Blackfriars Bridge Blackfriars Bridge was built in 1760. It cost £230,000 and was mainly paid for by fines which had accumulated from men refusing the post of Sheriff. Replaced by the present structure in 1860. Note the pulpits, a reminder of the religious significance of its name.

Blackfriars Railway Bridge Built in 1886 for the London, Chatham and Dover Railway, this elegant iron bridge, with its high parapet and decorative coat of arms at each end, can best be seen from the road bridge.

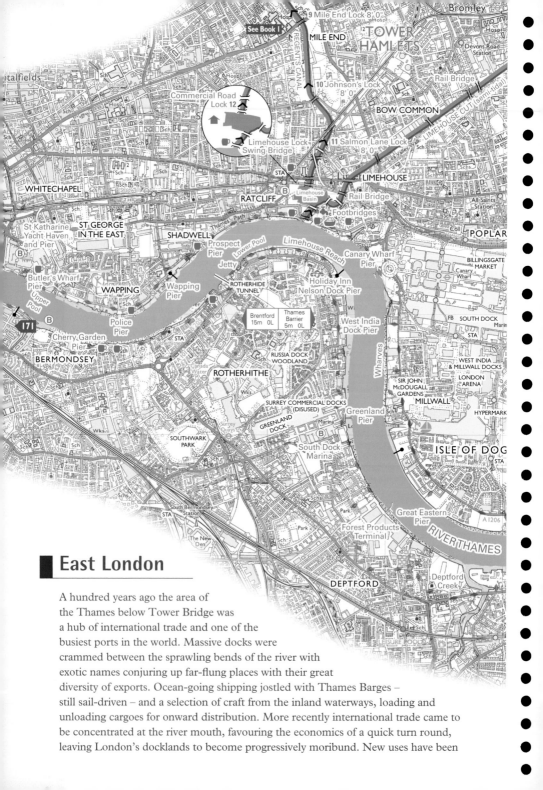

East London

A hundred years ago the area of
the Thames below Tower Bridge was
a hub of international trade and one of the
busiest ports in the world. Massive docks were
crammed between the sprawling bends of the river with
exotic names conjuring up far-flung places with their great
diversity of exports. Ocean-going shipping jostled with Thames Barges –
still sail-driven – and a selection of craft from the inland waterways, loading and
unloading cargoes for onward distribution. More recently international trade came to
be concentrated at the river mouth, favouring the economics of a quick turn round,
leaving London's docklands to become progressively moribund. New uses have been

NAVIGATIONAL NOTES

Boaters joining the tidal Thames
at Limehouse should read the
Navigational Notes on page 162,
and the Mooring Note on page 161.

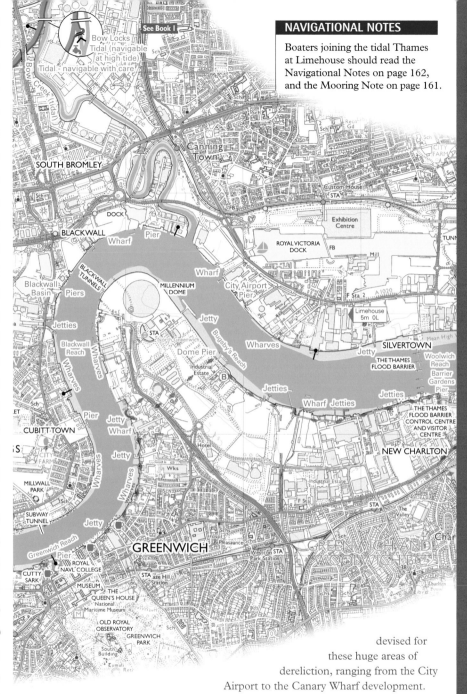

devised for
these huge areas of
dereliction, ranging from the City
Airport to the Canary Wharf development.
New housing and new industry have been drafted in, often
with scant regard for established communities and cultures. In converting
redundant warehouses the value of these solid symbols of a previous prosperity
and optimism has at least been recognised.

St Katharine Dock The first of the docks to be rejuvenated. Built on 23 acres in 1828, from a design by Thomas Telford, the original docks were closed in 1968. Five years later an £80 million building scheme was begun which included the Tower Thistle Hotel and the World Trade Centre.

Butler's Wharf Transformed from narrow alleys, where Oliver Twist's Bill Sikes met his end, into a smart resaurant, shopping and office complex including three Conran restaurants.

Cherry Garden Pier Where ships sound their signal if they want Tower Bridge to be raised. Turner sat here to paint *The Fighting Temeraire* as she returned from the Battle of Trafalgar.

Limehouse Basin *E14.* Formerly Regent's Canal Dock, this forms part of the Grand Union Canal system, opened in 1820 to allow barges to trade between London and Birmingham. The Limehouse Cut also provides access to the River Lea.

Royal Naval Victualling Yard Grove Street *SE8.* Founded in 1513 as the Royal Dock for Henry VIII's navy, the yard became the principal naval dockyard in the kingdom, rivalling Woolwich. Sir Francis Drake was knighted here after his world voyage on the *Golden Hind,* and it was from this yard that Captain Cook's *Discovery* set sail.

Docklands Stretching from Tower Pier to Beckton is London's Docklands. The area has undergone massive change from a thriving, commercial port through closure to regeneration. The London Docklands Development Corporation (LDDC) was set up in 1981 to create a new city for the 21st C incorporating riverside apartments, shops, restaurants and offices.

Canary Wharf Tower One Canada Square, Canary Wharf *E14.* Designed by Cesar Pelli, 1988–90, this 800ft building is the tallest in the UK. Clad in stainless steel and topped with a pyramid, the 50-storey building boasts a magnificent lobby finished in Italian and Guatemalan marble. Thirty-two passenger lifts operate from the lobby and are the fastest in the country. Canary Wharf itself is full of elegant architecture.

Isle of Dogs Until the industrialisation of the early 19th-C, the Isle of Dogs was mainly pastureland and marshes.

Greenwich Tunnel The Blackwall Tunnel, opened in 1897 as a road traffic tunnel. In 1902 it was decided to build a pedestrian subway to link Greenwich with the Isle of Dogs. There was opposition from the watermen and lightermen who, rightly, feared for their jobs. The southern entrance to the footway is in Cutty Sark Gardens, Greenwich; the northern entrance is in Island Gardens, Isle of Dogs.

Greenwich *SE10.* Once a small fishing village, the historic town of Greenwich marks the eastern approach to London. Its royal and naval past is illustrated by the magnificent riverside grouping of the Queen's House, the Royal Naval College, the National Maritime Museum and the Old Royal Observatory. From the Observatory the views are magnificent.

The Cutty Sark King William Walk *SE10.* One of the great 19th-C tea and wool sailing clippers, stands in dry dock. The history of the *Cutty Sark* is displayed in drawings and photographs. Close by stands *Gipsy Moth IV,* the yacht in which Sir Francis Chichester made his solo circumnavigation of the world in 1966.

Greenwich Park *SE10.* Laid out for Charles II by the French royal landscape gardener André Le Nôtre, the park commands a magnificent view of the Royal Naval College and of the river. It contains 13 acres of woodland and deer park, a bird sanctuary and archaeological sites. Crooms Hill lies to the west of the park, lined with a wealth of 17th- to 19th-C houses. Greenwich Theatre stands at the foot of the hill.

Old Royal Observatory Greenwich Park *SE10.* The original observatory, still standing, was built by Wren for Flamsteed, first Astronomer Royal, in the 17th C. Astronomical instruments and exhibits relating to the history of astronomy are displayed in the old observatory buildings and the time ball which provided the first public time signal in 1833 still operates. Home to the Meridian Line, interactive science stations and the largest refracting telescope in the UK.

Royal Naval College Greenwich *SE10.* Mary II commissioned Wren to rebuild the palace as a hospital for aged and disabled seamen. Designed in the Baroque style, it was completed in 1705. The Painted Hall, or Dining Hall, has a swirling Baroque ceiling by Thornhill, one of the finest of its period. The neo-classical chapel dates from 1789. In 1873 the hospital became the Royal Naval College to provide for the higher education of naval officers.

Queen's House Romney Road, Greenwich *SE10.* Now part of the National Maritime Museum, this delightful white house in the Palladian style was built for Queen Anne of Denmark by Inigo Jones, 1618.

Millennium Dome The centre piece of the country's Millennium celebrations, comprising a translucent canopy made from 328,100 square feet of fabric, held up with 43 miles of high-strength cable suspended from 12 vast 105-tonne yellow steel masts, visitor numbers failed to meet expectations, although an attempted diamond robbery did provide some unscripted excitement. As we go to press, the government plan to give it away to developers, with the possibility of a new river crossing also being discussed.

Thames Flood Barrier Best seen from the river. As you round the bend, the steel fins rise up from the water. Completed in 1982, it is the world's largest movable flood barrier and is designed to swing up from the river bed and create a stainless steel barrage to stem periodically dangerous high tides. Each gate weighs 3000 tonnes and is the equivalent of a five-storey building in height. The structures housing the machines which operate the gates seem to have been inspired by the 'sails' of Sydney Opera House.

WEY & GODALMING NAVIGATIONS

MAXIMUM DIMENSIONS
Length: 72' 0"
Beam: 13' 10"
Draught: 3' 0" to Guildford
2' 6" above Guildford
Headroom: 7' 0" to Guildford
6' 0" to Godalming (at normal levels)

MILEAGES
THAMES LOCK (junction with River Thames) *to*:
Woodham Junction: 3 miles
Cartbridge: 9 miles
Guildford: 15 miles
Guns Mouth: 17¼ miles
Godalming: 19½ miles

Locks: 16 (including Worsfold and Walsham Flood Gates)

Navigation Authority:
The National Trust
River Wey Navigations
Dapdune Wharf
Wharf Road
Guildford GU1 4RR
Visitor Services Manager:
01483 561389
swybeb@smtp.ntrust.org.uk

Annual or visitor's licences are issued at Dapdune Wharf, or at Thames Lock.
A copy of *Information for Boat User*s is supplied with each licence.
The speed limit is 4 knots – in practice, slower. Watch your wash. Use only the correct Wey Navigation lock handle, available from Thames Lock, the NT Navigation Office or Guildford and Farncombe Boat Houses. When leaving locks, exit gates should be left open, but with all the paddles *down*.
As a river navigation, the Wey is subject to flooding, increasing the speed of the current and pull of the weirs. Under certain conditions, locks may be padlocked and craft should moor up in a sheltered place and seek advice.
The towpath side of the navigation is available for mooring. Respect private property.

Boats have used the River Wey since medieval times, but the present navigation dates from the 17th C. In 1651 authorisation was given to make the river navigable for 15 miles from Weybridge to Guildford. This involved the building of 12 locks and 10 miles of artificial cut. This early navigation had the usual battles with mill owners, but gradually trade developed, predominantly local and agricultural in character. More unusual were the extensive Farnham Potteries, who shipped their wares to London along the Wey. In 1763 the Godalming Navigation was opened, adding another four miles to the waterway, and by the end of the 18th C considerable barge traffic was using the river. This was greatly increased by the building of the Basingstoke Canal in 1796, and the Wey & Arun Junction Canal in 1816; the latter offered a direct route from London to Portsmouth and the south coast. This canal closed in 1871, but trade continued to thrive on the Wey and as late as 1960 barges were still carrying timber to Guildford. Grain traffic to Coxes Mill continued until 1968, with a brief revival in the early 1980s. There is now no commercial carrying on the navigation.
In 1964 the Wey Navigation was given to the National Trust by Harry Stevens, its last private owner. In 1968 the Godalming Navigation Commissioners passed their section to Guildford Corporation, who in turn passed it on to the National Trust. It remains an artery of peace and tranquillity amidst the noise and bustle of Surrey, and will amply repay a visit.

Weybridge

The River Wey Navigation leaves the Thames by Shepperton Lock. The correct channel is clearly signposted. Just around the corner is the pound gate, used only when the water level is low or when a deep draughted vessel is passing through. The lock is in an attractive wooded setting, and the keeper here is available to advise you. An informative display can be seen in the stable by the lock. Just above, beyond the weirs, smart houses and gardens line the east bank; the west is wooded. There is a sharp westward turn (*see* Navigational Notes) followed immediately by Weybridge Town Lock, where Addlestone Road flanks the navigation on its way to Ham Moor. Note the towline roller on the corner, installed to allow towed craft to negotiate the bend. Just above the railway bridge is Coxes Mill, a very handsome and varied group of industrial buildings now tastefully converted into flats. Note the large mill pond to the west, owned and managed by the Trust as a wildlife habitat. The Wey then continues its quiet wooded passage south. Beyond Parvis Bridge the towpath skirts the old grist mill (*NT*), where all kinds of cattle and poultry food were produced. Much of New Haw consists of 20th-C Georgian-style commuter housing. Moored craft line the east bank above New Haw Lock (with its pretty lock cottage) as the cut makes a beeline for Byfleet, cowering under the massive concrete structures and earth embankments of the M25 motorway – there is no longer any peace to be had here. The Basingstoke Canal (*see* page 9) leaves the Wey Navigation in the midst of a flurry of bridges. Beyond Parvis Bridge the Wey Navigation becomes more rural – breaks in the waterside trees reveal open meadows and farmland.

NAVIGATIONAL NOTES

1 Thames Lock (01932 843106). Attended. Licences, free *Information for Boat Users*, plus visitor passes. Lock handles for sale or hire. All those wishing to enter the lock should consult the lock keeper. Craft with draught deeper than 1ft 9in coming up from the Thames should advise the lock keeper – who may then use the pound gate to increase the water level before they enter the lock. *Open 09.00–13.00 and 14.00–18.30 or sunset.*
2 Weybridge Old Bridge – the navigation channel is clearly marked, and is the most westerly bridge-hole (furthest right) when coming upstream. The lock is immediately above the bridge.

● **Weybridge**
Surrey. All shops and services, laundrette. A commuter town in the stockbroker belt, built around the confluence of the rivers Wey and Thames – the junction is marked by a pretty iron bridge dated 1865. Weybridge represents the frontier of the suburbia which now spreads almost unbroken to London. Behind the town lie the remains of Brooklands, the doyen of motor racing circuits in the early 20th C (*see* below).
Coxes Mill *Surrey.* Overlooking Coxes Lock is a magnificent group of mostly 19th-C mill buildings, partly brick, partly concrete and partly weather-board, the best industrial architecture on the river.
Brooklands Museum Brooklands Road, Weybridge (01932 857381; www.motor-software.co.uk/brooklands). A museum assembled around what remains of the Brooklands race track, the world's first purpose-built circuit, constructed by wealthy landowner Hugh Locke King in 1907. Its heyday was in the 1920s and 30s, when records were being set by the likes of Malcolm Campbell and John Cobb, driving vehicles with wonderfully evocative names, such as the Napier, Delage,

Bentley and Bugatti. It became very fashionable, and was known as the Ascot of Motorsport. It was also an aerodrome, and it was here that A. V. Roe made the first flight in a British aeroplane. The Sopwith Pup and Camel were developed here, and later the Hawker Hurricane and the Vickers Wellington were built here – the only surviving Wellington, salvaged in 1985 from Loch Ness and restored, is on display. The outbreak of war in 1939 brought an end to racing, and aircraft production ceased in 1987. Now you can walk on part of the legendary circuit, and see historic racing cars and aircraft in the museum. The clubhouse is listed as an ancient monument. A new addition is the Raleigh Cycle Museum, a reminder that cycle races were also held at Brooklands. *Open Tue–Sun 10.00–17.00 (16.00 winter). Closed G Fri, B Hol Mons and Xmas. Charge.*
● **Byfleet**
Surrey. PO, shops. Although buried by modern commuter housing, parts of the old village can be found. The church with its bellcote is mostly late 13th-C, and the 17th-C brick manor house is an elegant delight in the midst of so much dreariness.

Boatyards

Ⓑ **Weybridge Marine** 91 Thames Street, Weybridge (01932 847453). Long-term mooring, winter storage, slipway.

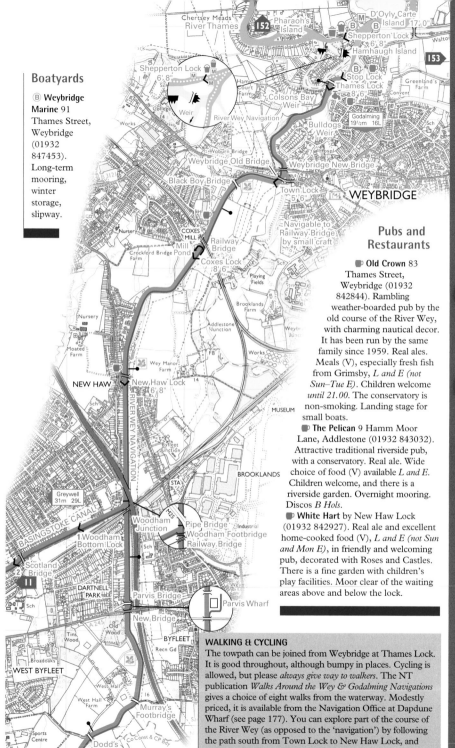

Pubs and Restaurants

🍺 **Old Crown** 83 Thames Street, Weybridge (01932 842844). Rambling weather-boarded pub by the old course of the River Wey, with charming nautical decor. It has been run by the same family since 1959. Real ales. Meals (V), especially fresh fish from Grimsby, *L and E (not Sun–Tue E)*. Children welcome *until 21.00*. The conservatory is non-smoking. Landing stage for small boats.

🍺 **The Pelican** 9 Hamm Moor Lane, Addlestone (01932 843032). Attractive traditional riverside pub, with a conservatory. Real ale. Wide choice of food (V) available *L and E*. Children welcome, and there is a riverside garden. Overnight mooring. Discos *B Hols*.

🍺 **White Hart** by New Haw Lock (01932 842927). Real ale and excellent home-cooked food (V), *L and E (not Sun and Mon E)*, in friendly and welcoming pub, decorated with Roses and Castles. There is a fine garden with children's play facilities. Moor clear of the waiting areas above and below the lock.

WALKING & CYCLING
The towpath can be joined from Weybridge at Thames Lock. It is good throughout, although bumpy in places. Cycling is allowed, but please *always give way to walkers*. The NT publication *Walks Around the Wey & Godalming Navigations* gives a choice of eight walks from the waterway. Modestly priced, it is available from the Navigation Office at Dapdune Wharf (see page 177). You can explore part of the course of the River Wey (as opposed to the 'navigation') by following the path south from Town Lock to New Haw Lock, and returning beside the Wey Navigation.

Pyrford

The popular Anchor pub is close to the bridge at Pyrford, with Pyrford Marina opposite; just beyond is Pyrford Lock and many colourful moored craft. The navigation then passes Pyrford Place, with its lovely old Elizabethen summer house with a pagoda roof, beside a charming little riverside terrace. Except in times of flood you may pass uninterrupted through Walsham Flood Gates, overlooked by the quaintly business-like lock cottage. The large weir is to the east. The river then becomes wider and strewn with lily pads, before it splits to form a trio of islands at Newark, where the remains of Newark Priory can be seen at the water's edge. The lock cut continues to Newark Lock – above here the river winds towards Papercourt Lock, arguably the prettiest on the river, with its stepped weir and charming garden. Factories and offices line the south bank as the navigation passes under High Bridge and approaches Cart Bridge, to the west of Send. It is, surprisingly, quite peaceful – a relief considering the boundless activity all around. The restored National Trust Workshop is by the lock, often with a few sturdy barges moored opposite. Then once again the Wey resumes its rural course, passing Triggs Lock, with another attractive lock cottage, this one dating from 1770. At one time it had a blacksmith's shop attached, and to the north there used to be a small wharf. William Stevens became lock keeper here in 1812 – it was one of his descendants, Harry Stevens, who was to give the navigation to the National Trust in 1964.

● Pyrford Village

Surrey. Tel. Surrounded by water meadows and trees, Pyrford is still a real village, an oasis in the ever-spreading suburban web. Brick cottages overlook the church, an almost intact Norman building 'built of puddingstone, dressed with clunch'; such a thing is rare in the Home Counties and is thus an even greater pleasure. The north porch is half-timbered and dates from the 16th C. Inside are wall paintings depicting scenes from the flagellation and the Passion, c.1200: the pulpit is 17th-C. There are many attractive 18th-C houses.

Royal Horticultural Society's Gardens Wisley (01483 224234; www.rhs.org.uk). By footpath south east of Pigeon House Bridge to Ockham Mill, then north east towards Wisley, or by footpath from Pyrford Lock. A 200-acre botanic garden acquired by the RHS in 1904 and famous for its trials and improvements of new varieties. Notable collections of old-fashioned and new roses, rhodo-dendrons, camellias, heathers and rock garden plants. Walled garden with tender perennial shrubs and climbers, Country Garden, Temperate Glasshouse and Garden of the Senses. *Open Mon–Fri (Sat 09.00) 10.00–sunset (closes 16.30 in winter). Members only on Sun.* Charge.

Newark Priory The tall broken flint walls of this 12th-C Augustinian priory stand in a meadow at the river's edge, an enticing and romantic ruin. Unfortunately there is no right of navigation up to the walls.

● Send

Surrey. Tel, shops, laundrette. An unremarkable linear village useful for supplies. The church, a muddled affair of all periods, lies close to the River Wey and well to the south west of the main centre. Although nicely sited amongst trees and 18th-C houses, it looks at its best from the river.

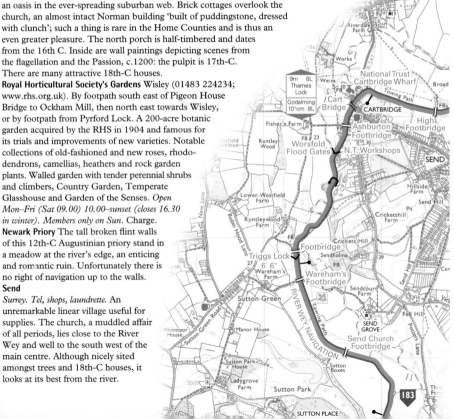

Boatyards

Ⓑ **Pyrford Marina** Lock Lane, Pyrford, Woking (01932 340739). 🛢 🛒 ⚙ **D** Pump out, gas, long-term mooring, winter storage, slipway, dry dock, boat and engine sales and repairs, boat building, telephone, toilets, showers, chandlery, solid fuel, DIY facilities. *Emergency call out.*

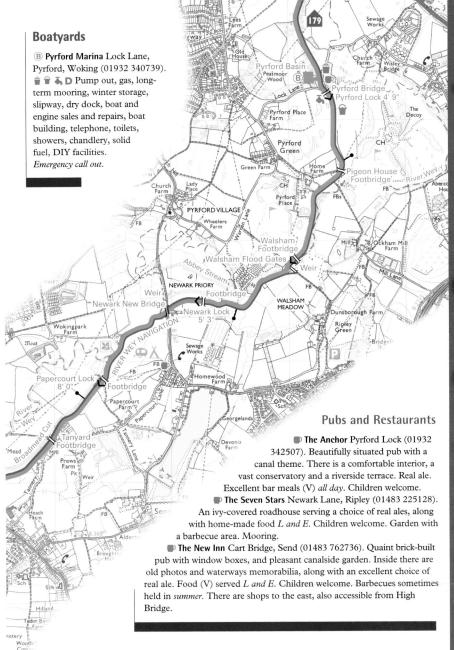

Pubs and Restaurants

🍺 **The Anchor** Pyrford Lock (01932 342507). Beautifully situated pub with a canal theme. There is a comfortable interior, a vast conservatory and a riverside terrace. Real ale. Excellent bar meals (V) *all day*. Children welcome.

🍺 **The Seven Stars** Newark Lane, Ripley (01483 225128). An ivy-covered roadhouse serving a choice of real ales, along with home-made food *L and E*. Children welcome. Garden with a barbecue area. Mooring.

🍺 **The New Inn** Cart Bridge, Send (01483 762736). Quaint brick-built pub with window boxes, and pleasant canalside garden. Inside there are old photos and waterways memorabilia, along with an excellent choice of real ale. Food (V) served *L and E*. Children welcome. Barbecues sometimes held in *summer*. There are shops to the east, also accessible from High Bridge.

NAVIGATIONAL NOTES

1 All the locks on this section are unattended.
2 Walsham and Worsfold Flood Gates are normally left open, except in times of flood. When closed the chamber should be used as a normal lock, unless flood boards instruct otherwise.
3 Be wary of the cross current below Papercourt Lock.

Guildford

The navigation now begins to sweep around Sutton Place, and comes very close to the A3, with its constant rumble of traffic. Care should be exercised at Broadoak Bridge (note the towline roller on the corner) and Bower's Lock (*see* below). The approach to Stoke Lock is tree-lined, a blessing in that it alleviates some of the noise from the nearby trunk road, but it is now very clear that Guildford is being approached and the scene is becoming increasingly urban. A few willows overhang by Stoke Bridge, but soon all is back gardens, roads and factories. The scene gradually improves, and at Dapdune Wharf, the National Trust has established a visitor centre, with a fine restored Wey barge amongst other exhibits. At Onslow Bridge the change of scene is completed: the town turns to face the water – and what a jolly scene it is – with riverside walks, a handsome mill, the theatre, a busy boatyard, pubs and restaurants, all overlooked by the castle. Note especially the rare treadwheel crane standing on what was the old Guildford Town Wharf: from here the Wey Navigation becomes the Godalming Navigation and leaves Guildford in an ideal setting, with parkland to the east and pleasant private gardens glimpsed over high walls to the west. A footbridge marks the site of the old St Catherine's Ferry on the Pilgrims' Way, and a small stream spills into the river here below a pretty grotto, where those who pass are 'treading the path trod by Geoffrey Chaucer's Canterbury Pilgrims in the reign of King Edward the Third'. Just beyond is St Catherine's Sands, a favourite haunt of the local children during warm school holidays.

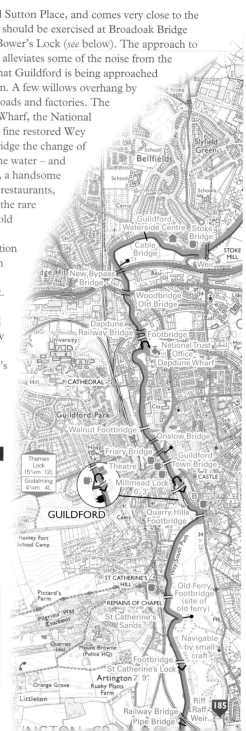

NAVIGATIONAL NOTES

1 At Broadoak Bridge pass through the arch closest to the towing path.
2 When approached from downstream Bower's Lock is to the left before the footbridge. When locking down, take the sharp blind turn to the right with care.
3 Keep clear of the weir above St Catherine's Lock.

BOAT TRIPS
Guildford Boat House Millbrook, Guildford (01483 504494; www.guildfordboats.co.uk). Regular trips on the *Harry Stevens* for up to 69 passengers, departing from Guildford Boat House or the Town Quay, from *Easter–end Oct*. Restaurant cruises on the *Alfred Leroy*, from *May–Oct*. Telephone for details.

185

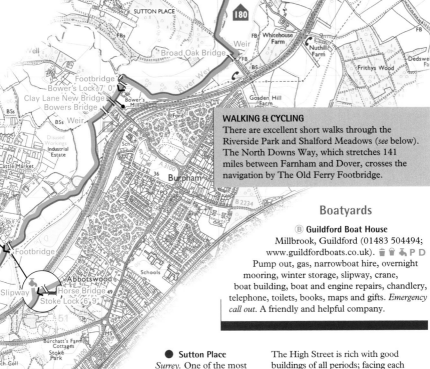

180

WALKING & CYCLING
There are excellent short walks through the Riverside Park and Shalford Meadows (*see* below). The North Downs Way, which stretches 141 miles between Farnham and Dover, crosses the navigation by The Old Ferry Footbridge.

Boatyards

Ⓑ **Guildford Boat House**
Millbrook, Guildford (01483 504494; www.guildfordboats.co.uk). 🚽 🚿 ♿ P D
Pump out, gas, narrowboat hire, overnight mooring, winter storage, slipway, crane, boat building, boat and engine repairs, chandlery, telephone, toilets, books, maps and gifts. *Emergency call out.* A friendly and helpful company.

● **Sutton Place**
Surrey. One of the most important early Tudor houses in England, Sutton Place was built by Sir Richard Weston, a Knight of Bath, Gentleman of the Privy Chamber and Under Treasurer of England. He died in 1652. It is a brick house, with terracotta ornamentation, built originally around a square; one side was demolished in 1786 leaving the plan more open. The house is an interesting mixture of Renaissance and English styles, and was once owned by the late Paul Getty. Private.

● **Guildford**
Surrey. All shops and services. The town is built on the steep sides of the Wey valley and so its centre is very compact, overlooked on the west by the bulk of the cathedral, and on the east by the castle ruins, where the public gardens contain a life-size statue of Alice Through the Looking Glass, celebrating the town's association with Lewis Carroll (*see* below). The castle grounds continue as Castle Cliffe Gardens: 'The Chestnuts', where the author once lived, is close by. The best parts of the town are around the traffic-free cobbled High Street, which leads steeply down to the river, where there are interesting mill and wharf buildings, including the last tread wheel operated crane in existence.

The High Street is rich with good buildings of all periods; facing each other at the top, the Baroque splendour of the 17th-C Guildhall and the 18th-C simplicity of Holy Trinity Church demonstrate this rich diversity. The University of Surrey has been developed on the slopes of the cathedral hill; the buildings show a better feeling for architecture than many other modern universities. The strength of Guildford as a cultural centre is shown by the modern Yvonne Arnaud Theatre, standing on an attractive riverside site, surrounded by trees but still in the town centre, and the number of festivals held here throughout the summer. Guildford seems to have been by tradition a popular and self-contained town, and this feeling still survives.

Riverside Park By Stoke Lock, Guildford (01483 444705). A natural countryside park containing oak, ash and chestnut, an assortment of reeds, sedges and grassland, with bluebells and red campions in the spring. Newts, frogs and toads, dragonflies and damselflies can be found near the lake, along with grass snakes (which are harmless), all managed with conservation in mind.

Guildford Cathedral (01483 565287) The brick mass of the cathedral overlooks the town – it is an uncompromising and unsubtle thing, the last fling of the Gothic revival. Designed by Edward Maufe in 1932, it was only completed in 1961, and sadly reveals its period all too clearly. From the outside it is a mixture of cinema, power station and church; the inside is a complete contrast – a wealth of detail, and delicate use of shape and form, far more genuinely Gothic in feeling. Interesting furniture, fittings, glass and statuary. *Open daily 08.30–17.30.* Gift shop, book shop and café.

Guildford House Gallery 155 High Street (01483 444740). The building dates from 1660, and contains fine decorative plasterwork, and a fine carved staircase. Permanent and visiting exhibitions. *Open Tue–Sat 10.00–16.45.* Free. Tea room.

Guildford Castle The huge motte dates from the 11th C, topped by a tower keep c.1170. It remains an imposing ruin.

Guildford Museum Castle Arch (01483 444750). Prehistoric, Roman and Saxon exhibits along with displays of Victorian life. Space is also devoted to Lewis Carroll. *Open Mon–Sat 11.00–17.00.* Free. Shop.

The Undercroft 72 High Street (01483 444755). A vaulted medieval basement dating from the 13th C, with an exhibition illustrating life in medieval Guildford. *Open Easter–Sep, Tue and Thur 14.00–16.00 and Sat 12.00–16.00.* Free.

Lewis Carroll's Grave You can find the grave of this Victorian author, who was born Charles Lutwidge Dodgson in Daresbury (*see* Book 5), near the chapel in the Mount Cemetery, which is to the south west of Onslow Bridge. *Open 09.00–20.00 (16.30 winter).*

Guided Walks Contact the TIC (*below*). Topics include Historic and Unknown Guildford, plus Ghosts and Legends, and Lewis Carroll. *May–Sep Sun, Mon and Wed 14.30 and Thur 19.30.*

Shalford Meadows East of St Catherine's Sands. There are rich plant communities in this riverside water-meadow.

Dapdune Wharf Visitor Centre Wharf Road, Guildford (01483 561389; swybeb@smtp.ntrust. org.uk). This was once the barge building centre of the River Wey Navigation, and has been tastefully restored with a stable, smithy, barge building shed and old cottages. Displays tell the story of the people who lived and worked here. Some handsome restored craft can be seen outside, including the barge *Reliance*, built 1931–2, one of 11 Wey barges built here by the Stevens family. It traded between the Wey and London Docks until it hit Cannon Street Bridge, in London, and sank. It languished on the mud flats at Leigh-on-Sea in Essex, to be later salvaged and returned to Dapdune for restoration. *Open Apr–Oct, Thur–Mon, 11.00–1700.* Charge. 🅰 You may visit by river bus from Guildford Town Quay or Guildford Boat House – details from Guildford Boat House (01483) 504494.

Tourist Information Centre 14 Tunsgate, Guildford (01483 444333).

● **Shalford**
Surrey. PO, tel. A meandering village built along the main road. It is at its best by the river, which is flanked by old wharf and warehouse buildings.

Pubs and Restaurants

🍺 **The Rowbarge** 7 Riverside, Guildford, by Stoke Bridge (01483 573358). Pleasant garden and moorings, close to the Guildford Waterside Centre. Real ale. Coffee and bar food (V) *L and E*. Children welcome. *Weekend* discos.

There are lots of pubs, restaurants and tearooms to choose from in Guildford. The following are all close to the navigation.

🍺 **The Plough** 16 Park Street, Guildford (01483 570167). Cosy and traditional one-bar town pub with an open fire. Real ale, and English food (V) *L Mon–Sat.* Quiet children welcome.

🍺 **The White House** 8 High Street, Guildford (01483 302006). A smart new pub in an attractive riverside building, with a shady terrace by the water and the largest pub garden in Guildford. Real ale. Meals (V) served *all day.* Children welcome.

🍺 **Scruffy Murphy's** Millmead, Guildford (01483 572160). Overlooking the lock, this handsome red brick pub has been converted into an Irish style bar, serving Guinness (of course) and real ale. Food served *L.* Children welcome *during the day.* Outside seating overlooking the river. Plenty of entertainment, including quizzes, theme nights and live music.

🍺 **The Weyside** Shalford Road, Millbrook, Guildford (01483 568024; theweyside@ punchgroup.co.uk). Large riverside pub with a garden, conservatory and terrace. Real ale. Meals (V) available *L and E.* Children welcome.

🍺 **Ye Olde Ship Inn** Ferry Lane, Guildford (01483 575731). Up the old Pilgrims' Way, this friendly pub serves real ale, and interesting food (V) cooked using a wood-burning oven *L and E.* Children welcome in the saloon, and there is a garden.

WALKING & CYCLING
Stretches of the towpath approaching Godalming consist of very soft sand, which is not very kind to bicycles! Be warned. You can explore a section of the Wey & Arun Canal on foot by following the path south east from Broadford Bridge and then returning across Bramley Common to the Godalming Navigation, where you cross Unstead Bridge and head north along the towpath.

Godalming

The river passes Shalford through flat meadow land, and by former riverside mills above the low Broadford Bridge. There are craft moored here and at Guns Mouth, the entrance to the unnavigable Wey & Arun Canal. A fine wooded stretch below Unstead Lock ends abruptly, an indication that the main roads are closer than you might think. The gardens of very smart residences line the Farncombe bank as the river approaches Catteshall Lock, the highest on the river and the furthest south on the linked navigable system. There are good moorings at Lammas Lands on the towpath side above here, and it is only a short walk to Town Bridge, the usual head of navigation and the end of the Godalming Navigation. Those who left the Thames to journey to Godalming will be sad their voyage is over, as the Wey Navigations provide a priceless rural lung, and one of the few local refuges from the stress of Surrey. Their preservation is of the highest priority.

BOAT TRIPS

Restaurant boat **Speedwell** is available for private charter from Godalming, for parties between 6 and 12 people. Bring your own wine. Details on 01483 421306.

nb Iona The Packet Boat Company (01483 414938). A horse drawn narrowboat based at Godalming, available for public trips *in summer* and private charter. It can carry up to 48 passengers, and cream teas and a licensed bar are available. Telephone for details.

Boatyards

Ⓑ **Farncombe Boat House** Catteshall Lock, Godalming (01483 421306; www.farncombeboats. co.uk). 🚽 💧 🛢 D Pump out, gas, narrowboat hire, day-boat hire, overnight mooring, (for long-term mooring, telephone 01483 239309), winter storage, boat building, boat and engine sales and repairs, public telephone, toilets, books and maps, gifts. Riverside tearoom.

1 Broadford Bridge is low, with only 6ft 4in maximum headroom.
2 In Godalming, at the last winding hole, navigators are advised to wind with their bows to the towpath side of the navigation.
3 Small, shallow draught craft may be able to pass under Town Bridge to reach Boarden Bridge – but note that it is beyond the navigable limit, and there is a weir just above the railway bridge.
4 A horse-drawn boat operates between Godalming Wharf and Unstead Bridge *from Easter–Sep*. Do not moor on bends in this area, and keep your cabin top clear.

Wey & Arun Canal

This navigation, built between 1816 and 1817, linked London with the south coast at Littlehampton, and Portsmouth, and has been romanticised as London's lost route to the sea. The first 100yds or so is still in water and used for moorings, but there is no turning space. A low bridge presently impedes further progress. Much of the rest of the route is still intact and The Wey & Arun Canal Trust is working towards restoration, a dream that one day may well become a reality. Meanwhile the canal makes a very attractive walk, linking the North and South Downs Way.

Godalming

Surrey. All shops and services. The head of navigation is near the heavy stone bridge to the north east of the town centre. By tradition a cloth-making town, Godalming has developed in a haphazard way over the years, but its confusion of streets has something to offer. The Market Hall, built in 1814 by John Perry, a local man, is a modestly handsome building with an open ground floor, and is ideally situated. The church of St Peter and St Paul, with its rare and tall leaded 13th-C spire, gives the town an interesting skyline.

Pubs and Restaurants

The Parrot Inn Broadford Road, Shalford (01483 561400; parrotriverwey@aol.com). East of Broadford Bridge. Victorian pub by the green, which has been a winner of the Guildford in Bloom Pub of the Year award. Real ales. Meals (V) available *L and E*. Attractive walled garden. Occasional theme nights, such as lobster, Greek or French. B & B.

The Manor Inn Farncombe (01483 427134). Riverside hotel with garden. Real ale. Bar and restaurant meals, including breakfast, (V) *all day*. Children welcome.

The Leathern Bottle 77 Meadrow, Godalming (01483 425642). Small locals pub serving real ale. Meals (V), such as steak and chips and *Sunday* roasts, *L and E*. Children welcome. Garden with a pool. Darts, cards and dominoes are played.

The Wey Inn 1 Meadrow, Farncombe (01483 416680). North of Town Bridge, and once called The Railway. A welcoming and friendly pub serving a range of real ales. Meals (V), speciality is bangers and mash with onion gravy, *L and E (not Sun)* Children welcome. Skittle alley, games room and a garden.

King's Arms & Royal Hotel High Street, Godalming (01483 421545). Traditional coaching inn which was visited by Peter the Great in 1698. Real ale. Food (V) including an all-day breakfast, *L and E*. Children welcome, and there is a garden.

Seafare 7–8 Bridge Street, Godalming (01483 416560). Award winning traditional fish & chips. *Open Mon–Fri 11.30–14.30 and 16.30–23.00, Sat 11.30–23.00, Sun 17.00–23.00.*

Millmead Lock, Guildford (see page 182)

INDEX